THE
STRUGGLE
FOR
CELIBACY

The Culture of
Catholic Seminary Life

PAUL STANOSZ

A Herder & Herder Book
The Crossroad Publishing Company
New York

The Crossroad Publishing Company
16 Penn Plaza – 481 Eighth Avenue, Suite 1550
New York, NY 10001

Printed in the United States of America
The text of this book is set in 11/14 Trump Mediaeval.

Library of Congress Cataloging-in-Publication Data

Stanosz, Paul.
    The struggle for celibacy : the culture of Catholic seminary life / Paul Stanosz.
       p. cm.
    Includes bibliographical references and index.
    ISBN-13: 978-0-8245-2381-7 (alk. paper)
    ISBN-10: 0-8245-2381-4 (alk. paper)
    1. Celibacy – Catholic Church. 2. Catholic Church – Clergy – Sexual behavior. 3. Clergy – Training of. 4. Theology – Study and teaching – Catholic Church. 5. Catholic Church – Education. I. Title.
BX1912.85.S73 2006
253'.25273 – dc22

                            2006013661

1 2 3 4 5 6 7 8 9 10   12 11 10 09 08 07 06

THE
STRUGGLE
FOR
CELIBACY

CONTENTS

ACKNOWLEDGMENTS

The Struggle for Celibacy is based on research performed for my doctoral degree in sociology at Fordham University. This effort is a modest expansion of my doctoral dissertation in which I was mentored by E. Doyle McCarthy of Fordham's Department of Sociology and Anthropology and Mark Massa, S.J., of its Theology Department. I have included more policy recommendations than found their way into the original dissertation with the hope that these recommendations will increase the value of my research to all those interested in the future of the priesthood and the Roman Catholic Church.

I am immensely grateful for those who helped me produce this volume, and I will acknowledge their particular contributions. In spring 2000, I began studying and interviewing New York priests in a course on qualitative research methods with Joseph Lella, a visiting professor from the Department of Sociology at King's College of the University of Western Ontario. Joseph Lella's initial enthusiasm and encouragement led me to continue my research with Michael Cuneo of Fordham's Department of Sociology and Anthropology in two courses the following year. Doing fieldwork in their courses contributed substantially to the research methodologies employed in my research.

Without Dr. McCarthy and Fr. Massa I would have had only a pile of tapes, transcripts, and fieldwork notes. Both brought much necessary keen historical and theoretical knowledge to my topic. Mark gracefully called for clarity in presentation of my thoughts and kept me honest regarding Church history. Doyle is a tireless worker and inspiration to those who know her. It was only after I started working on my dissertation with Doyle that I realized that some of her particular sociological interests and perspectives (culture, knowledge, emotions, symbolic interactionism) were also mine. Doyle demanded epistemological precision from me in my analysis of my interviews and field notes, as well as a theoretical sociological frame for my thoughts. While she never imposed a theoretical perspective on me, she provided great "leads" for my reading. Even while I was writing my dissertation nine hundred miles away, an intellectual kinship overcame the distance. I am deeply grateful to Doyle and Mark for their patience, comments, and everything they did to make this book possible.

I also wish to thank my dissertation readers, John Cecero, S.J., of Fordham's Psychology Department and Lynn Chancer of City University of New York. Lynn was significant in introducing me to the work of Michel Foucault, in whose works I retain a strong interest. I am also grateful to Fordham University for my University Fellowship and Alumni Dissertation Award, which provided financial support for my research. Special thanks to Mary Brauer for typing the interview transcripts and to Raymond Bedwell and Susan Petersen for proofreading my work. I also thank the administration, faculty, and students of all the seminaries where I did research for their cooperation in making this book possible. Lastly, I am extraordinarily grateful for John Jones, Rachel Greer, and John Eagleson at Crossroad Publishing Company for all their help in turning my dissertation into an accessible, readable volume.

INTRODUCTION

In January 2000, during my coursework at Fordham University, I began studying Roman Catholic priests' sexual practices and experiences of celibacy and seminary formation. In my interviews I was struck by the willingness of priests to share intimate details of their journey and their stories of loneliness, promiscuity, as well as contentment in celibacy. For none of them was sexual identity or celibacy an incidental feature of their priesthood. The following winter, I spoke with formators (faculty priests) in nine dioceses about how they trained candidates to live lives of celibacy. In spring 2001, I conducted on-site semi-structured interviews in two eastern dioceses to learn how men were admitted to the seminary and what kind of training they received regarding celibacy. I interviewed vocation directors, members of admission committees, and a psychologist about the recruitment and screening of candidates. Spiritual formation directors described their formation programs, and I talked with students about their vocations and seminary experiences. At one of these seminaries where I was invited to spend as much time as I wished with faculty and students, I began to formulate how I might do a case study of a seminary in which I would have the opportunity to spend several months getting to know students and faculty members.

My initial research led me to focus on the practices involved in the reproduction of celibacy in diocesan seminaries and to exclude the study of screening and admissions procedures. Practices engaged in by seminaries to reproduce celibacy include the spatial enclosure of seminarians, prayer, a prescribed rule of life, and rituals of membership. Learning how these practices produced the culture of seminaries would be more than enough to study. A detailed examination of both admission procedures and seminary formation was not feasible for one research project. A case study approach was chosen as a useful way to study the social processes involved in seminary formation for celibacy. A case study of a particular seminary would provide a representation of how the "sexual regime" of celibacy is reproduced in a diocesan seminary. My fieldwork would record through interviews and observations the practices that the seminary faculty members and students engage in to learn to live lives of celibacy. I would describe the "socialization" process seminarians undergo and provide an account of thoughts, feelings, and behaviors regarding sexuality and celibacy in the culture of the seminary examined. Not only would I seek to learn how celibacy is "taught," but also to learn how faculty and students internalize or give meaning to the practice in their own lives.

It is the contention of this study that seminary formation is a form of professional socialization that seeks to immerse students in Catholic culture (or various versions of it) and that students and faculty use culture in varying ways to make and legitimate their decisions and actions. However, the formation of Catholic priests differs from the training for other professions in its comprehensive scope and intensity. Students and faculty see priesthood as much more than a job or career. Training for priesthood involves more than learning how to perform a series of role-specific tasks (though it includes this as well). Rather, the socialization of religious personnel involves students internalizing and committing themselves in a comprehensive manner to a new social reality and way of life (Berger and Luckmann 1966:145). Seminary formation is an institutional initiation process into this new reality and ethos. This fact makes seminary formation particularly interesting to study and was part of its appeal to the men who enrolled in the seminary studied. Thus the scope of formation for the Catholic priesthood includes areas that in modern life are thought of as "private" or beyond a school or employer's legitimate concern and influence. Especially because of the Church's celibacy requirement, formation programs seek to cultivate the affective and sexual maturity of candidates. For these reasons, seminary formation is a very intense process. This socialization process occurs inside and outside the seminary classroom with seminarians and priest faculty living at the seminary so that a more complete immersion in Catholic culture is fostered.

Qualitative methods often are chosen over quantitative ones when researchers are seeking access to meaning and the culture of populations (Caceres 2000:246). A case study would explore how faculty and students draw on the cultural reservoir of Catholic beliefs and practices to find meaning for themselves and legitimate their own practice of celibacy. What I hoped to learn was the particular way students and faculty draw on Catholic culture (as well as other beliefs and practices) and exercise "agency" by appropriating culture for fashioning their own lives as seminarians and priests. This case study would not seek to render a "still life" picture of seminary culture as much as an account of how culture is used by priests and students to orient their lives toward particular courses of action, especially the practice of celibacy. What is offered in the succeeding chapters, then, is not a unified picture of seminary culture, but an account of how elements of culture are used at a particular site.

It is impossible to generalize from a single case study as to what occurs in all diocesan seminaries. This does not mean that all efforts to speak about other seminaries from my data are proscribed. Something of the general is always found in the particular (Arksey and Knight 1999:58). There are certain basic features that are found in all seminaries. Social processes at work in one seminary may or may not be present in all seminaries. However, this case study seeks to identify findings that have implications for other seminaries. Readers of this case study are encouraged to consider whether or not the social processes at work in the seminary examined here are found in the seminaries with which they are familiar. Readers of this research can then generalize on the basis of correspondence between this case study and seminaries and seminarians with which they are familiar (Arksey and Knight 1999:58–59). In addition, the findings in a single case study may challenge widely held theoretical assumptions or the empirical findings of other studies. A case study can contribute to the theorization of how to best train seminarians, as well as add to the rather limited empirical research on what seminaries actually do to form celibates. Thus, while findings cannot be generalized beyond what the research design can support, a case study can usefully add to our understanding of how celibacy is reproduced.

Based on earlier research done in several other seminaries, I did not find reason to believe that the seminary where the case study was conducted was radically atypical when compared to them. At least some of the behaviors and conflicts observed there are likely to be found in other seminaries.

My case study research was conducted during the fall semester of 2002, a few months after Roman Catholic clergy sexual abuse and its concealment by bishops made headlines across the country. Suddenly seminaries were under scrutiny and a subject of keen interest. People wanted to know if seminary formation somehow contributed to the behavior of abusive priests and how formation could prevent its occurrence. Seminaries quickly became targets of criticism by Catholics of a variety of ideological perspectives.

The Vatican had already ordered an "apostolic visitation" or review of the formation programs of all U.S. seminaries. Of particular concern to the Vatican was seminaries' teaching of Catholic moral doctrine and the means by which seminaries determined the suitability of candidates for ordination. I feared that seminaries, afraid of what I might write, would not grant me the complete access and freedom I needed to do my research. I felt very lucky to find one such seminary that allowed me to interview and observe faculty and students an entire semester.

In this book I attempt to make more transparent how Roman Catholic seminarians are currently trained to lives of celibacy. In chapter 1, I assert that celibacy has long been a means by which the Roman Catholic Church defined itself over and against the secular world. The 2002 revelations of clerical abuse by priests and the failure of many U.S. bishops to appropriately deal with abusive priests and to protect minors has contributed to the decline of celibacy as an esteemed ascetical practice. While only forty years earlier Catholics took it for granted that celibacy was a worthy sacrifice, now some saw the practice as breeding immaturity and pathology. Other Catholics viewed it as a needless obstacle in addressing the Church's acute shortage of priests. In this chapter, I will describe the changed status of celibacy in the American Catholic Church and how, as mandatory celibacy became more contested, training for celibacy became explicit, intentional, and systematic in seminaries. Then I will introduce culture and cultured capacities as a means by which seminaries encourage students to make celibacy a central aspect of their priestly identities. As seminarians are socialized to do so, they come to see themselves as set apart from the laity they will one day serve.

To understand seminary training today, some historical background regarding diocesan seminaries is helpful. In chapter 2, I describe the origins of the policy of mandatory celibacy in the medieval Church and the development of the diocesan seminary after the Council of Trent. Seminaries sought to remove candidates from worldly influence and reinforce the unique character and separateness of the ordained from the unordained. I will review ecclesial documents from the Second Vatican Council on the priesthood and priestly formation. I also will summarize more recent ecclesial documents that legitimate the practice of celibacy and regulate the training of candidates in diocesan seminaries, especially Pope John Paul II's *Pastores Dabo Vobis* (I Will Give You Shepherds) and the American bishops' *Program of Priestly Formation* (fourth edition). John Paul II, who enjoyed much popularity with seminarians, emphasized the distinctiveness of priestly identity consistent with Trent's teaching that ordination imparts an ontological character. His influence significantly shaped the formation programs that seminaries conduct. Then I will summarize spiritual writings on celibacy and empirical research on priesthood and seminary formation.

In chapter 3, I will consider contemporary cultural factors that I believe make a lifelong commitment more challenging. Prominent among these is modernity's privatization of life and heightened emphasis on romantic love and sexual intimacy. Given modern social currents, it is not surprising that celibacy is misunderstood and frequently unappreciated.

Next, I outline how I went about learning how seminarians prepare to live as celibate priests. Because I wanted to learn things that I didn't feel were possible to learn through survey methodologies, I describe how after initial research on several seminaries I came to do a case study of one diocesan seminary. I go into much detail because so little research on celibacy is empirically based, and I believe my objectivity and methodology are the strength of this study. In chapter 4, I specify the personnel involved in seminaries and what procedures I followed to conduct my research in the fall of 2002.

In chapter 5, I report how students came to study for the Catholic priesthood. Since the seminarians that I came to know undertook celibacy as a result of their perceived call to priesthood, it is important to understand the role of their vocation stories in their personal biographies. Through call narratives seminarians made sense of events in their lives and through these stories came to be who they were. These stories, though unique, were patterned or "scripted." In them, the tellers of these stories find reasons to begin to think of themselves as essentially different from those who have not received such calls. In this chapter, I report features of students' vocation narratives and how these are related to celibacy. In their promise of celibacy, diocesan priests make a lifelong commitment to forgo marriage and genital intimacy. However, priestly celibacy is much more than this behavioral expectation. Seminarians and their professors assigned various meanings, both theological and practical, to celibacy. These meanings are closely tied to how they conceived of priesthood. I describe these meanings and how students conceived of priesthood. For students, celibacy becomes a further way to mark themselves as different and unique as priests.

Based on the interviews and observations performed for this case study, I report in some detail in chapter 6 how the selected seminary was meticulously organized to produce commitment. In the sharing of a common residence and daily schedule of activities, little was left to chance in seeking to produce highly dedicated, qualified priests. Nearly every detail of students' lives was addressed by the seminary's formation program and was subject to scrutiny and formal evaluation by the faculty. However, students clearly exercised agency in forming their own identities by emphasizing certain activities over others.

While this was not a stated part of the curriculum, students also learned how to carefully manage the impressions that faculty members and their classmates had of them. This was essential so that they might be evaluated favorably. This skill would also be useful for them as priests, though it would create distance between themselves as religious professionals and the laity they served. However, such impression management also limited the seminary's ability to openly address issues of sexuality and students' freedom to honestly deal with their own thoughts and behaviors. While seminary administrators tout their formation programs as much more systematic and thorough than in the past, I perceive little progress in recent years in enabling students to explore their sexual thoughts and feelings in an honest manner. Church teaching and student discretion clearly continue to inhibit such exploration.

In chapter 7, I summarize my findings and suggest the role that celibacy plays in the formation of students' identities. Whether intended or not, celibacy still distinguishes priests as set apart from and superior to those who live otherwise. I also explore the practice's effects in the structuring of the Church. I suggest how seminary programs promote adjustment to the conditions of life in the seminary, but may not help students sustain themselves outside the highly structured life that seminaries provide. I conclude in chapter 8 with recommendations intended to improve formation for celibacy and possible deleterious effects of current priestly training.

Readers looking for a staunch defense of celibacy or an easy rebuking of the practice will likely be disappointed. I do hope readers will understand those who undertake the asceticism, as well as some of the consequences of its practice in the Church today.

One

PRIESTS, SEMINARIES, AND CELIBACY

PRIESTLY CELIBACY: A BRIEF HISTORY

Most writings in the Church on celibacy are understandably inspirational and idealistic since they operate to ideologize or legitimate celibacy's religious and spiritual values. For centuries, these writings extolled the virtues and superiority of celibacy over married life. In the century after Constantine's Edict of Toleration in 313 legalizing Christianity, martyrdom became much less frequent and was replaced by celibacy as the most celebrated state of Christian holiness. Generally, the Roman Catholic tradition has been ambivalent regarding sexual intercourse, which was often seen as incompatible with holiness and cultic ministry. By today's standards, patristic writings on celibacy appear misogynistic in the way they claim celibacy as a virtuoso form of holiness.[1] In time, celibacy among the Church's priests became a means of associating priests with the sacred realm, setting them apart from the profane everyday realm of sexual and reproductive activity and family life. Procreation tied men and women to the fallen, earthly realm from which Christians were delivered by the resurrection of Christ from the dead. Celibacy separated the priest from the earthly, fleshy realm of transitory things and was a strategy to live with an undivided heart, to represent and serve the eternal realm. In addition, during the patristic period (ending in the mid-seventh century in the West and in the mid-eighth century in the East), God was increasingly seen as non-passable or passionless. By their celibacy, Christians could distance themselves from the uncertainties of human passion and exhibit a detachment that imaged God (Sheldrake 1993:28).

9

Monastic ideals came to be expected of diocesan or secular clergy, though they did not withdraw from "the world" into the desert or monasteries as religious orders and monks did. The first ecclesiastical legislation that attempted to require celibacy of clerics was passed at the Council of Elvira in 306. Whether celibacy was practiced or imposed prior to the Council of Nicaea in 325 is a matter of speculation among scholars. A resolution to require celibacy of all clerics was rejected at the council (McBrien 2002:1).

Controversies regarding the licentiousness of clergy and the alienation of Church property in the tenth and eleventh centuries led to papal efforts to require celibacy.[2] Concerns regarding the children of clergy succeeding to their fathers' benefices increased support and legislation favoring mandatory celibacy for all priests. The Second Lateran Council (1139) made celibacy mandatory for all priests in Western Christianity. Canon 7 of the council pronounced:

> But that the law of continence and purity, so pleasing to God, may become more general among persons constituted in sacred orders, we agree that bishops, priests, deacons, subdeacons, canons regular, monks, and professed clerics who, transgressing the holy precept, have dared to contract marriage, shall be separated. For a union of this kind which has been contracted in violation of ecclesiastical law, we do not regard as matrimony. (Cited by Beaudette 1998:24):

Historian Paul Beaudette (1998) studied how ritual purity beliefs, which were the basis of clerical continence and celibacy, reflected boundary anxieties regarding the Church's relationship to "the world." Beaudette examined ecclesiastical legislation on continence and celibacy from the fourth through the twelfth centuries that led to priests being forbidden to marry at the First and Second Lateran Councils (1123, 1139). This legislation was enacted after the reforms of Pope Gregory VII (1073–85) had successfully begun to separate feudal ecclesiastical, political, and economic entanglements. Reform sought to end priests' and bishops' dependence on feudal lords and the treatment of Church property as secular property. The Gregorian Reform countered state control and interference in Church affairs by secular lords (Beaudette 1998:34). There also was increased stress upon the objective nature of the Real Presence of Christ in the Eucharist and a cultic understanding of priesthood (Beaudette 1998:37).

Not only did the Gregorian Reform establish a more distinct separation of the Church and the world, the sacred and the profane, but also there emerged an "increasingly sharp division of Christian society into two classes, the priestly above the lay" (Beaudette 1998:39). As R. W. Southern (cited by Beaudette 1998:39) states:

> In this view, the Church was a spiritual hierarchy culminating in the Pope; between clergy and laity there was a great gulf fixed; the lowest clerk in the hierarchy was superior to the greatest layman and this superiority had secular as well as spiritual consequences: he belonged to a privileged order, set apart by the conferring of spiritual gifts, judging laymen in his spiritual capacity but himself immune from secular judgment.

The Gregorian Reform also intensified the division of Church into two classes, with clergy above the laity. In this conception clergy were more closely associated with "the Church" and the laity with "the world." In summary, in the medieval period the Church was closely identified with organized society and eventually desired to erect boundaries to divest itself of its secular, feudal entanglements. By the twelfth century, the Church is conceived of as above and separate from the world. This conception of the Church's relationship to the world was maintained for eight hundred years until the Second Vatican Council (1962–65). The practice of celibacy, originating in anxieties regarding ritual impurity, served as a boundary marker between the Church and world and clergy and laity (Beaudette 1998:29). Priests were set apart from the profane realms of sexual, reproductive, familial, and economic activity. Instead, priests were tied to a sacred, heavenly realm through which otherworldly grace was mediated by their sacramental activities. Celibacy was a mark of the clergy's otherworldliness and superiority to the laity.

ORIGINS OF THE DIOCESAN SEMINARY

To counter the challenges of Protestant Reformers, who claimed that many clergy were poorly educated and morally lax, the Council of Trent (1545–63) mandated reforms in the training of candidates for the priesthood and the establishment of diocesan seminaries to better prepare them to live lives of celibacy (White 1989a:2–3). The council assumed a hierarchical worldview in which the Church was above and separated from the world (Beaudette 1998:40). Trent declared that ordination to the priesthood was a sacrament and its effect was to imprint an indelible character on the priest. Joseph White (1989a:3) summarized Trent's teaching on priesthood:

> The priest was distinguished from the unordained by the character of orders, called to a superior life by reason of celibacy. In an ontological, moral, and even social sense the priest's status was superior. The ministry of sacraments was the ordinary sphere of his activity.

Trent's teaching decisively shaped the goals and framework of seminaries for four centuries. Seminaries were to be established in dioceses as schools of perfection, but for the most part the content of their training was left for bishops to determine.

Charles Borromeo, cardinal archbishop of Milan, a vigorous and gifted reformer, was an early seminary founder and was thought to be a model Tridentine bishop. Borromeo opened different seminaries for candidates of various aptitudes for study. His example led to the founding of hundreds of seminaries throughout Italy (White 1989a:7). Though seminaries were slow to develop in France, the Tridentine reform produced figures that had a seminal influence in developing a model of priesthood and in establishing seminaries both in Europe and the United States. The French School, including founding Oratorian Cardinal Bérulle and Jean Jacques Olier, whose Sulpician order founded or staffed several of the earliest American seminaries for diocesan clergy, sought to have seminarians identify closely with the victimhood and priesthood of Christ (White 1989a:14). Sulpician Eugene Walsh summarizes the French School's identification of Jesus Christ and the priest (cited by White 1989a:15):

> The character of Holy Orders confers, as it were, a new nature, a new personality upon the priest. He is drawn by ordination into the personality of Christ, and with Him becomes by state, by ontological reality, an official person. ... According to the essential economy of sanctification the spirit of Jesus is given to the priest by the character of Sacred Orders to continue the life of Jesus, head and sanctifier of His mystical body. ... By this state of headship in which Holy Orders establishes him the priest is obliged to do on earth all [that] Christ does in heaven. He gives Christ's body to the Church to nourish it. ... The relations that the priest has to the Church by reason of Holy Orders is in every respect a created copy of the relation that Christ has to His mystical body, as head of that body.

The priests of the French School emphasized the sacramental character of the priest and his separateness from the laity (White 1989a:15). Their interpretation of Trent's teachings provided the basis for seminary training maintaining boundaries between seminarians and laity, boundaries that would persist after ordination. Olier envisioned seminaries as set apart from the world. This otherworldliness was cultivated by a variety of ascetical practices, which were prized above academic study. Olier's Seminary of Saint-Sulpice long remained the model for Sulpician seminaries in Europe and the United States.

In these seminaries a highly regulated day stressed self-denial and obedience to the house rule. The daily schedule included Eucharist, recitation of the Divine Office, the rosary, meditation, scripture reading, and examination of conscience. Individual spiritual direction played a key role in the student's spiritual development (Kauffman 1988:16). A hallmark of Sulpician seminaries was a method of mental prayer developed by the French School that encouraged identification with the states and attributes of Jesus (White 1989a:16). The seminarian's spiritual exercises were intended to make his identity conform to that of Jesus Christ as priest-victim. Training emphasized preparation for the *priestly state* rather than practical preparation for priestly ministry (Kauffman 1988:21). The seminary "was the means by which one was separated from the world, was elevated to the dignity of priesthood, and was prepared to return to the world fortified with a spirituality and outlook intended for the edification of the faithful" (Kauffman 1988:18). Emphasis on the spiritual disposition of candidates sought to develop a more highly motivated, less venal clergy in response to challenges by Protestant Reformers, who complained of the corruption of sixteenth-century clergy.

While the establishment of seminaries provided more rigorous academic and spiritual training for seminarians, it also "deliberately set out to inculcate students in the attitudes and behaviour patterns of a spirituality of separation, of a priestly caste spiritually superior to the laity" (Sheldrake 1993:29). As Kauffman (1988:20) points out, seminaries presented:

> the priestly vocation in a style of puritanical idealism, the priesthood was a call to the life of perfection, and celibacy was a necessary condition of such perfection in order to promote the kingdom of God. Sexuality was a necessary evil of the life of imperfection in order to promote and increase human population.

That seminaries should separate priesthood candidates from "the world" was not unique to U.S. Sulpician-founded diocesan seminaries. Commenting on seminary formation in the period 1910 to 1962, White observed, "At the beginning of the era, seminary methods appear to have been designed to isolate seminarians as much as possible from contact with the external and practical aspects of the priest's activities" (1989a:342). Developments in the 1940s and 1950s, and at the Second Vatican Council, led to changes in the training of seminarians. In the 1960s, seminary programs came under criticism for isolating seminarians from the world and limiting contact to other seminarians and priests. Formation programs were faulted for an "emphasis on obedience and docility" that allegedly "bred immature, passive, and apathetic personalities" (White 1989a:414). Even when seminaries began to admit a small number of lay students in the 1970s, a separate residential community for formation has remained the norm for diocesan seminaries.

ECCLESIAL STATEMENTS ON PRIESTLY CELIBACY AND SEMINARY FORMATION SINCE THE SECOND VATICAN COUNCIL

Prior to the pontificate of Pope John Paul II (1978–2005), the two most important recent statements of Church teachings on celibacy were the Second Vatican Council's *Presbyterorum Ordinis* (On the Life and Ministry of Priests, 1975b)[3] and Paul VI's *Sacerdotalis Caelibatus* (On Priestly Celibacy, 1967).

Presbyterorum Ordinis contains the most extensive treatment of celibacy of any of the Second Vatican Council's documents. In it, priestly celibacy is said to express and increase "pastoral charity," or the priest's generous service to others. Priests, it said,

> ... more readily cling to him [Christ] with an undivided heart and dedicate themselves more freely in him and though him to the service of God and men. They are less encumbered in their service to the kingdom and of the task of heavenly regeneration (Second Vatican Council 1975b: no. 16).

A priest's calling involved a complete "gift of self" to God and the Church that excluded exclusive relationships with men or women as well as family life. In *Sacerdotalis Caelibatus,* the advantages of celibacy also were reflected in the priest's sharing "in the dignity and mission of the Mediator and eternal Priest; this sharing will be more perfect the freer the sacred minister is from the bonds of flesh and blood" (Paul VI 1967: no. 21).

Besides enabling undivided pastoral service, *Presbyterorum Ordinis* asserted that there are several ways in which celibacy is fitting. The eschatological benefit of celibacy was that it acted as a reminder that Christians are ultimately destined for "resurrection in the Lord" when our earthly bodies are transformed in Christ.[4] Celibacy, it was reasoned, proclaimed the final stage of salvation where "in the Resurrection they neither marry or are given in marriage but are all like the angels in heaven" (Matt. 22:30). Celibacy was also viewed as a form of imitation of Christ's own celibacy (Second Vatican Council 1975b: no. 16). The decree, citing the Gospel of Matthew (19:12), asserted that Jesus himself recommended celibacy. Some exegetes have taken exception to this interpretation and hold that Jesus was recommending continence for marriages that have ended in separation or divorce (Schneiders 1986:10–21). The decree also underlined that celibacy was a gift freely given by God that can only properly be accepted by the priest's free choice (Second Vatican Council 1975b: no. 2). Significantly, avoidance of contact with women to preserve cultic purity was not an argument for celibacy used in the decree, a major departure from previous Catholic teachings.

Published amid increasing questions about mandatory celibacy for priests, Paul VI's *Sacerdotalis Caelibatus* (1967) recapitulated the themes found in *Presbyterorum Ordinis*. The christological reason offered for celibacy was that a priest's celibacy imitates Christ's example and is a response to follow Jesus so closely that a priest can belong to no one but Christ (Paul VI 1967: nos. 19–25). The ecclesiological reason for celibacy was that in sharing Christ's love for the Church, the priest seeks a bond with the Church that is exclusive (Paul VI 1967: nos. 26–31). The pastoral reason for celibacy was the greater freedom to serve God and the Church unencumbered (Paul VI 1967: no. 32). Celibacy's eschatological value was that it reminded Christians that their deepest attachments are beyond this world (Paul VI 1967: nos. 33–34). Paul VI (1967: nos. 65, 81) recommended that priests pray fervently to persevere in celibacy and expressed compassion for those who struggle with it. He added that dispensations from priestly ministry may be granted to those who for grave reasons are "not fit" to live celibately as priests (Paul VI 1967: nos. 83–90). Among the grave reasons cited by Paul VI are a lack of faith and immoral behavior, especially when they are a source of scandal to the Church.

Post–Second Vatican Council Church pronouncements on the training of priests called for increased attention to both the screening and formation of seminary candidates. The decline in the number of vocations in U.S. seminaries received particular attention from Pope John Paul II. In 1981, he mandated an apostolic visitation (official visit from a committee headed by a bishop) of all U.S. college and graduate-level seminaries. After examinations of all seminaries by teams of evaluators were completed, Cardinal William Baum of the Vatican Congregation for Catholic Education pronounced the work of most major seminaries as "generally satisfactory" but also voiced some concerns, calling for greater emphasis on "priestly identity" and caution about the mixing of clerical and lay students in seminaries, which began in some theologates and diocesan seminaries after the Second Vatican Council (Baum 1986:223). While not prohibiting lay students from attending seminaries in small numbers, Cardinal Baum called on seminaries to promote a better understanding of the distinctiveness of ordained ministry. He also praised the ways in which seminaries were forming students for "lifelong priestly celibacy" and encouraged them to strengthen their existing spiritual formation programs (Baum 1986:232).

In 1990, Pope John Paul II convened an international Synod of Bishops on "The Formation of Priests in the Circumstances of Today." If there was confusion regarding the identity and purpose of the priesthood, the synod sought to clarify these matters and their implications for seminary formation. As a follow-up to the Synod, John Paul issued *Pastores Dabo Vobis* (1993). It remains the definitive statement of John Paul II on the meaning of priesthood, celibacy, and the formation of priests. In this work he spoke of a need to "emerge from the crisis of priestly identity," which he said arose from a distortion of the Second Vatican Council's teachings and led to resignations from the priesthood and a decline in vocations (John Paul II 1993: no. 11). In the exhortation, he recalled the Synod's affirmation of the permanence of the Western Church's discipline of celibacy saying, "The Synod does not wish to leave any doubts in the mind of anyone regarding the Church's firm will to maintain the law that demands perpetual and freely chosen celibacy" (John Paul II 1993: no. 29).

John Paul II reiterated reasons for celibacy stated in *Presbyterorum Ordinis* and *Sacerdotalis Caelibatus*. He then highlighted another motivation for mandatory celibacy by linking it with a "nuptial relationship to Church." This well-known theological (and rhetorical) claim symbolizes the Church as the spouse of

Christ and the celibate priest as a figure, like Christ, given over to total love and sacrifice. In John Paul's words (1993: no. 29):

> The will of the Church finds its ultimate motivation in the *link between celibacy and sacred Ordination,* which configures the priest to Jesus Christ the Head and Spouse of the Church. The Church, as the Spouse of Christ, wishes to be loved by the priest in the total and exclusive manner in which Jesus Christ, her Head and Spouse loved her. Priestly celibacy, then, is the self *in* and *with* Christ *to* Church and expresses the priest's service to the Church in and with the Lord [emphasis in the original].

Seen as a form of spousal relationship, celibacy is a form of intimate communion and total dedication to the person of Christ and a sharing in the dedication of Christ to the Church. The love and care of the priest for those he serves was seen as analogously related to the love and care of a spouse for his family.

Pope John Paul II (1993: no. 43), for the first time in Church pronouncements, stated that besides intellectual, spiritual, and pastoral formation, seminaries should engage in "human formation." This dimension of formation is described as the foundation of all priestly formation and is associated with affective maturity and education regarding sexuality and chastity (John Paul II 1993: no. 44). Pope John Paul II said that the world today is not supportive of the celibate commitment and that training regarding sexuality has become "more difficult but also more urgent" (1993: no. 44).

The pope's exhortation led to the revision and publication of the fourth edition of the *Program of Priestly Formation* for U.S. seminaries (National Conference of Catholic Bishops [NCCB]: 1993). These guidelines are currently undergoing revision by the U.S. bishops for a fifth edition. The 1993 text provided guidelines for the formation of seminarians and the operation of seminaries based on *Pastores Dabo Vobis* and the *Ratio Fundamentalis Institutionis Sacerdotalis* (Basic Norms for Priestly Formation), the Holy See's guidelines for seminaries all over the world (Sacred Congregation for Catholic Education 1985). These guidelines enable the hierarchy of the Church to more closely regulate and coordinate the training of priests. They achieve this through greater standardization so that seminaries will accomplish the outcomes the Holy See has mandated. Guidelines for formation in celibacy are described in the document as receiving heightened attention since its last revision in 1981. This new emphasis was made because the "social climate in the United States often can hinder capacity for lifelong celibate commitment and undermine the social support system on which it depends" (NCCB 1993: no. 15). Formation for celibacy is also challenged by "a widespread tolerance of sexual behavior contrary to Catholic teaching" (NCCB 1993: no. 16). Compared to earlier editions, this edition paid greater attention in its guidelines to the meaning of celibacy, practical perspectives on spiritual formation and community life, and implications for admissions and evaluations.

These tasks are likely to be even more critical for seminaries today. In the past, candidates were often admitted into high school and college seminaries at much younger ages. They spent eight to twelve years in "formation," where they were observed and those not deemed appropriate for ordination by faculties were "weeded out" over time. Today's seminarians have fewer fixed points of familial, social, or religious reference, often having been away from the Church for several years. Odd as it may seem, they seek ordination but frequently have had little contact with the Church. Seminary candidates are more diverse than in the past. Today many seminarians are entering seminaries after college and with work experience of several years. They are likely to be thirty to forty years old and even older. Candidates bring a broad range of experiences. They are likely to have dated, had long-term relationships with women and men, including sexual relationships, and perhaps even have been married and divorced.

In November 2005, the Sacred Congregation for Catholic Education released an instruction on the admission of homosexuals to seminaries and holy orders (2005). While the document raised accusations of discrimination against gay men, some were left doubting that the document would significantly alter most seminaries' admission practices or formation programs. The instruction directed that sexually active homosexuals, those who participate in gay subcultures, and men with deep-seated homosexual tendencies be excluded from seminary. However, I believe that gay men who promise to live celibately and agree not to publicly identify themselves as gay are likely to continue to be admitted to U.S. seminaries. The instruction, nevertheless, is likely to drive gay candidates further into the "closet" and make it more difficult for formation programs to create an atmosphere where candidates can discuss sexual matters openly. By making homosexual seminarians fearful of appropriate self-disclosures, the policy may also inhibit gay seminarians and priests from developing supportive relationships necessary for living chastely and celibately. If gay seminarians are stigmatized, their homosexuality may become an even greater preoccupation, a source of shame, and lead to further isolation (Stanosz 2005b:8).

POST–SECOND VATICAN COUNCIL
SPIRITUAL WRITINGS ON CELIBACY

Post–Second Vatican Council authors often describe celibacy in personalist, psychological, and therapeutic terms. In the influential *The Sexual Celibate* by Donald Goergen (1975), "healthy" celibates are said to be sexual, though they do not engage in genital activity. Sexual celibates seek friendship and non-genital intimacy. Instead of renouncing their bodies, celibates are chastised if they fail to "get in touch with them [their bodies]" (Zullo n.d.:9). "Healthy" celibacy excluded genital intimacy, but included emotionally intimate relationships with men and women. While celibacy may still hold the possibility of a deeper relationship with God, this relationship was no longer seen as enhanced by withdrawing from transitory human relationships into an eternal sacred realm.

While genital activity is still prohibited, celibacy is commonly legitimated in therapeutic, humanistic terms as a strategy for self-actualization. Indeed, celibate priests are called to be "fully human" and to seek "intimacy, relationship, affirmation, and acceptance" (Zullo n.d.:9). In some respects, these contemporary constructions of celibacy may require more training, effort, and skill than disciplining seminarians to "renounce the world" and avoid women and sex. Whereas in the past, human attachments were seen as a barrier to holiness and emotionally intimate relationships were to be avoided, now a celibate priest is expected to cultivate them. Formators said priests were supposed to be capable of having close relationships in order to be a "healthy" celibate and "self-actualized person."[5] At the same time, with self-actualization and personal fulfillment as norms, it may be more difficult to legitimate the prohibition of genital intimacy. Conflicts with celibacy may arise if priests come to believe that genital expression rather than prohibition better serves their needs for self-actualization and intimacy. The expectation that priests ought to be adept at cultivating friendship and non-genital intimacy has likely increased the demands placed on seminary formators to form candidates with high levels of affective and psychosexual maturity.

George Aschenbrenner's *Quickening the Fire in Our Midst: The Challenge of Diocesan Priestly Spirituality* (2002) mixed new and more traditional approaches to celibacy and sought to respond to the postconciliar problems posed by what John Paul II called "a crisis of priestly identity" in *Pastores Dabo Vobis* (1993). The widely read spiritual writer drew on his experiences as Jesuit novice director and spiritual director of American seminarians at Rome's North American College. Aschenbrenner developed a fresh approach to the issue of priestly identity and offered practical help toward achieving that "renewed identity." He asserted that the diocesan priesthood has "its own distinctive configuration to Christ" and that this configuration "has its own unique empowerment" (Aschenbrenner 2002).

Aschenbrenner maintained that this identity is rooted in an affective relationship with Jesus and an active ministry performed in the midst of an everyday, increasingly secularized world. The purpose of the ordained priesthood is to affirm and enable the universal priesthood of all believers. Throughout the work, Aschenbrenner consistently sought to specify what is unique to the life and ministry of diocesan priests and to distinguish that life and ministry from religious life and the lay apostolate.

He developed the image of the diocesan priest as "mystagogue" aflame with "divine fire" (2002:5). By this he meant that a priest is a person who has experienced God's love and guides other believers into the mystery of God's love for them. Aschenbrenner believes that the priest through ordination "has a unique power to administer that fire, to call it down from heaven, to summon it forth into our midst" (5).

While priests are called to live a distinctively different lifestyle that includes the renunciation of genital activity, Aschenbrenner cautioned that celibacy should not be confused with isolation or loneliness. The celibate commitment of the diocesan priest is possible only when supported by a strong affective relationship with God and a life of faith and ministry shared with the priests of his diocese and with the laity to whom and with whom he ministers. As in *Pastores Dabo Vobis*, celibacy is linked to the evangelical virtues of simplicity, obedience, and prayerfulness.

Like many other post–Vatican II spiritual writers, including Pope John Paul II in *Pastores Dabo Vobis* (1993), Aschenbrenner insisted that celibacy, in itself, does not limit human affectivity. Nor should friendships be avoided. Rather, emotional intimacy and friendships are a confirmation of a vocation to priesthood (Aschenbrenner 2002:112–13). Celibacy should be lived in a communitarian fashion. Communitarian celibacy counters loneliness and is an antidote to the excessive individualism that Aschenbrenner says characterizes American society. A communitarian approach to celibacy is fostered by the presbyterate's collective vision and mission and guards against isolation and a "lone ranger" mentality in the priesthood and ministry.

Aschenbrenner's effort is an interesting one that seeks to integrate the humanistic orientation of early post–Vatican II writings on celibacy with John Paul II's spousal imagery and rationale for celibacy. In addition, Aschenbrenner promoted celibacy as a challenge to many of the negative cultural currents that John Paul II has criticized (excessive individualism and autonomy, secularism, promiscuity, among others). It is more critical and pessimistic in its orientation to the world than the early postconciliar spiritual writings.

EMPIRICAL RESEARCH ON
CELIBACY AND PRIESTHOOD

The period after the Second Vatican Council, particularly the 1980s and 1990s, produced an abundance of books about celibacy, which fall under the categories of "spirituality" and "self-help." However, there has been very little empirical study of how diocesan or religious priests actually live out their respective promises or vows. Clerical celibacy is a topic where rumors and anecdotal evidence exceed research and empirical findings.

Andrew Greeley and his colleagues at the National Opinion Research Center reported in 1972 that difficulties with the institutional structure of the Church and the desire to marry were the principal reasons for priests to resign (Greeley 1972:258–59) and that loneliness was a major factor in resignations (Greeley 1972:211). Priests who were dissatisfied with priestly ministry were most likely to report dissatisfaction with celibacy. Greeley (1972:244–47) also reported that there was no evidence to indicate that substantial numbers of priests were engaged in dating or courtship activities with men or women. Greeley did not address incidences of homosexual relations.

In *The Catholic Priest in the United States: Psychological Investigations* (1972), Eugene C. Kennedy and Victor J. Heckler reported the findings of a major study of U.S. priests, whose emotional maturation was assessed through a variety of psychological instruments and clinical interviews. A multistage developmental framework, based on the work of developmental psychologist Erik Erikson, was used for understanding and interpreting the lives of those studied. Out of 271 priests with whom clinical interviews were conducted, 179 were classified as "underdeveloped" and 23 as "maldeveloped" (Kennedy and Heckler 1972:51–52). The greatest difficulty underdeveloped priests faced was in their ability to form appropriate, intimate relationships (Kennedy and Heckler 1972:9). However, the emotional maturity of U.S. priests as measured by the Personality Orientation Inventory compared favorably with that of other American men (Kennedy and Heckler 1972:65). While priests as a group were no less healthy than other U.S. males, the failure of most to reach full maturity was seen as disappointing, given the careful selection and training process they had undergone.

Kennedy and Heckler also reported that Catholic priests engage in a variety of "defense mechanisms" to fend off unpleasant feelings and sexual thoughts. Among maldeveloped and underdeveloped priests, intellectualization was frequently used to manage feelings and distance themselves from people, especially in relationships with women (Kennedy and Heckler 1972:8, 60, 85). Kennedy and Heckler raised questions regarding the structuring of seminary programs. They suggested that the isolation and strictly adhered-to daily schedules of pre–Second Vatican Council seminaries encouraged dependency, passivity, and emotional immaturity (Kennedy and Heckler 1972:178–79, 202–3).

Sociologist Dean Hoge of Catholic University of America, who has extensively studied American Catholic priests, estimated that about one in seven priests ordained in the 1990s resigned from ministry within five years of ordination, up from 8 to 12 percent in the 1980s (2002:2). Hoge conducted a national survey of active and resigned priests and found that nearly half of those who resigned reported that loneliness and celibacy were their greatest problems. Among all priests surveyed, satisfaction or dissatisfaction with celibacy was the strongest variable affecting overall priestly satisfaction (Hoge 2002:37). Hoge claimed that many newly ordained priests felt ill-prepared to deal with the loneliness and isolation of priesthood after enjoying an active community life in seminary. "Seminary training hadn't prepared them for this type of life. The priests have to be told, have to be trained in leading this isolated life" (Briggs 2001:1).

Psychotherapist A. W. Richard Sipe's *A Secret World: Sexuality and the Search for Celibacy* (1990) was based largely on clinical interviews and reports with fifteen hundred people. One-third of the informants were priests receiving psychotherapy. Another third of the informants were not patients, but were clergy who shared information in meetings, interviews, and consultations individually and in small groups. The last third were laymen and laywomen, clergy, and professed women religious who had been in sexual relationships with priests, or were victims of clerical sexual abuse, or had directly observed such relationships and/or abuse (Sipe 1990:8). It is problematic that his research was not based on a random sample, but largely on those who were in therapy or were in relationships with priests. As psychologist John Allan Loftus (1999) noted regarding Sipe's work, "From a statistical point of view, there is still much rumor passing as fact" (13). Sipe defined celibacy as a lifelong growth process and much more than sexual abstinence. By his lofty criteria, only 2 percent of all priests "achieve celibacy" (Sipe 1990:263). In his subsequent work, *Sex, Priests, and Power: Anatomy of a Crisis,* Sipe (1995) described what he termed the Roman Catholic Church's "celibate/sexual system." While continuing to hold celibacy in high regard, Sipe denounced what he saw as deceptions in the way the Catholic Church dealt with sexuality and the misconduct of priests. Sipe construed mandatory celibacy as a strategy to concentrate power in the hands of men and subjugate women. Sipe and other critics of mandatory celibacy allege that this policy, combined with the denial of ordination to women, results in the concentration of ecclesiastical power in the hands of unmarried men. Sipe (1995:161–80) argued that these policies reinforced patriarchal structures in the Church and larger society and excluded women from positions of leadership.

Though written as an account of clinical findings, Sipe's work frequently departed from any pretense of value-neutrality in his examination of Church policy and practices. In addition to the other problems with Sipe's research cited above, his moral framework and high criteria as to what constitutes celibacy are not useful for a social scientist seeking an understanding of the behavior of most priests or an "average" diocesan priest. However, Sipe is noteworthy because he has been so widely cited and interviewed as an expert on clergy sexual abuse and can certainly provide insights into the difficulties inherent in celibate lives.

Raymond Hedin's *Married to the Church* (1995) is an absorbing ethnography based on interviews with the 1969 ordination class of Milwaukee's St. Francis Seminary. Hedin probed the experiences of both active and resigned priests to uncover their struggles with Church authority and celibacy and what they found satisfying in their ministry as priests. American society's tumult of the

1960s and the Roman Catholic Church's Second Vatican Council significantly marked these priests' lives. Those who remained priests (twenty-two of thirty) renegotiated their priesthood and relationship to the Church to find satisfaction in ministry in a church of which they were often suspicious and hostile.

Their journeys and "renegotiations" were usually articulated in the idiom of popular psychology and notions of self-actualization (Hedin 1995:119). Many reported feeling emasculated by a Church that they perceived to be controlling both their personal and ministerial lives. As a result, loneliness was their almost-constant companion (Hedin 1995:96–97). Feeling emasculated by mandatory celibacy, many of these priests sought more instrumental rewards in ministry, such as financial compensation and more training for a higher professional status (traditional masculine sources of self-esteem) (Hedin 1995:162,166). Thus, celibacy was generally not seen as an enhancement of their persons or ministry, but was accepted to varying degrees as part of "the terms of employment." Little effort was made by Hedin's informants to give meaning or legitimacy to their practice of celibacy, except as a legal requirement. Given this fact, it is little wonder that many expressed deep levels of resentment and anger. Hedin did not significantly explore what meaning celibacy had for his informants as seminarians or the degree to which they thought about it. While in seminary they appear to have focused primarily on what they would accomplish in ministry and their high hopes for a rapid transformation of the Church by the changes initiated by the Second Vatican Council.

RECENT EMPIRICAL RESEARCH ON SEMINARIES

Current studies have pointed to a decline in the academic abilities of students entering both Catholic and non-Catholic seminaries. The scores of prospective seminarians on the Graduate Record Exam (GRE) declined in the 1980s, though the scores of all test takers rose (Chaves 2003:39). Chaves reports a substantial gender gap in GRE scores, with females consistently outperforming males, a basis for optimism for religious groups whose clergy are increasingly female. This source of optimism for religious groups is not currently available, of course, to the Catholic Church (Chaves 2003:39).

Since the 1990s seminary formation for celibacy is said to be much more intentional and systematic. Psychology and more careful screening are thought to have brought improvements in training for celibacy (Schuth 2004). In seminaries today, psychotherapy has found a place alongside of (and sometimes jostling with) these and other traditional religious practices. At one large East Coast seminary I visited, all first-year seminarians were encouraged to undertake psychotherapy. Referral of seminarians to therapists for counseling is commonplace in some seminaries. In addition, seminaries use batteries of psychological testing to screen applicants prior to their admission.

Seminaries, Theologates, and the Future of Church Ministry by Katarina Schuth (1999) provided a useful overview of Roman Catholic seminary formation and education. The work was based on interviews and questionnaires in all forty-two U.S. seminaries and schools of theology that train laity and diocesan and religious order priests. Its aim was to provide a general picture and appraisal of the state of preparation for lay and ordained ministry, including strengths and weaknesses in seminary training. Schuth provided the best available account of changes and trends in Catholic ministerial formation since the late 1980s.

Among the strengths Schuth reported are improvements in the professionalism of management practices and the governance of seminaries (1999:98). She also found shifts in the academic curriculum and formation program that she believed will better prepare students to serve in an increasingly pluralistic and ethnically diverse American Catholic Church. Schuth (1999:90) also reported that education on sexuality greatly increased in the last ten years in seminaries, but provides hardly any information or details about this.

Among the critical concerns Schuth noted is the difficulty that seminaries reported in recruiting students with an aptitude for ministry. Many men seeking entrance to seminaries lacked the intellectual skills and familiarity with Church practices necessary to begin intellectual and pastoral formation for the priesthood

(Schuth 1999:79–85). Today's candidates are likely to be more eclectic and idiosyncratic in their spiritual practices than those before the Second Vatican Council.

Schuth found an increased diversity of ages, racial backgrounds, and experiences in the Church in the histories of the men entering seminaries. Men entering theologates were typically older than in the past and often described having had religious conversions and relatively little recent contact with parish communities. She did not address the particular motivations of seminarians to enter ministry and promise celibacy. Schuth (1999:74–79) offered a brief religious profile of men entering seminaries and theologates at the time of her research and found that at least one-third of the men had undergone a conversion or reconversion experience, while others are recent converts to Catholicism. Others of this group have returned to the Church after many years of non-practice. Some entered the seminary following a significant prayer experience, participation in a large rally celebrating a visit by Pope John Paul II, a pilgrimage to Medjugorie, or involvement in "pro-life" activities. Another fifth of the seminarians did not report a conversion experience, but said they had little contact with the Church in the past. However, they felt called to be priests. This group knew what it meant to be indifferent to religion, but now sought greater meaning and direction for their lives. They were "searchers" who hoped to find stability and purpose in life as priests. Another group that is small, but is reported to be having significant impact, Schuth (1999) characterizes as "those who have a rigid understanding of their faith, the Church, and their potential role in it" (77). They were seeking to "correct the wrongs of Second Vatican Council" and demand a return to a traditional Church that they had not grown up with themselves, but to which they claimed allegiance (Schuth 2001:19). The fourth group that Schuth described is those that are deeply rooted in the faith and in local faith communities. They had participated in worship and religious education in local parishes, had a long-term commitment to Catholicism, and possessed a sense of the larger Catholic tradition and universal Church. "Most theologates would be delighted to find one-third or even one-fourth of all their students with this profile, a striking change from thirty years ago when virtually all seminarians belonged to this group" (75).

The changed character of seminary populations is certain to pose new challenges to formators as they prepare seminarians to live celibate lives. Older candidates are more likely to have had a much broader variety of experience than candidates admitted to seminary high schools and colleges at age fourteen or eighteen, as most seminarians were in the 1940s and 1950s. At the same time, older candidates are frequently less adaptable in conforming to expectations of formators and may have greater difficulty addressing personal habits or dispositions that impede effective ministry and celibate living.

Because candidates are now likely to enter the seminary after graduating from college, they have only four to six years to be formed and evaluated by seminary administrators. In the past, "lifers" entered as freshmen in high school and spent twelve years in formation. In addition, seminarians with little prior recent experience with parish life might have made vocational decisions based on romanticized images of priesthood. Such seminarians have little familiarity with the actual day-to-day ministry of priests. They have sometimes made significant vocational decisions with little formal religious training or counsel. With seminarians' diverse experiences and contact with the Church before entering, seminary formation programs have had to adapt their efforts for changed populations.

A contested question was how to best promote the development of a priestly identity in seminarians (Schuth 1999:127–31). At issue, according to Schuth, is the question of choosing the best model of seminary. A distinction is made between "self-contained seminaries" and "interconnected seminaries" as contexts for theological education. Self-contained seminaries enroll only candidates for the priesthood and are more likely to be operated by dioceses. In them, contact with people beyond the seminary is minimized. Interconnected seminaries enroll both candidates for priesthood and for lay ministry. Schools conducted by religious orders are likely to be the interconnected model. Some dioceses operate interconnected schools as well. Schuth said these seminaries are characterized by greater contacts outside the seminary in parishes and the larger community. The alleged strength of the first model is that it inculcates a stronger sense of priestly identity and conveys the distinctiveness of the priest's role. The alleged strength of the latter model is that it prepares seminarians better for collaborative ministry with laity in local parishes. Supporters of the second model maintain that priestly identity is strengthened by contact with laity. Schuth does not address to what extent disagreements over what model is appropriate result from disagreements regarding the nature of priesthood.

In 2002, the U.S. bishops approved the Charter for the Protection of Children and Young People, a set of procedures to address allegations of sexual abuse, including guidelines for reconciliation, healing, accountability, and prevention. The Charter established a group of laypeople — the National Review Board for the Protection of Children and Young People — to study the causes of the crisis. For its *Report on the Crisis in the Catholic Church in the United States* (2004), the review board's research committee interviewed eighty-five individuals including bishops, priests, seminarians, theologians, victims of clergy abuse, psychiatrists, civil and canon lawyers, law enforcement officials, and other knowledgeable laypeople. It also consulted studies and public records relating to abuse, as well as several Church documents. Roughly one-fifth of the commission's report deals with seminary formation from the 1950s forward.

The report places the blame for some of the clerical misconduct on pre–Vatican II seminaries that were inundated with candidates who received too little attention and scrutiny. Of formation for celibacy, it asserts "sexuality was not meaningfully discussed" (National Review Board 2004:74). Formation was more exclusively intellectual, with less attention paid to issues of human maturity. On the other hand, the board cites the decline in vocations after the council as resulting in pressure to ordain unfit candidates. The report also claims that after the Second Vatican Council, formation in some seminaries sowed confusion due to moral relativism, neglect of the Church's moral teachings, an overreliance on psychology, inadequate attention to spiritual concerns, a growing homosexual subculture, and tolerance of sexual activity engaged in by seminarians and faculty (National Review Board 2004:75–77). The report's comments add credence to Michael Rose's (2002) scathing traditionalist indictment of 1970s and 1980s seminaries as heterodox hothouses of homosexuality. However, the report's recall of the period is largely based on the anecdotal recollections of bishops. At the same time, anecdotal accounts by disaffected seminarians of the period are consistent with the board's description of the era (Heinz 2004).

The report is confident that improved formation and screening is producing better-prepared candidates for ordination. Whether or not this is the case has not been empirically verified, and shortcomings in formation usually have been apparent only in retrospect. The National Review Board recommends that seminaries deal with "issues of sexual conduct more openly and more forthrightly" (2004:78). The report places great emphasis on the role of bishops in selecting and approving candidates, as well as being familiar with the personal struggles of their priests regarding celibacy. Psychological evaluations are "not a substitute for the exercise of good judgment by a bishop, who should get to know every potential candidate for the priesthood before the candidate is accepted into the seminary" (National Review Board 2004:71–72). He should know his seminaries and be involved in their formation programs. Bishops should also become familiar with their seminarians so that they can determine their suitability for ordination (National Review Board 2004:79). Bishops are expected to be familiar enough with their priests to be able to refer them for counseling or other forms of assistance. The review board squarely places responsibility on bishops for the quality and maturity of their seminarians and priests.

While such responsibility is rightly placed on bishops, one wonders how familiar bishops can truly be with their candidates and priests, especially with every applicant for the seminary. Now that one-quarter of all priests in U.S. seminaries come from foreign countries, it is unlikely that bishops would know these candidates well before acceptance by the diocese. The large number of foreign-born applicants presents greater challenges for all seminary and diocesan personnel in learning the background of applicants. Most priests see their bishops infrequently, and then usually at large public meetings and liturgical gatherings.

The failures in oversight and leadership by the bishops compounded the abuse problem and resulted in the current crisis. Priests experiencing personal difficulties may want to keep their distance from bishops and diocesan officials, fearing interference with their ability to minister. However, the board clearly wants to put the bishops on notice that it will hold them accountable for priests' future misconduct.

Two

CELIBACY AND CONTEMPORARY CATHOLICISM

Since the Second Vatican Council (1962–65), the policy of mandatory celibacy has frequently been challenged. I will describe here some of the issues and the parties involved in supporting and contesting requiring celibacy of priests. While formal training for celibacy receives much attention in seminaries today, this was not always the case. Prior to the 1970s, comparatively little time was spent in seminaries training students to live celibately. Seminarians knew the promise of celibacy was a prerequisite for ordination, and they were not permitted to "date" women or associate with women. They may have thought of celibacy as a "sacrifice," but in the Church of the 1940s and 1950s it was a highly esteemed and much lauded sacrifice. Marriage was an impediment to holy orders, but celibacy was no impediment to filling the many new or enlarged seminaries of the 1950s and 1960s with eager students.[6] Celibacy was taken for granted as an essential part of priesthood and was supported in the larger Catholic culture. For a number of important reasons, including the recent and very public crisis of the American Church regarding sexual abuse by priests, celibacy is no longer a widely esteemed commitment. In fact, celibates have become an increasingly suspect "sexual minority." Today celibacy is a distinctive but highly contested feature of the Catholic priesthood. This is clearly linked to the loss of priestly legitimacy due to the sexual scandals. But polls have also shown a public critical of the idea that priests cannot marry. A poll published in the March 6, 2002, issue of *Newsweek* found that 73 percent of U.S. Catholics believe that priests should be allowed to marry. Other research has associated the worldwide decline in the number of priests since the mid-1960s with the Church's policy of mandatory celibacy.[7]

CELIBACY: A CONTROVERSIAL ISSUE

The late Pope John Paul II and his successor, Pope Benedict XVI, along with other Church authorities have been unwavering in their defense of mandatory celibacy, considering the continuance of the practice a closed question. At the 1992 Synod of Bishops convened on the topic of the priesthood, John Paul II stated that "the Synod does not wish to leave any doubts in the mind of anyone regarding the Church's firm will to maintain the law that demands perpetual and freely chosen celibacy" (John Paul II 1993: no. 29). Furthermore, support for mandatory celibacy has been seen as a prerequisite for advancement in the Church's hierarchy (Bruni 2003:8). The more critics called for celibacy to be made optional, the more the Vatican appeared intent on safeguarding the requirement.

The need for sociological research into how seminaries train men to live celibately is suggested by several factors. Especially since the mid-1960s there is public evidence that many priests have failed to live the celibate ideal. Many priests have resigned from the priesthood in order to marry, though their exact number is difficult to calculate precisely. According to the *New York Times*, in the twenty years after the Second Vatican Council, between 70,000 and 100,000 priests worldwide "left the priesthood" in order to marry (Sweeney 1992:24). Resignations from the priesthood have continued in recent years, with an estimated 15 percent of those ordained in the 1990s resigning from active ministry within five years of ordination (Hoge 2002:2). Studies of both active and resigned priests have found dissatisfaction with formation for celibacy, especially faulting seminaries for a lack of depth and frankness regarding celibacy and sexuality (Walsh, Mayer, Castelli, Hemrick, Blanchette, and Theroux 1995; Hoge 2002).

The failure of some priests to live a life of celibacy has also been made public by priests dying from AIDS. Accurate estimates of the number of priests who have died from AIDS are difficult to obtain, because state death records are closed in two-thirds of the United States. However, a *Kansas City Star* investigation documented more than three hundred AIDS-related priests' deaths

(Thomas 2000:1). The *Star* examined death records and did family interviews to find the cases. The death rate of priests due to AIDS in the fourteen states studied was more than double that of all adult males and more than six times the general population (Thomas 2000:1). No other reliable data is available on the numbers of priests who have died of AIDS.

The widely publicized occurrences of clerical sexual misconduct, including the sexual abuse of children and youths by priests, has provided the most serious and public evidence of clerical failure to live celibately. Even more important, it shows a dark side of priestly authority: the willingness of bishops to conceal abuse to prevent scandal and protect the reputation of the Church and the priesthood. Bishops are reported to have routinely transferred perpetrators with little regard for the safety of children and youth in these priests' new assignments. Dioceses have been accused of being insensitive to victims of abuse and using "hardball" legal tactics to settle lawsuits with them. Large sums of money were paid to victims who were required to sign confidentiality statements, a legal practice that contributed to the further concealment of the problem.[8]

In June 2002, the U.S. bishops were pressed to take decisive action to address the problem. The bishops established a Charter for the Protection of Children and Young People that called for the removal of all priests with any substantiated allegations of abuse of minors. Within two months of the adoption of a "zero tolerance" policy, 114 U.S. priests were removed by 31 bishops, according to a *New York Times* survey (Goodstein and Dillon 2002). The removal of additional priests has continued. The bishops also commissioned two independent groups to comprehensively study clerical sexual abuse of minors and the way in which dioceses dealt with abusive priests and their victims. One group studied the causes and ecclesiastical context of the abuse crisis. The other group audited diocesan records to assess the numbers of clergy and minors involved in sexual abuse between 1950 and 2002. In 2004, researchers reported that 4,392 U.S. priests (or 4 percent) abused 10,667 minors (National Review Board 2004:22). Since the figures rely on self-reporting, and abuse victims frequently do not come forward until years after the abuse occurred, the actual incidence of abusive priests and victims is likely to be even higher.

Among the causes of the abuse crisis, researchers faulted inadequate screening and formation of seminarians for celibacy. In calling for seminaries to review and improve their screening and formation of seminarians, the group affirmed the Vatican's decision in 2002 to investigate the screening and training of seminarians at all of the nation's seminaries and theologates (Gill 2002:10). The review board's strong criticisms of recent formation for celibacy will be considered in the next chapter.

Celibacy has been a symbolic means for the Church to mark a boundary between itself and the world. Today, some advocates of optional celibacy support change in the policy of mandatory celibacy on the basis of the need for more priests. However, if celibacy is truly an important organizing symbol for the Church that expresses its relationship to the world, then more is at stake than only the number of priests. But in the face of the sexual scandal, policy on celibacy and Church reform on the treatment of criminal priests make this issue an urgent one. However, the fact that priestly celibacy is so central to Catholicism and its governance means that changes in this requirement could bring other significant changes to the Church, its authority, and its legitimacy (Schoenherr 2002).

Critics within the Church, both "traditionalists" and "progressive" reformers, have used the clergy sexual abuse crisis to call for changes in other Church policies and the training of seminarians. Those seeking to end mandatory celibacy assign at least partial blame to the policy for the steep decline in the number of priests (Schoenherr 2002). Allegations of sexual misconduct have been used by some Catholics to criticize mandatory celibacy and to portray the Catholic Church as out-of-date on other teachings related to sexuality, such as artificial contraception, premarital sex, the ordination of women, and homosexuality (Wills 2000). Theologian Richard McBrien (Hoge, Potvin, Ferry 1984:76–77) alleged that mandatory celibacy has reduced the pool of high-quality candidates for seminaries and also leads to the admission of weaker candidates. McBrien (2002:8) also speculates that mandatory celibacy has resulted in a greater percentage of homosexuals and immature candidates to be ordained. Jenkins (1996) reported that some critics claim that the only way to "purge the Church" is to permit priests to marry and admit women to seminaries and the priesthood (109). Some critics maintain that mandatory celibacy encourages clerical superiority and gender exclusivity to the detriment of theological, ministerial, and management concerns (Sipe 1995:161–80). Schoenherr (2002:205–7) asserts that mandatory celibacy and an exclusively male priesthood provide sacred legitimation for a patriarchal social order.

Other critics charge that allegations of clergy sexual misconduct are the result of a loss of authority and a resulting moral laxity among clergy (Weigel 2002). Traditionalists have accused bishops and seminary rectors of being "soft" on homosexuality and tolerating sexually active priests and seminarians (Rose 2002). These critics call for a "crackdown" on gay seminarians and stronger measures to censure homosexual activity and subcultures alleged to occur in seminaries. Other critics have expressed concerns that seminaries have become breeding grounds for pedophiles run by those who dissent from Church teaching (Rose 2002). Supporters of mandatory celibacy say that it fittingly emphasizes the otherworldliness of priests. In addition, celibacy is said to provide a countercultural witness in a hedonistic and sexually permissive society. These advocates of mandatory celibacy assert that celibacy retains an attractive distinctiveness for the Catholic Church and its priesthood when compared to ordained ministry in Protestant denominations (Jenkins 1996:95–112).

This study of how seminarians are trained to live the celibate life can also be important for providing knowledge regarding some of the most divisive, contested issues facing Roman Catholicism. Several of the most widely disputed issues among Roman Catholics, including artificial contraception, abortion, marriage, divorce, homosexuality, women's ordination, and celibacy, involve matters of sexuality and the human body. Bryan S. Turner (1992:12) asserts that ours is the "somatic society" because the human body has become "the principal field of political and cultural activity" (12). If ours is the "somatic society," then it is not surprising that several of Catholicism's most hotly debated issues deal with the human body. Pope John Paul II's theology of the body has been hailed as revolutionary by George Weigel (2002:54), who praised John Paul II's sexual ethic for taking seriously human embodiment and stressing that sexual love involves the complete gift of one's self. Others see the pope's moral theology, especially his opposition to artificial contraception, as the Church's "Achilles' heel" (Kissling 2000:27). Johnson (2001) criticizes John Paul II's theology of the body for its use of scripture, for reverting to a pre–Vatican II act-centered morality, and for neglecting to draw on the actual experiences of human beings: in the pope's teaching, sexual passion "appears mainly as an obstacle to authentic love," and sexual activity is seen as having little value apart from procreation (11). Dubbed by its critics Rome's "pelvic theology," the Roman magisterium is said to be preoccupied with sexual matters. Besides stirring controversy within the Church, Catholic teachings have frequently shaped public debates on sexual matters. Rosemary Ruether (2000) notes that these teachings have "come to be seen as a major obstacle to liberalized laws on contraception, legal abortion, divorce and remarriage, and the acceptance of homosexuality as a normal human variant of sexual orientation" (9).

Examining how seminarians view their own sexuality and celibacy provides insights into how they as future Church leaders will address these contested issues. How they are trained to live celibately surely colors what these future priests will tell their flocks about sexuality. The personal lapses of priests to live celibately and the failure of bishops to responsibly deal with these priests has surely undermined the Church's ability to teach credibly on sexual matters.

Seeing formation from the cultural perspective that I use in this book highlights the challenge seminary formators face today in training men to live celibately. Prior to the 1960s, the Catholic symbol system legitimated the practice of celibacy, and little attention was paid to it during the years of a candidate's formation. Catholicism's symbol system objectified celibacy as a worthy moral and aesthetic calling. Its symbols were used to induce moods and motivations that made celibacy a sacrifice that

was part of a higher calling. These symbols mediated a hierarchical worldview that opposed "this" world and the spiritual
realm. Chaste celibacy imaged the purity and perfection of the
spiritual realm. Set apart from the everyday realm of sexual and
reproductive activity and family life, priests were able to perform
sacramental rituals and become mediators of grace between the
heavenly realm and this fallen, sinful earthly realm.

FORMATION IN DIOCESAN SEMINARIES

Priests in religious orders live in religious houses sharing (to
varying degrees) prayer, meals, recreation, a common spirituality,
charism, and purpose. Ideally, their common life and spirituality
aid them in living lives of chaste celibacy. Their religious order
provides members some of the benefits (as well as costs) of a
family. Diocesan (or "secular") priests are not normally the ben-
eficiaries of these supports to living lives of celibacy. Nor are they
subject to the accountability that living with others can bring. As
there are fewer diocesan priests, increasingly they live alone and
have fewer other priests to turn to for support.

Diocesan priests number about 30,500 of the 46,000 priests in
the United States (Froehle and Gautier 2000:111). They are not
members of a religious institute or society of apostolic life and
work in a given place under the authority of a bishop and a diocese, usually ministering in parishes.[9] Their celibacy is lived out
in a different context than that of consecrated religious (priests,
brothers, and sisters who are members of religious orders like Do-
minicans, Jesuits, Augustinians, etc.). In 2000, 16,000 priests in
the United States belonged to religious orders (Froehle and Gautier 2000:111). Members of religious orders take vows and usually
serve and live in community.

Diocesan priests' practice of celibacy is shaped by the flexible
availability required of a parish priest (Aschenbrenner 2002:11).
Though celibacy became mandatory for diocesan priests in the
twelfth century, they do not follow a formal rule as religious order
priests do. They also promise obedience to a local bishop. Their
ministry is usually directed toward the mission and spirituality
of laypeople. As their numbers dwindle and parishes increasingly

have only one priest, they are even more likely to live alone. This contrasts with religious order priests, who live in groups regulated by their order's rule. Diocesan priests are referred to as secular priests because they do not withdraw from "the world" into monasteries or religious houses, but rather live among the people whom they serve in parishes. The local parish has been routinely cited as a key to understanding the vitality of American Catholicism and the average Catholic's experience of faith and Church (Morris 1998:301; Dolan 2002:255). While many Catholics find fault with the Church's hierarchy and its teachings, through parish celebrations of sacramental rituals Catholics continue to draw meaning for their lives and enjoy social support from the parish communities they form (Greeley 2004b:105). Studying the training of diocesan priests is especially relevant for understanding Catholicism: parish priests are on the "front lines" of dealing with laity and are those in the best position to understand the controversies that have riled the Church since the Second Vatican Council (Aschenbrenner 2002:29).

How diocesan seminaries train candidates today cannot be understood apart from the origins of the diocesan seminary at the Council of Trent (1545–63). Today's seminaries continue to be significantly shaped by their Tridentine origins. The council's decree *Cum Adolescentium Aetas* called for bishops to establish seminaries as specialized institutions for training youths to be diocesan priests (White 1995:1181).[10] Trent's legislation sought to address the perceived "moral laxity" and "ignorance" among clergy by establishing minimal standards for the training of diocesan priests (Kauffman 1988:12).[11] Graduate-level seminaries (also known as theologates) are responsible for the proximate preparation of candidates before their ordination. In the years after the Second Vatican Council, dozens of seminaries closed across the country, including most high school seminaries. In 1999, there were only 43 U.S. theologates training diocesan and religious order candidates for the priesthood (Schuth 1999:245–48). According to the Center for Applied Research in the Apostolate, in the 2002–3 school year, the number of men studying for the priesthood in U.S. theologates declined by 170 students from the previous year to 3,414 (Donovan 2003:8). As recently as 1968, more than

8,000 men were enrolled in major seminaries and theologates in the United States (Froehle and Gautier 2000:119).

Church law explicitly requires seminaries to prepare their students to live celibately. Canon 247 states that "students are to be prepared through suitable education to observe the state of celibacy, and they are to learn to honor it as a special gift of God" (NCCB 1987: III-9). Recent ecclesial documents have called for more attention to formation for celibacy in the training of priests. The most recent *Program of Priestly Formation* calls for seminaries to "more consciously and persuasively" state the purpose of celibacy to candidates (NCCB 1993: no. 60). It acknowledges the difficulty of this task in a sexually permissive social environment and calls for increased attention to formation for celibacy (NCCB 1993: nos. 16–17). Schuth (1999:138) reported that in the 1990s seminaries increased their attention to formation for celibacy. Formation for celibacy includes attention to sexual and psychological maturity, as well as prayer, spirituality, and theology (Schuth 1999:138). In his influential *Pastores Dabo Vobis*, John Paul II (1993: no. 50) summed up the goal of formation for celibacy as training seminarians to *"know, appreciate, love and live celibacy according to its true nature* and according to its real purpose, that is, for evangelical, spiritual, and pastoral motives" (emphasis in the original). Not surprisingly, this requirement has contributed to seminary formation different from that of other forms of professional socialization in the degree of its attention to the development of human maturity, sexuality, character, and morals. Few organizations place as great a premium on the training of its personnel as the Roman Catholic Church does. How diocesan seminarians give meaning to celibacy, and how seminaries train men for this practice, is the subject of this study.

My research about how celibacy is "reproduced" in one seminary is intended to aid both seminarians and their formators in asking worthwhile questions about celibacy and how people come to practice it. In fact it could be described as an exercise in institutional reflexivity, and it is hoped that it will contribute in a small way to the improvement of seminary formation for celibacy. I also place special emphasis on how the culture of this particular seminary sought to build "commitment" to the practice of celibacy and the Roman Catholic Church. I see the building of commitment and devotion to God and the Church as occurring through very human processes, and that social action is both structured and intelligible.

The use of psychology in seminaries has been viewed with caution and even condemnation by some commentators (Bleichner 2004:34–35, 40; Weigel 2002:163–66; Rose 2002:183–206). It may seem odd or even sacrilegious to some people to subject vocational discernment and training for celibacy to sociological inquiry as I do in my research. Seminarians are especially likely to view their "calls" in a supernatural and extraordinary light. Mature priests I know do so too; however, they are also likely to look back and see very human reasons, good ones and bad ones, for their becoming priests. Believers commonly view priesthood and religious celibacy as "vocations," both mysterious and beyond the comprehension of the social scientist, but in my view the use of the social sciences to study seminary formation constitutes a "rationalization" (in Max Weber's terms) of priesthood.[12] Formators' use of the social sciences in seminary formation constitutes a rationalization of formation for priesthood and perhaps of the vocations of celibacy and priesthood themselves. However ironic it may seem, I believe that by subjecting seminary education to the lens of sociology, something is added to our understanding of religion and institutions, however debunking and demystifying that something is. There has been little sociological research compared to other professions, so that the problems of seminarians and seminaries are not widely understood.

Obviously, the findings of this case study of how celibacy is reproduced in one Catholic seminary cannot be generalized to all Catholic seminaries. However, the findings may help to reveal something important about the culture at work in reproduction of a Catholic and religious sexual regime. Because there is little empirical research on formation for celibacy, this study is both exploratory and descriptive. However, I believe this study can contribute to an understanding of how social institutions organize and shape the sexual lives of individuals and how individuals, like these seminarians, shape their own lives. Besides the case study I report on here, I did preliminary research on several seminaries on the East Coast and in the Midwest. In doing so I was provided with access to a social world that few outsiders are privileged to encounter. From the voices of those I talked with, I hope to reveal something of the meaning-making process religious individuals and institutions engage in.

Three

REPRODUCING CELIBACY
AS A CULTURAL PROCESS

This study of how Roman Catholic seminarians are trained to live a life of celibacy is largely based on a diocesan seminary in a Midwestern state. My particular research focus is to understand the various meanings these candidates for priesthood give to facets of sexuality, celibacy, and priesthood, also focusing on how they are trained and perceive their training for celibacy by seminary faculty.

Using the vocabulary of sociology and anthropology, I emphasize the active "agency" both of seminarians and formators (faculty priests) in receiving and producing the various meanings of priesthood and celibacy, viewing this process as part of an institutional "culture," and exploring how seminarians and formators together produce a culture in which the practice of celibacy itself is deemed valuable. In doing so, the culture enables them to invest the practice of celibacy itself with meaning and significance. For example, leading a celibate life is associated with the positive religious value of bodily asceticism; it is viewed as "freeing" priests from the close and intimate ties and relations of marriage and parenting; celibacy is also seen as a condition for a certain type of spiritual life and active religious life, and so forth. Borrowing from a well-known writer on culture, I interpret the "webs" of meaning and significance that both seminarians and formators "spin" (Geertz 1973:5).

Another dimension I consider is how commitment to this culture and to celibacy is developed. These processes of commitment are themselves constitutive of the culture in the seminary I studied. Sociologically speaking, seminary formation is treated as a form of professional socialization that involves all aspects of a candidate's life. This formation is a lengthy rite of passage. The

44

definition of "rite of passage" that Becker et al. (1961) applied to medical school is equally applicable to seminaries:

> A rite of passage is that series of instructions, ceremonies, and ordeals by which those already in a special status initiate neophytes into their charmed circle, by which men turn boys into fellow men, fit to be their own companions and successors. (4)

Seminary training as a rite of passage is intended to confer a substantially new identity with an extraordinary depth of commitment to the Church's mission. An examination of a particularly intense form of professional socialization, this study explores the processes by which commitment to the role of priest occurs, especially the requirement to live celibately. "Commitment" is understood in the way Rosabeth Moss Kanter (1968) used it to mean the process by which individual interests are joined to socially organized behavior patterns and are seen by the individual as fulfilling his or her interests and needs. I use the concept to show how institutional purposes and individual interests are linked. Commitment to celibacy occurs as seminarians come to identify their interests with what they view as the mission of the Roman Catholic Church (hereafter referred to as the Church).

I contend that seminarians evaluate the rewards and costs of celibacy and priesthood as they weigh their commitment to the Church. In addition, this study views the development of commitment to celibacy and the role of priesthood as occurring through the acquisition of what Roger Finke and Kevin D. Dougherty (2002) have called "religious capital," by which I mean learning the Roman Catholic narratives, symbols, rituals, ethos, and worldview necessary to assume the role of priest. Acquisition of this capital and these capacities is seen as providing rewards to seminarians that result in a deepening of commitment to the Catholic Church and its various cultures (international, national, local) — a culture that has historically valued the practice of celibacy as a "worthy" practice for priests and the Church as a whole. By examining how commitment to celibacy and the Church is developed, this work describes some of the ways in which a particular "sexual regime" is institutionally reproduced (Giddens 1991:63).

ASCETICISM, IDENTITY, AND SOCIAL THEORY

In the following pages, I will identify some of the principal works used in this study: the works of sociologist Anthony Giddens, anthropologist Mary Douglas, and historian Paul Beaudette are reviewed to consider the relationship between the body, sexuality, and identity — central themes of this study. Some of these authors' theories will be used to help understand how seminarians use celibacy to fashion distinctive identities for themselves. Thus, I emphasize that seminary formation is not something that students are simply subjected to as passive subjects. Rather, they are active participants and agents in shaping their own identities and creating the culture of their seminary.

The Body's Use for Religious Practices

I use the term "regime" or sexual regime in the way introduced by Anthony Giddens (1991:61–63) in *Modernity and Self-Identity: Self and Society in the Late Modern Age*. Giddens uses the term in a relatively neutral and descriptive way to mean socially and culturally organized ways of providing for, or regulating, organic necessities. He cites celibacy as an example of a sexual regime; diet and dress are other types of regimes, as are all learned regulative practices that reflect personal dispositions of social actors. They are more than mere habits or routines of living, since they always concern ascetic practice or actions having to do with controlling one's personal gratification. Regimes are "the focus of motivational energies" and operate in actors as "unconscious conditioning elements of conduct" (Giddens 1991:62). I take this to mean that regimes provide security and identity and are internalized as a form of self-discipline. While regimes reflect social conventions, actors modify them according to their personal inclinations. By performing these bodily practices actors are shaping how they present themselves to others. This work sees individuals' decisions to engage in particular sexual practices as an important way they give meaning to their lives and shape an identity for themselves. Priestly celibacy is viewed as a practice that is *learned* by individuals. In addition, it is not an incidental feature of a priest's identity, but rather is a practice used by the Church and individuals dedicated to its mission to cultivate a particular identity and self-understanding.

It is well known that religions have long utilized regimes of sexuality, diet, and dress as aspects of asceticism emphasizing renunciation, mortification, and penance. In recent studies of religious practice, bodily practices have received renewed attention. As Colleen McDannell (1995:14) points out, the human body is "the primary mediator of religious experience," being more than simply a medium of religious expression. The body's sickness, pain, suffering, and death are implicated in the most basic problems of meaning that religions address. Forms of sexual renunciation including virginity, continence (abstaining from sexual intercourse within marriage), and celibacy (abstaining from marriage) date to the first centuries of Christianity. After Christianity acquired legal status in 313, fewer Christians suffered the torture and pain of martyrdom, and sexual renunciation gradually became the hallmark of a life devoted completely to God. The history of this Christian sexual asceticism was treated more fully in chapter 2.

Asceticism and Works of Douglas and Beaudette

The human body and asceticism have received attention from a variety of disciplines in recent years.[13] In particular, I will consider aspects of the works of anthropologist Mary Douglas and the use of her theories by historian Paul Beaudette to suggest how the human body can be used to establish social boundaries and categories that individuals utilize in shaping identities for themselves. In *Natural Symbols: Explorations in Cosmology,* Douglas (1970) argues that organic systems, including the human body, provide an analogy for social systems so that the human body is a symbol for the social body. From her anthropological perspective, the body is used as a classification system that expresses beliefs about the social order. Bodily practices reveal what a group highly values or holds as sacred. As Douglas (1970) points out:

> The social body constrains the way the physical body is perceived. The physical experience of the body, always modified by the social categories through which it is known, sustains a particular view of society. There is a continual exchange of meanings between the two forms of bodily experience so that each reinforces the categories of the other. (69)

From this perspective, the meanings given to the body in ascetical practices and beliefs about the social body reinforce each other. Rules about bodily pollution and boundaries are efforts to deal with social disorder and accompanying anxieties (Douglas 1966). Societies develop classificatory schemes in which purity is associated with the sacred and dirt or disorder is linked with the profane. When a group is threatened, concerns with bodily purity are heightened.

Applying Douglas's insights to this study of seminarians raises questions regarding the significance of celibacy as a boundary marker for the Church's relationship to the world, as well as a boundary marker between laity and clergy within the Church. Peter Brown argues that as Christianity spread in its first centuries within a Greco-Roman environment, its sexual ethos distinguished it from pagan practice. "Lacking the clear ritual boundaries provided in Judaism by circumcision and dietary laws, Christians tended to make their exceptional sexual discipline bear the full burden of expressing the difference between themselves and the pagan world" (Brown 1987:263). Historian Paul Beaudette has developed Douglas's insight to consider how ritual purity beliefs, which were a basis of clerical continence and celibacy, reflected boundary anxieties regarding the Catholic Church's relationship to "the world" (1998). Beaudette studied ecclesiastical legislation on continence and celibacy from the fourth through the twelfth centuries that led to the Church's requirement of celibacy for priests. This legislation followed the reforms of Pope Gregory VII (1073–85), which sought to reduce state interference in Church affairs. At this time there also was greater emphasis upon the objective nature of the Real Presence of Christ in the Eucharist and an increase in the belief that priests were set apart for work "at the altar" (Beaudette 1998:37). Not only did

the Gregorian Reform establish a more distinct separation between the Church and the world, the sacred and profane, but there
also emerged an "increasingly sharp division of Christian society
into two classes, the priestly above the lay" (Beaudette 1998:39).
The Gregorian Reform intensified the division of Church into two
classes, with clergy above the laity. In this conception clergy were
more closely associated with "the Church" and the laity with "the
world."

Beaudette maintains that this conception of the Church's relationship to the world was constant for eight hundred years —
until the Second Vatican Council. The practice of celibacy, originating in anxieties regarding ritual impurity, served as a boundary
marker between the Church and world and clergy and laity
(Beaudette 1998:29). By their celibacy, priests were set apart
from the profane realms of sexual, reproductive, familial, and
economic activity. Instead, they were associated with a sacred,
heavenly realm through which otherworldly grace was mediated
by their sacramental activities. Celibacy was a mark of the clergy's
otherworldliness and superiority.

The works of Douglas and Beaudette help us understand how
celibacy functions as a critical organizing symbol for the Church.
Besides being linked to the example of the celibacy of Jesus,
celibacy also is a prerequisite for officiating at most sacraments
and holding the Church's most powerful administrative offices.
Douglas's work can be used to show how sexual intercourse
has sometimes been understood as a polluting practice for religious virtuosi in light of the fact that groups shape identities for
themselves by establishing boundaries that protect their purity.

I contend that while seminarians exercise their own agency
and give meaning to celibacy in varying ways, the heritage of the
Church, including meanings assigned to ascetical practices in the
past, are an obvious resource that seminarians draw on. I am also
attentive to the ways in which boundaries are used to structure
seminary life to produce commitment to celibacy. For example,
diocesan seminaries enforce a degree of separation from laity by
requiring students to live together with priest faculty members
on the seminary campus. This practice reduces interaction with

laity and allows seminarians to engage in practices through which they develop an identity that sets them apart from lay Catholics.

The Body and Identity Formation
in the Work of Anthony Giddens

Under the conditions of late modernity, Giddens (1991:99–103) rightly observes that the body has heightened significance for construction of identity. This significance is seen by contrasting modern societies with traditional societies. Modernity emerged from postfeudal Europe. The institutional dimensions that characterize modernity are industrialization, capitalism, administrative surveillance, and control of the means of violence within the nation-state (Giddens 1990:55–63). In late or high modernity these forces are intensified and extended in the globalization of worldwide social relations evaporating the remnants of premodern traditional orders (Giddens 1990:63–78). In traditional societies, lineage, gender, social status, and other personal attributes were relatively fixed. In modernity, custom weighs less heavily on individuals. Individual choice becomes central in the construction of "lifestyles" and narratives of self-identity (1991:80–88). As Giddens (1991:70) points out, individuals today, more than in traditional societies, are continually pressed to answer questions regarding what to do, how to act, and who to be. No longer is it assumed that sons will make a living in the way their fathers did and share their social status all their lives. Individuals today are faced with more choices about where they will live, whom they will live with, and what they will make of themselves.

Seminarians form identities for themselves and see their "formation" of identities as a central task of seminary training. More so than in most other professions, their identity as priests encompasses the most significant aspects of their lives, including sexuality. Today the trajectory of seminary, priesthood, and chaste celibacy is no longer as popular or highly esteemed by Catholics as in the past. However, to be motivated to enter seminary and prepare for priesthood, seminarians are pressed to conceptualize celibacy and priesthood in a manner that makes it worthy of their commitment. Seminarians *conceive* of celibacy and priesthood, as well as how seminarians *become* priests, by fashioning a priestly, celibate identity for themselves. Catholic beliefs, narratives, symbols, and practices are cultural resources that seminarians draw on to form identities for themselves. Seminary formation is not a process seminarians passively submit to. Nor is it presented as the acquisition of a monolithic, unitary Catholic culture. Rather, seminarians master particular Catholic practices, give them meaning, and fashion an identity for themselves.

As Giddens (1991:75) says, in late modernity individuals see themselves as responsible for building a self-identity. This process proceeds as a "reflexive project." By this I understand him to mean that individuals engage in a process of continual self-monitoring and self-mastering in which identity is always open or unfinished, due to an individual's continual self-monitoring. From this perspective, psychological counseling and spiritual direction are tools by which seminarians exercise agency and actively form who they are. From another perspective, these practices could be seen as means of social control. However, therapy and counseling need not be negatively evaluated as an "adjustment device," since they can be useful to individuals as forms of "life-planning" (Giddens 1991:180).

While I view counseling, spiritual direction, student evaluations, formation conferences, and other practices as devices used to build commitment to the Church's mission, seminarians can use these same practices to reflexively fashion an identity for themselves as priests. These tools may not always have the result seminary faculty members seek, since students will appropriate their training in ways they choose to. However, because individuals are engaged in a process of continual self-monitoring and reflection on incoming information about themselves, identity is an ongoing project. If the self is always open to revision, a lifelong commitment to celibacy and priesthood might be more difficult to make. However, this chronic flow of incoming information does not mean that a person's identity is fragmented or unstable. Giddens (1991:53) argues that a stable identity is reflexively understood by a person through the narrative biography that he or she develops. In my research, seminarians' vocation or "call" stories emerged as an essential feature of their own bi-ographies. In these stories, a seminarian's call to priesthood is typically seen as received from God rather than being an expression of the seminarian's own choice or preference. Seminarians easily recounted vocation stories that ordered and gave coherence to the biographies they constructed. Without being able to tell such a story, it appeared unlikely that a seminarian would believe he was "called" to priesthood, and subsequently be willing to undertake the challenges of seminary training. Thus, seminarians' stories came to be constitutive of the calls they claimed to have received. It is through their vocation stories that students came to see themselves as priests.

SEMINARY FORMATION: SOCIALIZATION AND THE ACQUISITION OF RELIGIOUS CAPITAL

Peter Berger and Thomas Luckmann (1966) cite the training of religious personnel as an instance of "secondary socialization," a "process that inducts an already socialized individual into new sectors of the objective world of his society" (130).[14] As a form of secondary socialization, seminary formation involves the acquisition of role-specific knowledge and prepares candidates to become religious specialists. This socialization involves the subjective internalization of objects of Catholic culture by seminarians. Culture is the primary lens through which I examine how men are formed to live celibately as priests. From this perspective, the process of acquiring Catholic knowledge and culture and becoming religious specialists can be understood as a process of developing mastery of and commitment to Catholic culture.

Finke and Dougherty (2002) have developed a religious capital approach to seminary formation that is useful for understanding some dimensions of seminary formation. They theorize that religious capital consists of "the degree of *mastery of* and *attachment to* a particular religious culture" (Finke and Dougherty 2002:106; emphasis in the original). For Catholics, developing this mastery involves learning about Catholic doctrines, worship, how to pray, devotional practices, and Catholic moral teachings. Mastery of this culture provides believers with a worldview that they come to accept as reality and that constitutes the world as a sacred cosmos (Berger 1967:33). For seminarians, mastery of Catholic culture enables them to orient their actions in the world and progress toward priesthood. Commitment to a religious culture has an emotional or affective component that is developed through religious experiences and engagement in practices such as prayer, liturgy, and other rituals that strengthen attachment to a religious tradition over a lifetime. These practices invest daily life in the seminary with meaning and help seminarians situate themselves in the Church as a sacred order.

Priests are one variety of religious specialists within Roman Catholicism. Given the sacramental emphasis of Catholicism, their work of officiating at sacramental celebrations is critical. Catholicism places great emphasis on a hierarchical, ordained priesthood (Schoenherr 2002:61). Training for the Catholic priesthood normally involves at least four years of human, spiritual, academic, and pastoral formation. Great care is exercised in the selection and training of candidates for priesthood. These four kinds of formation cultivate by promoting the acquisition of the knowledge of Catholic culture and attachment to that culture. The "role-specific" knowledge Catholic seminarians must acquire includes learning how to perform sacramental rites and preaching. Seminarians are expected to master this knowledge in order to perform their specialized priestly functions, especially presiding at sacramental celebrations. Intellectual and pastoral formation are the areas especially designed to emphasize the acquisition of Catholic knowledge and expertise that seminarians need to effectively perform their priestly duties.

Because religious organizations expect their ministers to perform their duties with dedication, a high degree of emotional attachment and commitment to a religious culture is desirable. Of the four kinds of formation conducted in Catholic seminaries, the spiritual formation component of seminary training especially cultivates an emotional attachment to Catholic culture so priests become willing to make sacrifices in their ministry. Spiritual formation helps candidates clarify their vocations. It also teaches them how to deepen their relationship with God through personal and communal prayer, spiritual direction, and other religious practices. These devices mediate meanings to seminarians who seek to identify with and internalize the role of priest. An affective attachment to Catholic culture is essential if a seminarian is to understand himself as having an authentic vocation to the priesthood and subjectively identify with the role of priest.

A unique prerequisite for ordination to the Catholic priesthood is a public promise by the candidate not to marry. As noted previously, earlier in the twentieth century it was taken for granted that a seminarian would live celibately after ordination and little was said about it. Especially since the late 1980s, training for celibacy became an explicit and systematic part of formation programs. Human and spiritual formation are the two primary types of formation that help prepare candidates to make this promise and live as celibate priests. Priestly formation seen as socialization involves the internalization of elements of Catholic culture and a worldview in which celibacy is esteemed as a worthwhile practice.

CULTURE AND CULTURED CAPACITIES

Since "culture" is the lens through which the organization and dynamics of the seminaries are examined here, I will review some of the contemporary approaches to "culture" that I will use. The term has been long debated and variously defined by social scientists. Clifford Geertz (1973:89) has been influential in conceiving of culture as "a historically transmitted pattern of meanings embodied in symbols, a system of inherited conceptions expressed in symbolic forms by means of which men communicate, perpetuate, and develop their knowledge about and attitudes toward life." Geertz emphasized the publicly available quality of the symbolic forms through which people experience and express meaning. To say that culture is publicly available means that culture is not merely an idea that is subjectively held by two or more individuals that can be privately inferred by another person. Beliefs and belief systems, including religious ones, are cultural phenomena existing independently of one or more believers. Beliefs are an instance of what Emile Durkheim ([1915] 1965) called "social facts" and require explanation in terms of other social facts.[15]

Ann Swidler (1986:273) has usefully built on Geertz's public conception of culture. She asserts that culture consists of "symbolic vehicles of meaning, including beliefs, ritual practices, art forms, and ceremonies, as well as informal cultural practices such as language, gossip, stories, and rituals of daily life." With Geertz, she underlined the public, shared quality of culture as something that exists between individuals. However, like most other contemporary writers on the subject, she does not see culture as a unified, coherent system, as had Geertz and others. Instead of being viewed holistically, "culture" is understood as a set of "practices" with multiple sites and sometimes conflicting purposes (McCarthy 1996:24–25). Religious culture, therefore, is found not only in the official teachings and rites of religious organizations, but also in the varied everyday practices of believers. Culture is conceptualized as a set of resources containing symbols, stories, rituals, and worldviews that social actors use to address different kinds of problems (Swidler 1986:273). Seminary formation builds the religious capital of candidates for the priesthood by imparting certain cultural capacities.

Seminary Formation as the Acquisition of Cultural Capacities and Culture

Culture produces a kind of self. The first capacity culture imparts is to be a kind of self or person (Swidler 2001:73). Seminary formation does not seek to make the candidate merely a religious functionary but rather to produce a particular kind of person. As a bodily regime, a priest's celibacy involves a particular kind of relationship to the body. A celibate priest's non-marriage and abstention from sexual intimacy is an external expression in practice of what is said to be an inner disposition and a means of self-transformation. Formation for celibacy enables seminarians to fashion themselves as a certain kind of person with particular dispositions. Seminary students draw upon the resources of the Catholic heritage as it is taught and practiced in the seminary to conceive of themselves "as growing in holiness and likeness to Jesus Christ." For instance, formation encourages students to subordinate their needs to those of others as a form of pastoral charity. I also will show how rituals, especially prayer and liturgy, are used by seminarians to create a priestly self. Not only do official documents cite the liturgical life as the most important element of formation, these rituals were essential for students to come to view themselves as future priests.

How seminary formation is intended to develop a particular kind of person is outlined in John Paul II's apostolic exhortation *Pastores Dabo Vobis* (1993). From his election as pope in 1978 to his death in 2005, John Paul II was particularly influential in shaping how celibacy is thought of and how seminarians are trained. He emphasized that the goal and desirable effect of seminary formation and ordination are nothing less than for a seminarian "to take on the likeness of Christ" (no. 45). In this process the priest is said to become an *alter Christus,* "another Christ." Of course, how seminarians understand who Christ is and how each priest should be "another Christ" will vary. John Paul II insisted that celibacy is fitting for the ministry of priests. Seminary faculties and students construct a culture that will produce a self that views celibacy as an enhancement of oneself and ministry. According to Swidler (2001), these ways of thinking and feeling are what Geertz called "moods and motivations" (73). Formation programs are viewed in this study as seeking to cultivate "moods and motivations" that lead seminarians to embrace celibacy as a worthwhile practice.

Culture imparts skills, styles, and habits. Second, as Swidler (2001:72–73) points out, culture aids people in internalizing skills, styles, and habits. Seminaries build the capital of candidates by teaching them a variety of skills, styles, and habits appropriate to the role of priest. Many of these "role expectations" are specific and formal and require specialized expertise, such as how to perform sacramental rites or conduct an adult education class. Professional socialization also includes more subtle matters, such as how to show deference to the bishop, how to avoid coarse language with parishioners, and how to place the needs of the ecclesial institution or parishioners before one's own needs. Other skills, styles, and habits relate to the most intimate and interior details of a seminarian's life, such as developing a personal relationship to God. For seminarians, the habits imparted are cultivated for professional and personal reasons. For instance, seminarians are encouraged to develop a piety that finds great satisfaction in the sacraments. Regarding the sacrament of penance, the *Program of Priestly Formation* states that "seminarians will not be formed into effective ministers of the sacrament unless they themselves have discovered its value in their own life" (NCCB 1993: no. 276). Seminaries are to encourage students to confess regularly so that they appreciate the sacrament's value and develop a habit of humble self-examination. The practice also trains seminarians to submit themselves routinely to clerical and ecclesiastical authority.

Culture marks group membership. Third, culture marks group membership (Swidler 2001:74–75) to produce social bonds and a positive "we-sentiment" within a group. It also can produce tensions within the group, as well as tensions with those outside the group. Boundaries between groups reinforce the construction of particular kinds of selves. Group membership also is a basis for the pursuit of common interests.

As a form of socialization, seminary formation sets clergy apart from the laity (Sheldrake 1993). In different historical periods, the separation and relationship between clergy and laity has been evaluated differently. Especially since the Second Vatican Council, there have been efforts to downplay clericalism and a "spirituality of separation," which sees priests as part of a superior group. At the same time, by proscribing sexual or family ties, the celibacy of priests, perhaps, is their most significant boundary marker from the laity and subordinates the service and loyalties of priests to the Church. The Second Vatican Council reconsidered and softened the boundary between the Church and the world (McSweeney 1980). In the nineteenth and twentieth centuries, a fortress-like Church resisted the frequently hostile encroachments of Protestants, the Enlightenment, and the French Revolution. The Church condemned Protestantism and opposed Enlightenment rationalism, modern science, democracy, and the secular world as godless. The Second Vatican Council's stress on the unity of all Christians (acknowledging other Christians as part of the Church of Christ), cooperation with non-Christians and atheists, and dialogue with the modern world was a significant shift from the Church's stance at the First Vatican Council a hundred years earlier.

The conflicts over mandatory celibacy are one of the many unintended consequences of the Second Vatican Council's reforms. However, it is not surprising that just as the Second Vatican Council was altering the Church's relationship to the world, the meaning and usefulness of mandatory celibacy would be widely called into question. In the years after the Second Vatican Council, a Church that many people thought to be immutable now appeared to be rapidly changing and more "open" to aspects of the world that it had opposed for centuries. Long-held teachings and practices were questioned and in some cases revised. Not only was the secular world more positively evaluated, the council also improved the status of the laity by using the less hierarchical image for the Church — "the People of God" — and highlighted the laity's own distinctive mission.[16] The effect of these changes was to soften the boundaries between the Church and the world, as well as clergy and laity, decreasing the functional usefulness of celibacy as a boundary marker. For Catholics alarmed at a perceived relaxation of creedal and moral boundaries, celibacy can be construed as a strategy to reaffirm Catholicism's distinctive identity.

Culture shapes a worldview. Lastly, as Swidler (2001:75) says, culture provides images that shape a worldview. Seminaries expose students to the Catholic intellectual, liturgical, and moral traditions, providing a rich set of ideas and images that are the basis for a particular view of the world. This worldview constitutes "reality" as having meaningful order or *nomos*, and enables individuals to situate themselves in it. Worldviews "give persons the continuing conviction that they know enough about how the world works to act with confidence within it" (Swidler 2001:75). The worldview that seminaries mediate allows seminarians to locate themselves in the world and invest the orientation of their lives and the practice of celibacy with meaning. The reasons for Catholic beliefs and practices are part of the cultural "toolkit" seminaries provide. An example of how a seminary seeks to enact a worldview can be seen in its celebration of the Liturgy of the Hours, in which Christ's paschal mystery is the focus and foundation of a believer's life. By praying the "Hours," all moments of the day and seasons of the year are understood as expressing that mystery. In my research, I found that seminaries are currently attracting individuals seeking a lavishly rich, religiously saturated subculture at variance with the secular world. Seminary activities imbue the everyday world with meaning and promise seminarians a high status within it after ordination.

Seminary Formation Seen through the Lens of Culture

Through the lens of culture, seminary formation involves both producing and mediating culture. "Seminaries inherit, embody, transform, dramatize, and pass on particular traditions, beliefs, perspectives, ideas, and practices" (Carroll, Wheeler, Aleshire, and Marler 1997:254). The cultures of Catholic seminaries obviously are shaped by the historical traditions of Catholicism that have their authoritative interpreters and ideological specialists. Together the Church's hierarchical magisterium and theological scholars produce a distinct Catholic knowledge of God that is both innovative and attentive to Catholicism's heritage. That the Holy See seeks to significantly shape and monitor how priestly formation proceeds is clear since it approves the guidelines episcopal conferences develop for their seminaries. American seminaries appear to have received special scrutiny during John Paul II's episcopacy. He authorized visitations of U.S. seminaries twice during his pontificate, one in 1981 and another in 2002 that is being completed now. On-site visitations have been conducted by bishops, religious superiors, and formation personnel from other seminaries and include interviews with faculty, students, and recent graduates. The last such review of U.S. seminaries was conducted twenty-five years ago. While acknowledging the seminaries were uneven in quality, the Vatican's previous report was generally praiseworthy. Given this fact and that seminary administrations are eager to put their best face on for the visitation teams, one wonders what real effect the latest review will have.

Through the *Program of Priestly Formation* of the National Conference of Catholic Bishops (1993), the hierarchy of the Church authorizes guidelines for the formation of priests and the transmission of Catholic knowledge.[17] The *Program* provides norms for the elements that are required of all seminary formation programs (NCCB 1993: no. 25). Seminaries necessarily give great attention to constructing and maintaining a normative culture with a worldview and ethos in which celibacy is a meaningful and valued practice worthy of a student's commitment. Seminarians' experiences are intended to internalize such a worldview and ethos.

While the guidelines of the *Program* influence what occurs in all seminaries, the culture of any particular seminary results from successive generations of faculty interacting with generations of students to shape a school's worldview and ethos (Carroll et al. 1997:255). This culture is daily produced and reproduced intersubjectively. The guidelines of the *Program* are only one element of the culture of seminaries, which means, among other things, that the *Program* structures the practices of seminaries; it also means that faculty members and students in everyday life appropriate and shape Catholic beliefs, symbols, and rituals in their own ways.

Shifts in religious worldview can bring renewal to a religious tradition, as well as increase tensions within a group. The Second Vatican Council significantly altered the worldview of Catholicism, especially as to how it understands its relationship to the rest of the world (McSweeney 1980). Since the council, differences in how Catholics believe and practice their faith have sometimes produced conflicts within the Church that have spilled over into seminaries. The council's 1965 decree *Optatam Totius* (On the Training of Priests) called for changes in the training of priests in seminaries and opened the door to a flood of reforms in schools that in some respects had changed little in four centuries. In the United States in the 1950s, seminaries focused mostly on intellectual and theological training (Schuth 2004:17). Spirituality of candidates was accessed by their attendance at public prayer. In the late 1970s pastoral formation involving internships and field learning was increased. As noted earlier, the use of psychology also came into vogue. Formation came to be more individualized with less emphasis on external appearances (Schuth 2004:17).

Schuth (1999:66) reported that one-third of the seminary rectors or presidents she interviewed were concerned about theological polarization in the Church and among their seminarians. Such polarization was viewed as a grave matter that must be addressed in seminaries. Sociologically, this polarization challenges seminaries' efforts to build a coherent worldview with its accompanying rituals and norms. Amid such polarization, Catholic seminaries seek to enable students to build an affective attachment to Catholic culture. Faculty and students may appropriate Catholic beliefs, symbols, and rituals in different ways, but the *Program of Priestly Formation* is clearly intended to prescribe a normative process for the training of priests by promoting a particular set of practices.

From a cultural perspective, seminary formation also imparts the capital of cultural capacities, which students use in varying ways. Drawing on interviews with faculty and students at one seminary, in the following chapters I will show what capacities the culture of one seminary seeks to impart and how it develops these capacities in order to build commitment to its Catholic culture. Seminary formation also seeks to form students into a particular kind of person or self. Students' descriptions of priesthood, ministry, celibacy, and sexuality shed light on how seminarians use, produce, and are produced by culture. Furthermore, the social processes for engendering commitment to celibacy is inextricably an enterprise of forming a self.

This study also examines how formation works to internalize skills, styles, and habits among students and considers how formation for celibacy marks group membership and enables priests and students to see themselves as "set apart" in their vocation, examining how boundary markers are used in formation. Since culture offers beliefs and symbols that constitute a worldview, the beliefs and symbols students and faculty use will be described. How one seminary helped students develop a commitment to celibacy by developing these moods and motivations is a principal focus of this study.

CELIBACY CHALLENGED:
REPRODUCING CELIBACY TODAY

I assume that the relationships between religious practices and society are contingent and variable. In this section, works describing the historical and cultural framework in which seminaries seek to reproduce celibacy will be considered. How celibacy is reproduced and support or challenges to its reproduction will vary over time and place. I contend that particular social and cultural conditions contribute an ethos that is unfriendly to celibacy in the United States. While priests and seminarians continue to find ways to make celibacy a worthwhile endeavor, contemporary cultural currents frequently militate against a positive evaluation of a life of celibacy.

I first consider works that theorize a growing privatization of life under the conditions of modernity and late modernity. These works assert that there has been an impoverishment of life in the public realm and a corresponding shift toward an emphasis on finding meaning in private life, especially intimate relationships. These works suggest reasons why romantic love and sexual intimacy are increasingly viewed as essential for a satisfying human life. If these authors are correct, they contribute some understanding of why there is less cultural support for a celibate priesthood today than in some earlier eras. The lives of celibate priests are viewed as unfulfilled lives because they do not share in the realm of romantic love and sexual expression. Second, I examine works that suggest why people are less willing to make lifelong permanent commitments today. The last section considers works that suggest that the Second Vatican Council effectively weakened the ecclesial institutional and disciplinary framework for celibacy or for a functionally successful "sexual regime" in which celibacy is mandated.

Privatization and the Increased Importance of Emotion and Intimacy in Everyday Life

Contemporary studies of late modern culture as well as works in social history provide a wealth of ideas for assembling a portrait of personal life in contemporary America — the context in which men are choosing to live a celibate priestly life.[18] Sociologists have identified the terrain of modern and contemporary life as lived out in the separate domains of "private" and "public" life, where the private sphere of family and intimate relations is identified as the locus of personal fulfillment, meaning, identity, and the expression of emotionality. The public realm is characterized by rational role behavior set by the standards of the market and workplace, bureaucracy, and the legal and technical ethos of public institutions.

Studies of the making of modern identity emphasize the rise of "personal life" as well as accompanying changes in structure and meaning of families and "married life" as an intimate compassionate institution, one where children have become the emotional center of households. These developments — occurring over centuries, from the early modern to the contemporary period — have been documented by historians of the family as well as social historians tracing the transformation of traditional social and communal institutions into "modern societies."[19]

An important theme in these studies of personal life and modern identity has been the rise of sentiment and emotion surrounding personal life, marriage, and the family. Contemporary studies of late modernity also focus on the sociocultural importance of material life, pleasure, and emotion, topics addressed in multiple forms and contexts of social life today: in consumer cultures and mass media; in the rise and growing influence and popularization of "therapeutic culture"; in the changing standards of behavior and feeling ushered in by globalization; in the role of emotions in "identity movements" of races, nations, sexualities; in studies of intense emotions involved in social movements, in sport, and leisure. "Capitalist culture" (Bell 1996) is examined as a powerful carrier of a culture of hedonism, pleasure, and release. Mass media have become vital transmitters of sex, romance, and love. The domain of "personal life" has probably never been more vulnerable to the power and technologies of public institutions.[20]

Using these studies to portray, however broadly, the sociocultural context for priestly celibacy today, one is immediately struck by the highly marginal and alienated role of priests in contemporary culture. In fact, priesthood and celibacy may be construed as a more costly sacrifice and burden than in the past. Simply put: a priest gives up participation in the private realm of life where fulfillment is supposed to be found. Furthermore, in late capitalism, priests are excluded from the entire role of consumption and material culture so central to the dominant capitalist culture where identity is increasingly derived from consumption and a particular "style of life," for a priest's calling and low salary usually do not allow him to participate in consumer culture. At the same time, institutional religion's decline within the secular culture is significant because a priest receives a smaller reward in prestige for his "sacrifice." If romance, sexuality, and consumption have increased prominence in culture and identity formation, it is not surprising that many people would consider priesthood a dehumanized or impoverished form of existence. Indeed many hold that celibates cannot be "fully human," because they are not engaged in emotionally and physically intimate exclusive romantic relationships. As fragile and provisional as romantic and intimate relationships are, they are seen by the mass media that drives capitalist culture as the only thing that makes life worthwhile. It is little wonder that celibacy is seen as neither attainable nor laudable. In fact, the view of priesthood and celibacy advocated by the Church is at odds with the dominant material and secular culture. More importantly, the Church has provided little support and motivation to men willing to enter the priesthood, while the dominant culture rebukes them (or merely finds them incomprehensible) in their turn away from pleasure, intimacy, and sexual love.

Central to this conflict is the unresolved question whether the mutuality and intimacy of marriage is a distraction or enabling vehicle for intimacy with Christ and ministerial effectiveness. If exclusive relationships are seen only in terms of sex and desire, they are more likely to be seen as distractions from intimacy with Christ. If exclusive intimate relations are seen in terms of mutuality, communication, and collaboration, they may be more positively evaluated. In this case, such relationships may be an aid to intimacy with Christ and collaborative ministerial efforts. No empirical studies are available to clarify whether exclusive relations aid or impair effective pastoral ministry. It is a significant question whether sexuality is characterized as primarily involving sexual desire or, on the other hand, mutuality, communication, and collaboration. The characterization of sexuality affects the evaluation of the appropriateness of marriage for ministry. In addition, ordained ministry since the Second Vatican Council is increasingly seen in terms of collaborative service with and to the laity rather than the juridical use of power. The mutuality and communicative aspects of relationships (exclusive or not) would likely enhance ordained ministerial effectiveness as envisioned by the Second Vatican Council.

Cultural Factors Affecting Willingness to Make Permanent Commitments

The Church holds that once a man is ordained, he is a priest forever. (Roman Catholic Church 1997: no. 1583). However, as noted earlier, resignations and laicizations from the priesthood have been common since the Second Vatican Council. In *The New Men: Inside the Vatican's Elite School for American Priests,* a seminary rector expressed concern with seminarians who "drift" or "are rolling toward ordination" without a sense of lifelong commitment to priesthood (Murphy 1997:40). The work described the inner struggles and challenges of first-year students to discern whether they are called to be priests at this "West Point" for diocesan priests. Particularly in cases of recent conversions to Catholicism, the rector observed, "One of the challenges we face today deals with making sure the vocation is interiorized" (Murphy 1997:41). A vocation must not be a "burst of enthusiasm ... but has to be borne out in fidelity for half a century" (Murphy 1997:41).

Two recent sociological works, *Talk of Love: How Culture Matters* by Ann Swidler (2001) and *Moral Freedom: The Search for Virtue in a World of Choice* by Alan Wolfe (2001) suggest reasons why such a lifelong commitment to priesthood and celibacy may be extraordinarily challenging to seminarians. Swidler's work was based on eighty interviews with middle-class Americans. From her interviews, Swidler (2001:104–6) attempted to show how culture functions as a repertoire of meanings that individuals appropriate in varying ways to orient and justify their actions. A common belief among her interviewees was the "principle of voluntarism," or the assumption that social ties should be created by individual free choice (Swidler 2001:136). Among her sample, she classified a large number of informants as "utilitarian individualists." Choices are right because of the benefits accrued to the actor. Utilitarian individualists clarified their wants and then sought to maximize their self-interest and fulfillment of these wants by their actions (Swidler 2001:137).

This tendency, if found among Catholic seminarians, surely conflicts with Catholic thinking about the call to priesthood and the charism of celibacy in at least three ways. Voluntarism places great emphasis on the choice of the individual. Actions are legitimate only when they are the free choice of the individual. Yet, while seminarians seek ordination, they are not simply making an autonomous choice among many career options. In a vocation to priesthood it is traditionally understood as God who chooses priests.

Second, "voluntarist utilitarians" make choices that maximize their self-interest. Celibacy, involving a renunciation of sexual activity and exclusive intimate relationships, may be perceived as no longer maximizing one's interests or meeting one's needs. Traditionally priesthood is seen as a calling that involves service and sacrifice for others, with Jesus' death on the cross as the supreme example. Self-interest and maximizing fulfillment may not coincide with the demands of the priesthood and obedience to the priest's superiors. A priest with a utilitarian individualist orientation would have to construe the sacrifices of celibacy in such a way that somehow they are consistent with maximizing his self-interests.

Finally, voluntarist strategies to maximize an individual's interests are subject to change over time, as an individual's wants change. Agreements made freely are not binding when they no longer maximize interests or interests change. Alan Wolfe, director of Boston College's Boisi Center for Religion and American Public Life, studied the virtue of loyalty to determine what it means to Americans. His research was based on a March 2000 poll by the *New York Times* and two hundred interviews with Americans from eight diverse communities. As Wolfe notes, in the name of efficiency and profit, businesses now frequently lay off or terminate longtime workers. American corporations' lack of loyalty to workers has led Americans to decrease their loyalty in personal relationships, including marriage. Institutions are seen as increasingly disloyal and people are treated as disposable. This perception colors the way people see relationships. Marriage vows are still taken seriously, but when the relationship creates suffering and happiness is not attainable, vows can be put aside (Wolfe 2001:51–52). Priests may face many periods in their lives when celibacy is not fulfilling or it is perceived as a source of undue loneliness or pain. If they share the perception that their promise can easily be put aside, they may engage in romantic and sexual behaviors or leave active ministry altogether. Wolfe reported that loyalty remained important to Americans. At the same time, however, they believe "people have to consider their own solution and decide what works best for them" (Wolfe 2001:55). Seminarians may pursue celibacy and priesthood as long as it "works" for them. The promises of priesthood, like marriage, may not be seen as binding. The former rector of the North American College indicated that he believes this is the attitude of some seminarians today (Murphy 1997:40).

Seminary formators have frequently decried postmodern notions of the self. Aschenbrenner claimed that the notion that the self as highly pliable or infinitely changeable could certainly undermine the seminarian's long-term faith in Jesus and his commitment to celibacy. He wrote, "Such belief in the radical changeability of the self affects even the possibility of a permanent profession of this 'self'" (Aschenbrenner 2002:70). Aschenbrenner derided postmodern theories that deny the possibility of the permanent profession of the self. As noted previously, sociologist Anthony Giddens (1991:54) maintained that in late modernity a stable self-identity is not sustained by a person's behaviors, but rather by the biography he or she constructs. Individual reflexivity is theorized as a continual process of self-monitoring and reflection upon a chronic flow of psychological and social information about possible paths in life. Identity is no longer seen as "a given" or the result of ascribed statuses, but an ongoing project. In late modernity, the body has heightened significance in the construction of self through choice. The body is no longer seen as a "given," but is increasingly analyzed, dissected, eroticized, and celebrated. Through exercise, diet, pills, and surgery, the body is less something one is born with and increasingly something to be "worked upon" as central to the construction of self.

In such a society, seminarians are likely to see their own bodily practices, including sexual behaviors, as central in their identity. Like their peers, they grow up in a society where bodily and sexual experience is exalted. Like others in societies with a high level of reflexivity, their identities may be perceived as having "open" character. Their self-identities must be continually reconstituted by choices as they reflect on their pasts, presents, and futures. According to the dominant form of self in late modernity, new information received in new experiences can lead individuals to orient their life along a new trajectory. Reflection may help priests and seminarians monitor themselves, aid in their practice of celibacy, and confirm their clerical, celibate identity. However, in late modernity, there is also a sense in which an individual identity is always provisional, because it is always reflexively open to new experiences and information about the self. A commitment to live the asceticism of celibacy is subject to monitoring, evaluation, and reevaluation. The practice can then be more easily put aside if it no longer serves the project of constructing and confirming one's identity.

Decreasing Institutional and Disciplinary Support for Celibacy within the Roman Catholic Church

Pluralism and choice. Under the conditions of late modernity, seminarians do not necessarily experience the Church and its teachings and practices as inherited "givens" that are shared by all and have always been understood and practiced in the same way. The historical consciousness of post–Second Vatican Council theology no longer sees the Church as an unchanging reality (McBrien 1994:610). In addition, U.S. vocations are no longer recruited primarily from Catholic immigrant enclaves. For groups such as the Irish, entering the priesthood was a means of upward mobility and a source of family pride. Nor do most Catholics any longer live in ethnic ghettoes where they interact primarily with other Catholics. Seminarians are aware of competing belief systems and secular worldviews. As Peter Berger points out, such pluralism is a central characteristic of modern societies, exhibiting the coexistence in a society of multiple symbolic universes, with different beliefs, values, and moral evaluations (Berger 1969:127, 137–38). Pluralism heightens the role of choice in modern life and undermines the "taken for granted" quality of beliefs (Berger 1969:138). Others maintain that one of the effects of the Second Vatican Council was to legitimate theological and liturgical pluralism in the Church (McSweeney 1980:166–80, 192–95). As noted earlier, Schuth reported that polarization was a problem in many U.S. seminaries. Seminarians know that celibacy and other Catholic beliefs and practices are contested even within the Church. From Berger's perspective, this situation would tend to challenge the plausibility of the beliefs and practices of Catholic culture that seminarians are suppose to internalize. The result is that formation and commitment to a life of celibacy become more precarious.

Sociologist Patricia Wittberg (1994) has maintained that the teachings of the Second Vatican Council undermined the importance of celibacy. For most of Catholicism's history, "celibacy has been the essential precondition for embarking on any true search for sanctity, as well as the source of the virtuoso's spiritual power" (120). The pre–Second Vatican Council Catholic worldview organized the Church into three hierarchically ranked states: clerical, religious, and lay. The chaste celibacy practiced by clergy and religious gave them a superior status. Their lifestyle was modeled on the purity and perfection of a higher spiritual realm. By contrast, attention to the body, sexual desire, and familial connections tied the laity to the sinful, fallen world and its polluting influences. As late as 1954, Pope Pius XII's *Sacra Virginitas* (Sacred Virginity) taught that chaste celibacy was a superior state to the married life (Wittberg 1994:120).

However, the Second Vatican Council contributed to a delegitimation of celibate chastity and religious life as an elite calling. Wittberg claims the council *"nullified the basic ideological foundation for 18 centuries of Roman Catholic religious life"* (214;

emphasis in the original). Non-ordained religious were now classed as laity. The fact that their chaste celibacy no longer gave religious a privileged status also may have devalued the chaste celibacy of diocesan priests. As Wittberg laments, "the universal call to holiness" of *Lumen Gentium* removed chaste celibacy from its pedestal as a prerequisite for spiritual perfection. In addition, Wittberg sees *Gaudium et Spes* as "proclaiming the Church to be in *solidarity* with the very world its religious leaders had shunned for so long" (Wittberg 1994:214; emphasis in the original). The Church shifted its position from seeing holiness as a rejection of the world to one of affirming the positive elements of the modern world.

Worldly renunciation, including the renunciation of sexual activity as a means to holiness, is no longer unambiguously endorsed by the Church. I contend that this shift in normative Catholic documents removes some of the motivation that seminarians and priests might enjoy by living lives of celibacy. Marriage and family life are no longer viewed as obstacles to holiness, and spiritual perfection is now possible in any state or walk of life. Since the council, in the particular seminary examined in this case study, the number of priesthood candidates has plunged and lay ministry candidates, who are usually married, outnumber seminarians.

Declining stigmatization of resignation. The negative sanctions for resigning from the priesthood have also declined since the Second Vatican Council. The easing of restrictions on the laicization (official permission to cease ordained ministry and marry) resulted in seventy thousand priests being laicized since the mid-1960s (Cornwell 2001:155). As the number of priests' resignations has increased, the stigma of resigning from the priesthood has decreased. This lessening of the stigma may have contributed to more priests deciding to leave. As Cornwell (2001:15) speculates, these departures had a negative impact on those who remained as priests. In addition, as the number of priests declined, many more diocesan priests found themselves living alone. Diocesan priests in rural areas increasingly find themselves many miles from another priest. Priests have found themselves potentially more isolated from one another, and this may have weakened bonds of priestly fraternity. Not only are there smaller numbers of priests, but changes in liturgical theology and practices resulted in there being fewer opportunities for priests to gather for prayer and socializing. The traditional Forty Hours and Eucharistic Days of Adoration (which often included elaborate meals, card playing, and cocktails for clerics) are much less frequent since the Second Vatican Council. However, based on the analysis of survey data compiled in 1970 and 2002, and despite their lack of sexual relationships and family life, Greeley has argued that priests are happier with their lives and work than most American men (Greeley 2004a:48–53). In 2002, 90 percent said they would choose priesthood again (Greeley 2004a:49). I now conclude this chapter by considering some sociological works that theorize how religious commitment groups and institutions develop.

PRIESTHOOD, CELIBACY, AND COMMITMENT PRODUCTION

Seminary formation is a particularly intense form of professional socialization. To be effective, the Catholic Church, like other formal organizations, must engage in practices that build commitment to sets of role expectations for their personnel. In order for organizations to fulfill their purposes, they require that participants "become positively involved with the system...loyal, loving, dedicated, and obedient" (Kanter 1968:499). Seminary formation programs necessarily and deliberately engage in practices to build seminarians' commitments to the Church and to the practice of celibacy. Seminaries do not simply impart a body of knowledge to their students; they are "schools of commitment" that seek to engage the deepest loyalties of their students. Celibacy itself constitutes one such "commitment strategy" that the Roman Catholic Church has used for centuries to build loyalty and dedication to its mission and to effect a distance between its priests and its laity, a distance that effectively legitimates the priest's authority in relation to lay Catholics (young and old) and all women, religious or lay.

A number of sociologists have addressed the question of the social processes by which organizations validate and maintain commitment to beliefs. Borhek and Curtis (1974) describe several activities that members of organizations typically engage in to develop commitment to and validate beliefs. They argue that social sanctions are commonly used to produce elements of an organization's culture in general and commitment to systems of belief in particular (1974:86). This argument might appear to contradict my study's emphasis on the agency of both faculty and students in using cultural practices to build a culture where celibacy is esteemed. However, my research also examined the way in which seminary life is structured to produce commitment to celibacy. This structuring of seminary life includes formal sanctions and a sense of "not fitting in" for seminarians who do not conform to the expectations that faculty and students together create. Besides motivating commitment, Borhek and Curtis also specify the social processes through which organizations seek social support for beliefs through their consensual validation by group members. Several of the processes that Borhek and Curtis say are used to develop commitment and validate beliefs were observed at the seminary where research for this study was conducted. For example, I witnessed how rituals of membership, such as a priestly ordination ceremony, maintained consensual support for Catholicism's worldview and aided seminarians in acquiring a new social identity as priests.

In their examination of commitment to the role of priest, Schoenherr and Greeley (1974) studied a sample of 3,045 U.S. priests collected from a survey by the National Opinion Research Center. Studying the reasons for priests' resignations from the priesthood, Schoenherr and Greeley demonstrated the usefulness of understanding commitment to priesthood as a process in which actors seek a net balance of rewards over costs. They found that for younger, inner-directed priests, if the costs of celibacy, such as loneliness, outweighed perceived rewards, they frequently resigned from the priesthood (Schoenherr and Greeley 1974:422). They concluded that the cost of celibacy is the greatest factor in the commitment process (Schoenherr and Greeley 1974:417).

Among the ways in which cultural practices of seminary life are examined in this case study is in terms of the costs and benefits students and faculty members reported. Students engaged in practices that provided rewards and also served to deepen their commitment to the Catholic Church's work and mission. Kanter defined "commitment" as "the process through which an individual becomes attached to carrying out the socially organized patterns of behavior which are seen as fulfilling those interests, as expressing the nature and needs of the person" (1968:500). Kanter used historical materials to study ninety-one utopian communities founded between 1780 and 1860 in the United States. She assessed to what extent these communities used a variety of different commitment organizational strategies. Like Becker (1960) and Schoenherr and Greeley (1974), Kanter (1968:504) also saw commitment as involving a weighing of costs and rewards by group members.

Among the devices used by the groups Kanter studied were "sacrifices," practices involving austerity or renunciation. Sacrifices deepen group cohesion. Cohesion was said to involve actors forming positive "cathetic orientations" or affective ties among members (1968:500). As Kanter notes, individuals make sacrifices when there is a net balance of rewards over costs. Groups have frequently conceived of sacrifice as a means of consecration to God and a sacred action that brings the individual closer to God. These sacrifices raise a group's cause to a sacred level and also bind the individual to the group and its cause (Kanter 1968:504–5).

Sacrifices take a variety of forms, including abstinence and austerity. Abstention from oral gratification can include abstaining from alcohol, tobacco, and meat. Austerity also included the mechanism of material poverty (1968:505). Material poverty and abstention from sexual activity have been common commitment mechanisms used by Roman Catholic groups, and both continue to be used by the Church's religious orders of men and women. Kanter reported that celibacy was a frequent commitment mechanism used by utopian groups she studied. Successful utopian communities (defined as lasting at least twenty-five years) were more likely to use celibacy as a commitment mechanism than unsuccessful groups. Of the successful communities, 89 percent employed celibacy at some point. Only 9 percent of the unsuccessful communities used the mechanism (1968:505). Kanter theorized that celibacy was used to build cohesion and intensify affective ties in the groups she studied.

In my study, I view the daily life and the formation program of one seminary as constituted by the practice faculty members and students engage in to develop students' commitments to the seminary, priesthood, and the Church. Celibacy is a "sacrifice" and one cultural practice that is used to bind students' interests to the mission and purposes of the Church; other practices such as prayer, spiritual direction, and annual student evaluations, are described. Celibacy and other seminary practices provide students with particular costs and rewards that they weigh before proceeding to ordination to priesthood.

Stark and Finke (2000:181) theorize that celibacy is a "high cost" for Catholic seminarians that has kept all but the most motivated or committed persons from seeking ordination. They studied differences in commitments between seminary students who had promised celibacy and those who had not (were preparing for lay ministry). Stark and Finke examined data compiled by the Educational Testing Service on 416 students who entered Catholic seminaries from 1992 to 1994. They reported that the reasons for entering the seminary differed between students who were living celibately and those who were not. Celibates gave greatest emphasis to "a call from God" and a "desire to serve others" in explaining why they entered seminary (2000:181). Non-celibates were more likely to emphasize "intellectual interest" and the "opportunity for study and growth." Stark and Finke (2000:181) concluded that celibates are more dedicated and that mandatory celibacy keeps less committed persons from seeking ordination. However, Stark and Finke neglected the possibility that celibates may be motivated to enter seminaries more out of a commitment to serving others because they are virtually assured an opportunity to minister as a priest. Even the least gifted newly ordained is virtually assured of a lifetime of work, including being a pastor. Lay ministers face a much more uncertain career path and are not assured of a position in ministry. They may substitute personal reasons for study (intellectual satisfaction and opportunity for growth) because they may have more difficulty finding work after completion of their degree.

Stark and Finke assert that there has been a decline in religious vocations since the mid-1960s because particular Second Vatican Council decrees (*Lumen Gentium, Gaudium et Spes,* and *Perfectae Caritas*) decreased the elevated status of chaste celibacy. They maintain that the result was a decrease in the perceived reward for the costly sacrifice of celibacy (2000:178). Stark and Finke (2000:182) assert that restoring the traditional rewards of priesthood, such as high status, would likely yield an increase in vocations. In this study, how celibacy might serve to elevate the status of priests in the eyes of seminarians, priests, and laity will be explored. For people who see celibacy as edifying or even heroic, it is possible that requiring diocesan priests to engage in the practice enhances the status of priests. On the other hand, if individuals evaluate celibacy negatively, as leading to immaturity or even pathological behaviors, then the policy of mandatory celibacy would likely decrease the status of priests in the eyes of people who hold such views. The 2002 revelations of clerical sexual abuse of the young have certainly given ammunition to those who hold the latter view. Increasingly celibacy and priests have become popularly stereotyped objects of suspicion and the butt of jokes even among Catholics.

Four

OBSERVING CELIBACY
METHODOLOGY FOR A STUDY

SEMI-STRUCTURED INTERVIEWS

The core of my case study is semi-structured interviews with faculty and students. Rather than producing measures, rates, and scores, I sought to produce an account of seminary faculty and students' thoughts in a language faithful to their lived experience. Interviews are better able to represent the conceptual world of the informants in a detailed way. Only by interviewing seminarians and faculty could I hope to find out in their own words (and worlds) how they resist, internalize, and give meaning to celibacy. Semi-structured interviews with open-ended questions were chosen over written surveys or verbal questionnaires with closed questions with the hope that my probes would elicit more detailed data regarding how faculty and students actually use culture in a particular setting.

Social desirability bias is problematic in all research regarding sexuality, especially face-to-face interviews. Social desirability bias occurs when informants gauge their responses to the perceived expectations of the interviewer. It results in false answers that conform to perceived norms rather than revealing the informants' actual thoughts and behaviors. Understandably, informants might not respond with candor about the very personal aspects of their lives about which I was inquiring. Though informants were assured of anonymity, their possible tendency to give socially desirable responses was a critical issue throughout this case study. Students seeking ordination may have felt vulnerable if they responded in ways that called into question their ability to live lives of celibacy or become priests. Also, faculty may have been protective of their school's reputation. At the same time, it is my contention that priests and seminarians generally exhibit two traits that would enhance the trustworthiness of the interviews: a desire to be helpful to others (including the priest–graduate student conducting interviews) and a desire to be honest if at all possible (that is, if they perceived no negative sanctions for their honesty). I found faculty and seminarians enthusiastic about the fact that I was researching seminary formation and helpful and cooperative throughout the period of data collection. The social desirability of their answers is more difficult to assess.

It could be argued that one of the purposes of all professional training programs, from medical schools to seminaries, is to teach practitioners how to maintain a mystique and "public face" that distances themselves from the clientele they serve. If this were the case, seminaries would train students not only to live lives of celibacy, but also how to "manage" their public sexual identities and practices to please ecclesiastical superiors, as well as the laity they serve. I found that seminarians did manage their identities in the presence of faculty and other students in order to be deemed worthy of ordination, increasing the likelihood of socially desirable responses. Goffman has described the elaborate ways in which stigmatized individuals manage their public identities (1963). Homosexual seminarians would have a particularly strong incentive to manage their public sexual identity. If the sexual scandals have managed to paint all priests with the broad brushstroke of "sexual predator," then both homosexual and heterosexual faculty and seminarians may have felt more pressure to manage their public sexual identities as heterosexual and celibate. Assuming this to be a strong likelihood, my interviews also hoped to reveal the ways in which seminarians learn to manage their public sexual selves. It also is likely that informants were managing their identities for the interviewer as well. Efforts by informants to manage their identities for the interviewer then necessarily became part of the data collected.

It is difficult to estimate the extent to which recent scandals and reports of a possible policy forbidding ordination of homosexuals affected the informants' abilities to speak freely and be helpful. (Both the scandals and this possible policy are described below under "Site Selection for Case Study," p. 84.) These same scandals and reports also were likely to have affected the conditions under which formators conduct their programs. Reports of the policy on the ordination of homosexuals could have a particularly chilling effect on the ability of homosexual students to be open among themselves or with faculty. As these national events unfolded, both the object of my study (seminary reproduction of celibacy) and my ability to conduct the research were changing. These events could affect the openness and attitudes of my informants. Measures to develop rapport with informants and overcome socially desirable responses are addressed below in the "Procedures" section (p. 90).

Because of the sensitive nature of the sexual content of my interviews, the vulnerability of seminarians scrutinized for their fitness for ordination, and the political climate in the Catholic Church and seminaries, written informed consent of all informants was critical. In addition, seminarians are a vulnerable population because they spend so much time with professors who evaluate them annually (besides course grades) regarding their fitness for ordination. Much time would have to be spent by the researcher on campus attending meals and liturgies so that rapport with students and faculty could be gained and they would consent to interviews.

I also sought permission from each informant to make an audiotape of the interview. Audiorecordings provided more likelihood of a complete record of the interview than extensive note taking during and after interviews. Audiorecording provided the opportunity to review tapes as often as necessary so that more understanding could be gained from each informant. Pauses and emotional tone could also be easily reviewed. Taping freed me from extensive note taking during the interview and enabled me to focus and attend to the informant and the flow of conversation. I also sought permission to take brief notes (words and phrases) during the interview to focus my own attention and to indicate attention and interest to the informant. I was aware that audiotaping could hinder informants' candidness and increased the likelihood of socially desirable responses. These were significant concerns in this project and for all research on sexuality. However, it was decided that the advantages of audiotaping outweighed the disadvantages. Interviews would be transcribed verbatim within a few days of the interview. Field notes from each interview were written up after each interview as soon as possible, usually within twenty-four hours.

Selection of Faculty Informants

For this case study, I sought to conduct semi-structured interviews with both students and faculty of the seminary studied. I also sought to interview the head of the seminary's governing board or the person most responsible for oversight of the operation of the seminary. In the case of seminaries operated by a diocese, the local ordinary is ultimately responsible for the school's governance, in accordance with canon law, whether or not he is on the governing board (Schuth 1999:95).[21] The local ordinary is responsible for seeing that the seminary operates according to the decrees of the Second Vatican Council and canon law (NCCB 1993: no. 446). Because the ordinary is to maintain a close relationship with the seminary, he is likely to be influential in shaping its policies and faculty appointments.

Among faculty, I chose to interview both those responsible for the overall operation of the seminary and those most intimately involved in seminary formation for celibacy. Priests normally hold major administrative positions (NCCB 1993: no. 458). To learn from those responsible for and most involved in formation for celibacy, I needed to interview the rector (or rector-president), the academic dean, the dean of students, and the faculty member who oversees the spiritual formation program (variously known as the dean of formation, director of spiritual formation, or the spiritual formation director).[22]

The appropriateness of interviewing these administrators was determined by the functions they perform in seminaries. The rector guides the overall operation of the seminary, and seminary statutes determine who appoints the rector. In those dioceses operated by a single archdiocese (accounting for seventeen of the thirty-three seminaries training diocesan priests), rectors are appointed by and are accountable to the bishop of the diocese that owns and operates the seminary. However, if seminaries are run by religious orders or are autonomous corporations, the local or-dinary still must approve the appointment of the rector (NCCB 1993: no. 460). The rector is the seminary's chief administrative officer. He is responsible for implementation of the seminary program and the well-being of faculty and students (NCCB 1993: nos. 461–62). He should be schooled in "sound doctrine" and "be an exemplary model of priestly virtue" (NCCB 1993: no. 463). The rector is expected to address the topic of celibacy periodically and not less than once a year (NCCB 1993: no. 290). He is also responsible for clearly stating behavioral expectations for students regarding sexual conduct (NCCB 1993: no. 330).

The academic dean assists the rector by administering the academic program of the seminary. This includes overseeing its curriculum, the work of the faculty, and the academic progress of students. The academic dean may be assisted in maintaining academic records by a registrar. From the academic dean I would learn how student coursework contributed to students' formation for celibacy.

The dean of students assists the rector with a variety of tasks. He may oversee the annual student evaluation process (NCCB: 1993 no. 470). He coordinates access of students to psychological services and assures that counselors are "supportive of the Church's expectations of candidates for the priesthood" (NCCB 1993: no. 471). The dean of students also "holds seminarians accountable in the external forum for their conduct as men preparing for the priesthood, whose actions contribute to a whole-some spirit in the community" (NCCB 1993: no. 469).[23] The dean of students functions as the seminary disciplinarian. He is responsible for punishing rule infractions, from missing mass to dating. All of these responsibilities make the dean of students a key administrator to interview.

The director of spiritual formation (also known as the dean of formation or simply the spiritual director) assists the rector by overseeing the spiritual formation program for priesthood students. He is responsible for planning weekly formation conferences. He also coordinates days of recollection and retreats. He works with the director of liturgy to assure that the Liturgy of the Hours and the Eucharist are celebrated daily (NCCB 1993:

no. 481). He sees that each student has a personal spiritual director. He supervises the students' personal spiritual directors (who may or may not be faculty members), making sure that they are priests who have been adequately prepared to be spiritual guides (NCCB 1993: no. 480). Students' particular spiritual directors should be "exemplary priests who are dedicated to the Church's service and to the total ministerial priesthood" (NCCB 1993: no. 482). It was necessary to interview the director of spiritual formation because he is the person that most immediately designs and oversees the implementation of formation for celibacy.

Besides these administrative positions, the other positions described by the *Program of Priestly Formation* are the director of the pre-theology program, the director of field education, the director of development and public relations, and the business manager (NCCB 1993: no. 468, 472–78). Because they are less intimately involved in and responsible for areas related to formation for celibacy, these personnel were not interviewed. The *Program of Priestly Formation* carefully specifies the spiritual, academic, and professional preparation and responsibilities of faculty members who teach in seminaries and theologates. Particular attention is directed toward their doctrinal responsibilities (NCCB 1993: nos. 502–4). While lay faculty members are permitted, "Priest faculty members should teach significant portions of the course of studies in the major theological disciplines" (NCCB: 1993 no. 487). In addition to the rector, academic dean, dean of students, and director of spiritual formation, I sought to interview two additional faculty members to learn how faculty members contributed to the reproduction of celibacy in diocesan seminaries, as well as to verify what administrators say is done. I selected these two faculty members after having spent time on campus and acquainting myself with the faculty in the semester I was doing the interviewing. Two criteria were used to select which two teaching faculty members were interviewed. The professors who were selected were based on my evaluation of their willingness to talk freely about seminary formation. This subjective evaluation was based on exchanges with faculty prior to beginning my interviews. Second, professors teaching courses related to celibacy and sexual morality were favored for selection. The teaching of sexual morality has drawn the particular attention of Vatican officials (Gill 2002:10). The detailed way in which the *Program of Priestly Formation* specifies formators' responsibilities and requires that they be exemplary priests reflects the great care that is taken in the training of Catholic priests. Faculty members are expected to be models of priesthood and ministry for seminarians.

Selection of Student Informants

Students were selected on the basis of three main criteria. First, I selected students whom I perceived to be more open and willing to share their experiences with me. This was a form of purposive sampling. My subjective evaluation was made based on interactions with students at meals and observations during the orientation for first-year students. This way of selecting informants had both advantages and disadvantages. A potential advantage was that more outgoing informants provide lengthier, richer interviews. A disadvantage is that the data from these informants may have differed from those that were not selected, and their responses may not have been representative of all seminarians in that school. It is possible that less outgoing students had different experiences and attitudes. However, they likely would be less willing to share these with me. The students I selected were those with whom I felt there was the greatest likelihood of rapport and openness necessary for strong interviews. I believed the advantages of interviewing these students outweighed potential disadvantages.

Second, due to the possibility that experiences and attitudes of students differed by years spent in formation, I interviewed two seminarians from each of the four or five years in the graduate theological program.[24] A third factor in selection of students was ethnicity. I wished to interview both native-born and foreign-born students (likely to be Hispanic or Asian). Foreign-born students are increasing in number and I was open to the possibility that their attitudes and experiences may differ from those of native-born students. The precise ethnic mix of students chosen to be interviewed would depend on the ethnic composition of the school selected. I preferred that the selected students together reflect the ethnic make-up of the school and at the same time wanted the opportunity to interview both native- and foreign-born students to assess any differences in their attitudes and experiences.

OTHER DATA SOURCES

While interviews were the primary data collection method utilized in this project, observation of formation activities and daily life, as well as document analysis, were seen as useful ways to verify what informants said and add to the richness of my account of the reproduction of celibacy. On-site observation and document analysis were means for the triangulation of data by methods of data collection other than interviewing. In this case study, triangulation of data refers to using multiple methods of data collection to confirm accuracy of the research and to increase the completeness of the data or picture of seminary life. Observations of formation activities and daily life were a means to verify what students *said* occurs in interviews. Observation provided another way to learn about seminary culture and how students and faculty interact with themselves and one another. Observed activities included formation conferences, classes, masses, prayer services, meals, and days of recollection. Field notes were taken as soon as possible after all observation periods.

Document analysis provided a means for learning how seminary practices and culture were codified in the seminary academic bulletin, handbook, and especially the rule of life. The seminary catalogue and handbook were read to see how the institution presented an account of itself, as well as pertinent policies. In addition, all seminaries are required by the *Program of Priestly Formation* (1993) to have a written rule of life. It is intended "to establish the basic patterns and expectations of community living" (NCCB 1993: no. 202). It is the seminary's rulebook for priesthood students and thus would be helpful in understanding the expectations of students and the ways that administrators sought to regulate student behavior. Concrete behavioral expectations, proscribed activities, and their sanctions are described in each seminary's rule of life.

Site Selection for Case Study

My search for a seminary for a case study was made more challenging by the news events of early 2002. In January, the *Boston Globe* began to publish a series of articles revealing that dozens of the Archdiocese of Boston's priests had sexually abused minors over many years. Offending priests had been frequently transferred to new parishes, where they molested more minors. Secret payments were made to silence victims and prevent scandal. Soon media across the country began to reveal hundreds of cases of alleged clergy abuse, with the failure of diocesan personnel to assure that perpetrators did not repeat their actions. Most of the victims were adolescent boys. In the first four months of 2002, the *Boston Globe* alone published nearly three hundred articles on clergy sexual abuse (Investigative Staff of the *Boston Globe* 2002). The revelations of still-unfolding clergy sexual abuse provoked the American Roman Catholic Church's greatest crisis ever. In April, the Vatican announced that investigating teams would be sent to all American seminaries. Their inquiry would focus on two areas: "the need for fidelity to the church's teaching, especially in the area of morality, and the need for deeper study of the criteria of suitability for candidates to the priesthood" (quoted by Gill 2002:10). In October 2002, it was reported that the Vatican Congregation for Education was circulating draft proposals that would forbid the ordination of homosexuals to the priesthood (Williams and Cooperman 2002:5B). Newspaper stories were raising the question of what role seminary formation played in clergy sexual abuse (Goodstein 2002:A1).

While some maintained that seminaries in the 1950s fostered sexual repression and immaturity, others blamed the abuse crisis on moral laxity in their operation in the 1970s and 1980s. Seminary officials were stung that spring of 2002 by new charges that heterosexual men who adhered to traditional Church teachings and morality were discriminated against in U.S. seminaries. As I began to look for a seminary for my research, the poorly documented but widely read *Goodbye, Good Men: How Catholic Seminaries Turned Away Two Generations of Vocations from the*

Priesthood by Michael Rose (2002) was published. Rose maintained that openly gay subcultures have flourished in a largely dysfunctional seminary system. Rose interviewed many disaffected seminarians, but didn't allow seminary administrators to defend their policies or practices. Seminary administrators have been quick to challenge Rose's allegations (Canary and Cameli 2002:6). Though highly biased, Rose's contentions appeared to be well received among traditionalist Catholics searching for explanations for the plunge in seminary enrollments after the Second Vatican Council. Seminary formation was quickly becoming a battleground for supporters and critics of celibacy.

Educational institutions, including seminaries, are understandably protective of their reputations. However, I needed to be free to write up my findings without any interference. A seminary's effective training and good reputation may help laity to develop trusting ministerial relationships with their clergy. Seminaries also protect their reputations so that they can attract students. Seminaries operated by a single diocese or religious order depend on bishops in dioceses that do not operate a seminary to send them students. Seminary administrators must please the bishops of other dioceses if those bishops are going to have their students trained there. Seminaries also depend on alumni/ae for donations. Seminaries owned by dioceses must raise funds among the laity of that diocese in order to pay for their expense. These factors would likely contribute to caution on the part of seminary administrators in granting access to do research.

Amid these news events and the controversy regarding Rose's book, I sought a seminary for a case study. Schuth's study of all U.S. theologates and seminaries lists forty-three all-graduate-level theologates and seminaries in the United States. The listing remains accurate and was cross-checked with the Center for Applied Research in the Apostolate's listing of theologates and graduate-level seminaries (Froehle and Gautier 2000:184–85). Schools that trained primarily religious order students were eliminated from consideration since the focus of my research was diocesan seminaries. Schuth lists thirty-three seminaries that train candidates for diocesan priesthood. Most of these seminaries are owned and operated by a single diocese or religious order. Autonomous corporations operate three. In addition, St. Vincent de Paul Regional Seminary is jointly owned and conducted by five Florida dioceses. The Pontifical North American College (Rome) is jointly owned and operated by the U.S. bishops. The American College of the Catholic University of Louvain (Belgium) is cooperatively owned and operated by the bishops of the United States and Canada (Schuth 1999:245–48). Among these thirty-three seminaries, the two European seminaries for U.S. diocesan seminarians were eliminated as possible sites because many visits over several months would be necessary and studying an overseas seminary would be costly and cumbersome.

I was left with thirty-one seminaries from which to find one that would permit me to do a case study. For all the above stated reasons, I was fearful no seminary would grant me permission to do my research and allow me free access. The selection of a seminary for a case study hinged on finding a seminary that would permit me to have free, unencumbered access to students and faculty. I would need to interview any and all students and faculty of my choosing. I wanted the freedom to attend seminary formation sessions, liturgies, and meals, and to observe daily life within a seminary.

In a case study, the selected site obviously greatly affects what the findings of the research project will be. It is also obvious that no single seminary could meaningfully be held to be typical or representative of all diocesan seminaries. Since an ethnographic study is necessarily local and particular, it was not necessary to seek the most "representative" seminary (if one could be meaningfully said to exist). The Vatican-approved *Program of Priestly Formation* guides all these seminaries, but of course they are not all the same. Seminaries vary in myriad ways. Some seminaries enroll only men studying for priesthood. Increasingly, seminaries also enroll men and women in lay formation programs. As noted earlier, in her study of all U.S. seminaries and theologates, Schuth described the varying contexts of academic and spiritual formation by distinguishing between these two models: the self-contained seminary (only priesthood students) and the

interconnected seminary (priesthood and lay ministry students). A case study of a single seminary cannot in itself offer contrasts between these two models.

Some student bodies are made up mostly of men in their mid-to-late twenties and thirties, while a few specialize in training older "second career vocations." Seminary students in their sixties are not uncommon. Men of European descent comprise the majority of the students in some seminaries. Other seminaries are enrolling more native- and foreign-born Hispanic and Asian students. Some seminaries are located on the campuses of large urban universities. Others are located in remote rural areas. Schuth (1999:99–116) noted the varieties of their administrative structures, differences in faculty academic credentials, and responsibilities.

In my own previous visits I had sensed much diversity among seminaries. I have observed students attending mass in blue jeans. At another that I visited, students were required to wear cassocks and surplices at mass. Eastern seminaries are purported by some to be more "traditional." Midwestern seminaries by reputation are more "progressive." However, generally it is difficult to categorize seminaries ideologically.

While seminaries surely vary, the trends that characterize their student populations (older, more ethnically diverse, more theologically conservative, less previous association with parish life) have been seen throughout the country (Schuth 2000:19–21). There is no typical seminary that in a privileged way could explicate formation for celibacy in all seminaries. Even if it were possible to have the time to develop the trust of informants in several seminaries, there is no coherent way to select a seminary or seminaries that would be representative of all U.S. diocesan seminaries. As a case study, my research is necessarily local and specific and cannot claim to represent the essence of all seminary cultures. What is much more important in ethnographic research is selecting a site where the researcher will have free and unencumbered access to converse with and observe his or her informants.

Across the country, newspapers and television news programs were awash in reports of clergy sexual abuse. It was my contention that my status as a priest was among my greatest assets in gaining

access and trust to do my research. I decided to contact a seminary where I personally knew several faculty members and sought to parlay this familiarity into trust and access for my research. In March, I wrote to the rector of what I call in this book "St. Mark's Seminary in the Archdiocese of Middlefield." Since "St. Mark's" was one of a relatively small number of seminaries, it is referred to by this pseudonym. Likewise, "Middlefield" is a pseudonym. Some details of seminary life and informants' interviews were omitted or modestly altered. All names of faculty and students are pseudonyms. Identifying features of the school, faculty, and students have been altered to protect anonymity. Like dioceses across the country, Middlefield faced much negative publicity and the removal of several priests after the U.S. Conference of Catholic Bishops adopted a "zero-tolerance policy" in June 2000 for all priests who have ever abused minors. I suggested in my letter that the recent misdeeds of clergy made research into the training of priests to live lives of celibacy more necessary than ever. I stipulated that I needed to be free to confidentially interview whomever I wished. I promised to conceal the identity of the informants and of the seminary at which the case study was conducted. Four weeks later, I received a friendly affirmative reply to my request. The rector, Fr. Dahman, mentioned that a student advisory committee was also amenable to my desire to do research at St. Mark's.

I was glad to receive permission to conduct my research but was concerned about the effect of the clergy abuse scandal on the openness of faculty and students in response to my interview questions. Since St. Mark's was one of only a relatively small number of seminaries, some details of the seminary life and informants' interviews would have to be omitted or modestly altered. Stories of clergy misconduct had already harmed the fund-raising efforts of the Middlefield archdiocese. With a Vatican investigation of all U.S. seminaries pending, faculty might be even more inclined to put the best face on their formation efforts. Homosexual students, faced with the possibility of being barred from ordination, would have more incentive to be evasive regarding their sexual thoughts and feelings. I remained hopeful that my

status as a priest and former seminarian would merit my informants' trust as an "insider" and discourage evasive or socially desirable responses to my questions. Before beginning interviews, I would spend seven weeks on campus attending liturgies and meals to become familiar with faculty and students. In all my interactions with students and faculty, I wanted them to know I was a sympathetic member of their clerical "tribe."

Research Site

St. Mark's Seminary is the primary center of ministerial formation for the Archdiocese of Middlefield. Originally founded more than a hundred years ago, the seminary conducts programs of intellectual, spiritual, and pastoral formation for diocesan priests. In recent years, a graduate program for lay ministers was added. Most of these students are women. The lay formation program prepares laity to minister in parishes, schools, hospitals and hospices, prisons, and other settings. St. Mark's is fully accredited by the Association of Theological Schools. The seminary also offers separate non-degree programs for permanent deacons and lay ministers.

St. Mark's is one of the nation's smaller seminaries. Fewer than thirty-five students were enrolled in the five-year priesthood program at the beginning of the fall 2002 semester. An additional student was in the English as a Second Language Program. More than forty students are in the lay ministry degree program. Students without an adequate background in philosophy and theology spend a minimum of a year in a pre-theology program. International students (nearly half of the students in the priestly formation program) are most often recruited from Latin America. Non-English-speaking students must pass the *Test of English as a Foreign Language* (TOEFL) before they can begin their theological studies. Priesthood students earn a master of divinity degree. Lay formation students may earn a master of arts in pastoral studies or the more comprehensive master of divinity degree. The master of divinity degree requires four years of full-time study, plus an internship year for priesthood candidates. After the second year of study, priesthood students do a quarter of Clinical Pastoral Education, usually in a hospital setting. This is followed by

a full-time eight-month internship in a parish. Upon completion of their fourth and fifth years of study, students are ordained to the priesthood.

Only priests and candidates for the priesthood live on campus. The seminary approximates Erving Goffman's account of a total institution in that seminarians studied, recreated, ate, and slept in the same place (1961). Unlike the mental hospital Goffman studied, St. Mark's is not coercively organized. Several priest faculty members, including the rector, vice-rector/dean of resident students, and spiritual formation director lived on campus. Other priests and all lay faculty members lived off campus. This living arrangement meant that faculty (especially resident priest faculty) and priesthood students interacted regularly throughout the day at Morning Prayer and Evening Prayer, Eucharist, classes, meals, and during "off-hours." This arrangement contributed to the intensity of the socialization experience that seminarians underwent.

PROCEDURES

Initial Steps in Conducting Research

In July 2002, I called Fr. Gerald Dahman, the rector, to arrange to meet to discuss details of how my research would proceed in the coming school year. In mid-July, I had a friendly, nearly hour-long conversation with him about these matters. I was a bit surprised when he greeted me in his office in shorts and a golf shirt, but I was to learn that this was a part of the informality at St. Mark's. We discussed the impact of the recent clergy abuse scandals in the diocese and details about how to best proceed with my research that fall. Fr. Dahman was encouraging of the research project and clearly pleased to have me conducting research at St. Mark's. I reaffirmed my commitment to protecting the identity of the seminary I was studying and the anonymity of those I would interview. I also stipulated that I had to be free to write up my findings without the interference of St. Mark's or Middlefield diocese. Fr. Dahman agreed to these conditions. We also agreed that I would provide information for a letter from

Fr. Dahman that would be placed in all students' mailboxes at the beginning of the fall semester. The letter briefly described my research, informed them of my anticipated presence on campus, and invited them to consider being interviewed if asked.

Toward the end of our talk, Fr. Dahman took me down the hall to see St. Mark's academic dean, Dr. Nathan Litkowiak. Fr. Dahman and Dr. Litkowiak suggested that I send a longer letter to the faculty describing my project and inviting their cooperation. It was also agreed that I would present an overview of my research project to them at the next faculty meeting, which was scheduled for the third week in August, just before the beginning of the academic year. I would also be introduced to the student body at a community liturgy at the beginning of the term. It was then agreed that when attending a class or formation conference, I would gain permission of the faculty member conducting the class or conference prior to its occurrence. Otherwise, I was free to come and go on campus as I wished. Fr. Dahman suggested I meet with Fr. Francis Blatsky, the director of spiritual formation for the priesthood program. Fr. Blatsky provided me with a list of all the students with their corresponding year in the five-year formation program. From him I could learn what components of the priestly formation program I wanted to observe in the coming semester. A couple of weeks later, I met with Fr. Blatsky to learn what formation events it would be helpful for me to observe. He gave me a booklet outlining the fall formation schedule.

During the third week of August, I spent a half hour at a faculty meeting. I introduced myself and described my interest in celibacy and seminary formation. I then outlined my research project and invited their cooperation. I informed the fifteen full-time faculty members in attendance that I would regularly be on campus in the next semester and that I might seek to interview them and attend one of their classes. They listened very attentively and then I fielded questions, including one on how would the identity of the informants and seminary be protected. I explained my confidentiality procedures. I also expressed a willingness to present my research findings to the faculty and students after the completion of my dissertation. My summer meetings with Fr. Dahman, Fr. Blatsky, Dr. Litkowiak, and the entire full-time faculty all paved the way for me to begin my research with students. I was receiving excellent cooperation from the St. Mark's faculty and the access to students for which I had hoped.

I began my research at St. Mark's the first week in August, sitting in on several sessions of a month-long orientation period for new priesthood students, as well as attending masses and meals. The last week in August, all students, both priesthood and lay ministry candidates, returned to school and began classes. The second week of classes, I was introduced to the student body at the conclusion of weekday liturgy. From then on I would visit the campus about three times a week to observe the daily life in the seminary.

Interviewing Students

By the third week of September, I had decided which ten students (two from each formation year) I wanted to interview. By interviewing ten students, I was interviewing almost half of the priesthood students. The ethnicity of students was obtained from Fr. Blatsky. Just over half are native-born. Because of attrition, there were only two students in the fourth and fifth year classes, so both would have to be interviewed. All the fourth and fifth year students were foreign-born. I chose five native-born students and five foreign-born students from these classes so that the ethnic background of the students interviewed would be more representative of the student body. These two factors did not leave much room for my third criterion, perceived openness and willingness to be interviewed. However, this criterion was used when it was necessary to select one student over another. This criterion was not applied absolutely. In one case, I chose to interview a student who appeared to interact less with students and be a bit of a "loner." I thought that he might bring another perspective to my research.

I wrote letters to the ten students selected as informants. I asked them if they would be willing to be interviewed for my research project. I requested that they call me at my personal phone number within two weeks to indicate whether they were willing to participate. I used a telephone answering machine to take messages in the event that I was not present to receive their call. I returned their calls and informed them that I would call again to set up an interview with them in October or November. All but two students were prompt in returning my calls. Another student who was doing his internship year in a parish seemed hesitant to agree to be interviewed and asked that he first receive the permission of the pastor in the parish where he was interning. After a second call and my telling him that I did not think his pastor would mind, he agreed to the interview with some hesitation. To some degree, agreement to be interviewed may be an expression of deference to the researcher as a priest. It may have also been an expression of compliance, since the ethos of seminaries calls for students to be helpful to others and cooperative with authority figures (I shared the same priest status with several faculty members). I now had ten students who agreed to be interviewed. I began the student interviews in mid-October and completed them in November. I intentionally spread the interviews over several weeks, but they were not done in any particular order.

About two weeks before I hoped to interview a student, I called the student to let him know where we would meet. The interviews needed to be done in quiet, private rooms where audiotaping was easily done. The proposed St. Mark's rule of life stated that only fellow seminarians and faculty are permitted in student rooms. The rector said that the school's building usage coordinator would handle arranging a room for me if I notified her when I would be interviewing students. The rooms I conducted the interviews varied depending on the class schedule and campus events for any particular day. Most of my interviews were conducted in the same airy, high-ceilinged classroom with oblong, rectangular wooden tables and padded wooden chairs. The room was nondescript, except for a very large oil painting of the seminary's patron, St. Mark. Such paintings of saints were frequent throughout the seminary. At the suggestion of one student, the other seminarian doing a parish internship, his interview was conducted at Middlefield's college seminary residence. The residence was much closer to the parish where he was interning. That interview was conducted in the building's small chapel, the student reasoning that we would be undisturbed there.

At the beginning of each interview, I spent about ten minutes introducing myself, asking how their semesters were going, and generally seeking to put them at ease. Then I described to them how I came to be interested in research on celibacy, priests, and seminarians. Then I explained the purpose of my current interviews and how their interviews could contribute to a better understanding of celibacy training and possibly lead to improvements in the formation of priests in the future. I explained the project's confidentiality procedures, including the use of pseudonyms and the removal of identifying features from the interviews. I asked informants to sign two copies of the Informed Consent Form. I returned a copy to them and kept one copy for myself. I also let them know that they could contact me at the phone number on the consent form if they had any additional thoughts regarding the interview topics or if they had second thoughts about having their interview used in the research. I also asked the informants if I could tape the interviews, as well as take notes while we talked. None expressed reservations regarding my audiorecording the interview or note taking or asked questions about the consent form or confidentiality procedures. I took brief notes of their attire, manner, and non-verbal behaviors, as well as key points or phrases used by students. I did not engage in extensive note taking during the interviews since they were recorded and I did not want to take my attention away from my informant's responses.

Although the questions were open-ended, I used a questionnaire guide so that all the areas I thought necessary were covered. The guide included a cover sheet with questions regarding biographical information (age, birthplace, education, previous career, number of years in seminary, and previous seminaries attended). The biographical questions were the first ones that were asked of the participants. The interview guide included questions regarding how they came to be interested in priesthood and entered the seminary, their experiences dating, their impressions of seminary life, and their thoughts regarding formation for celibacy (Appendix A). The use of the interview guide assured that I would cover all the areas that I thought were important but would permit a conversational tone that allowed flexibility for students to describe experiences in their own terms and raise issues of importance to them. Because of the conversational tone of the discussions, questions were not always covered in the order listed on the guide or asked with the same wording. This flexibility also allowed me to depart from the scripted questions when necessary. This format was used to build rapport and enhance the openness I hoped for from informants.

Consistent with naturalistic modes of research, while interviewing students I encouraged them to describe their experiences in their own vocabulary and categories. For instance, early in the interview I always asked students how they came to be interested in priesthood. I never phrased the question, "When did you learn you had a vocation or call to the priesthood?" since this would be introducing particular categories into how they think about themselves.

Students appeared to accept my role as priest–graduate student conducting research on formation for celibacy. I believe that being a priest established a rapport and trust that might not have as easily been granted to a layperson. I saw myself as both an insider and outsider to the St. Mark's community. I was an insider in that I was Catholic, a former seminarian, and a celibate priest. While I presumed they shared similar aspirations, I was distanced from them from having already been ordained for eighteen years. I avoided sharing my own impressions and experiences of seminary and celibacy. I did find that it was easier to talk to informants than to a friend about an issue close to my heart. I was an outsider in that I was not a part of this small group of people that interacted several times daily, living in the same building and sharing meals, prayer, classes, and recreation. I let the students know that it had been many years since I was in seminary and that things may be different today. They should not presume I had much knowledge of their particular seminary. While my status as priest surely colored their perception of me, I preferred that they know as little about me as possible. However, since I shared many meals with students and attended a weekend human development workshop at a retreat center, it was inevitable that students came to know me somewhat. I hope that my congeniality and limited familiarity enhanced the openness and trustworthiness of students rather than contributing to their guardedness or socially desirable interview responses. I began and ended interviews assuring students that nothing they said would be shared with the faculty in an identifiable way.

I sought to demonstrate a "critical empathy" in my interviews and interactions with students. This meant trying to understand their own personal biography and the context of their experiences without necessarily internally agreeing with them. Generally, I expressed agreement with whatever informants said to me. I wore dress slacks, an open-collared dress shirt, and sometimes a sweater during the interviews. Except in the cases of two students who wore blue jeans and sweatshirts, students were similarly attired. I purposely avoided wearing a clerical collar shirt to try to disassociate myself from my status as a priest, though this status provided rapport with faculty and students. I believed that avoidance of clerical clothing might indicate a less judgmental attitude and decrease the likelihood that students would feel compelled to respond in ways consistent with official school or Church policies.

The interviews lasted fifty-five minutes to ninety-five minutes. Most ended with the student expressing interest in the results of my research and wishing me well. I let them know I would continue to visit the campus if they wished to see me. One student contacted me to set up a time to meet to add further thoughts on one of his responses. We met one evening in a student lounge for another half-hour.

This study's interviews were conducted in the autumn of 2002 following the previous winter-spring revelations of clergy sexual abuse. Even as the interviews were conducted, local media continued to present new stories on the old local abuse cases uncovered in the spring.

INTERVIEWING FACULTY
AND THE ARCHBISHOP

The administrators interviewed were those who were responsible for and most closely involved in formation for celibacy. These faculty members were the rector, dean of resident (priesthood) students (who was also the vice-rector), the academic dean, and the spiritual director (director of formation for the priesthood students). All of them also had some teaching duties at the school. I also interviewed three additional professors from the school. The first two were chosen based on two criteria. First, in interactions on campus they seemed knowledgeable and willing to talk about formation for celibacy. These professors had previously served as the rector and vice-rector of St. Mark's. Second, they were chosen because they both taught moral theology. My research design did not call for interviewing a third faculty member. However, another professor was added when I learned that he was seriously considering leaving the priesthood due to the policy of mandatory celibacy and would be on sabbatical the following semester contemplating his future. This situation, and that he told me he was gay, provided an opportunity to interview someone with a different perspective on formation for celibacy. Since he told me he was likely to be leaving the faculty and the priesthood, he might not be as protective of the official positions of the school and the Catholic Church.

I contacted all faculty members by telephone, in the same manner that I contacted students. Most of the faculty were interviewed in November. A second interview with the vice-rector/dean of resident students was conducted the first week of the second semester in January. The faculty interviews were not conducted in any particular order, except that the vice-rector/dean of resident students was interviewed second to last because of his significant role in formation for celibacy at St. Mark's, and I thought he could fill in some of the "holes" regarding a few matters that seemed unclear. I taped the final interview in January at the home of the professor who was considering leaving the priesthood and who was then on sabbatical. I kept in touch with some faculty members by telephone in the following semester when questions arose as I was writing up the first semester's interviews. All other faculty interviews were conducted in the faculty members' offices, except for one person who asked that his interview be held in an empty classroom. These offices were, without exception, cramped and filled with books. All faculty members agreed to be interviewed and to audiotaping without hesitation. The same confidentiality and informed consent procedures were followed with faculty as were used with students. As with the student interviews and for the same reasons, I wore dress slacks and a dress shirt in my faculty interviews. Faculty at St. Mark's alternated clerical and "civilian" dress, and so my not wearing clergy clothing did not seem inappropriate.[25] A questionnaire guide was used in the same manner as in student interviews. Interview themes included formation approaches and practices used, changes in practices, behavioral expectations of students, indicators of student success, perceptions of students, and difficulties working with students (Appendix B). During the course of the research, it became necessary to contact the Middlefield archdiocese's vocation director, Rev. Michael Moto, and the director of the lay formation program, Jason Fox. For these brief interviews notes were taken, but no audiotaping was performed.

As with students, I saw myself having an insider/outsider status when interviewing faculty. I shared the status of priest with the faculty, with the exception of the academic dean, who is a layman. I sensed an enthusiasm for my research from every faculty member as they felt that the research could improve formation for celibacy. Assuming that my research would help students, faculty appeared to respond freely to my questions. At the same time I was an outsider and not a part of the seminary community. I did not share the faculty members' potential interest in protecting the reputation of the school. At times I was surprised by the frankness of faculty members, especially regarding difficulties with Church teachings and policies, and their criticism of students (although not by name). Interviews with faculty varied from 55 minutes to 155 minutes. If an interview took more than 90 minutes, another was scheduled. In one case (the vice-rector/dean of students), I had to arrange for an additional hour-long interview.

I contacted the appointment secretary of the archbishop of Middlefield by telephone in October to schedule a December interview. The archbishop of Middlefield was interviewed in December and January at diocesan headquarters in suburban Middlefield. We met in his comfortable (but not elaborate) window-lined office. The same confidentiality procedures were used with the archbishop that had been used with students and faculty. He also agreed to be audiotaped and to my taking notes.

A questionnaire guide was used to assure that I covered all my areas of interest, though questions were not used in the same order. Out of deference for his position, I felt it appropriate to wear clergy clothing to conduct the interview. The two interviews totaled 125 minutes. Interviews were professionally and confidentially transcribed. Field notes were written up as soon as possible.

PARTICIPANT OBSERVATION
AND DOCUMENT ANALYSIS

My immediate priority when I began participant observations at the seminary was to spend time with faculty members and students so that I would know which faculty members and students I sought to use as informants in my research. I began my observation of seminary formation activities the first week in August by attending several sessions of St. Mark's month-long "Intensive," or four-week introduction to seminary life for first-year priesthood students. The second week of the Intensive was focused on celibacy, so I arranged with Fr. Blatsky to attend the lecture-discussion sessions that are a part of the week. I also attended masses and meals during this week, plus a session the following week on human development by Fr. Schrieter. During the regular school year, I also attended one formation conference on human development for the fourth-year students conducted by Fr. Schrieter.[26] I attended two days of a three-day workshop on human development that was held for all students at a retreat center away from the seminary.[27] Photocopied handouts from faculty were offered and collected by me at formation sessions and the human development workshop.

Though not called for in my research design, I received permission from the rector to live on campus for one week in December. This allowed me to complete my interviews, observe some classes, and have additional time to observe daily seminary life. Previous visits to the campus had been made to interview faculty and students and attend a meal, mass, or evening prayer if these occurred while I was on campus. I wondered what life was like in the early morning and later evening at St. Mark's and thought that living at the seminary could fill out my data collection efforts. During this week, I would also begin to analyze and code the nearly completed interviews. I hoped that analyzing the interviews in the setting in which I had conducted them might stimulate my analysis of the data. During this week, I also accompanied the priesthood students and priest faculty one evening to a Christmas party at the archbishop's residence. I continued to take field notes after such periods of observation. During my week living at the seminary, a room in the guest wing of the main building was provided for me. In July 2002, I obtained copies of the St. Mark's catalogue and the student handbook.

A faculty committee was drafting the first edition of St. Mark's rule of life when I began my research. No formal rule of life had been in use. It was being drafted to comply with the *Program of Priestly Formation*'s requirement that all seminaries have one to codify the expectations of student conduct. For background I also read a history of the seminary that had been written by one of its professors to mark its hundredth anniversary.

Besides these seminary publications, two unsolicited five-page letters written by two different groups of students were examined. Five first- and second-year native students wrote one letter; six international students from four different years wrote the other. The letters were written in the semester after this research was conducted. An administrator made a point of providing the letters to me because of the observations and suggested changes their authors made for the school.

DATA ANALYSIS

Transcribed interviews, along with field notes, were read and re-read several times to identify emergent themes. Copies of the transcripts were literally cut apart and filed so that responses of informants on a particular theme could be more easily compared. By comparing and contrasting informant responses to interview questions, categories of analysis were derived. Automated searches of transcripts also were made for keywords and combinations of keywords to identify patterns of informant responses, including differences and commonalties in responses.

Five

CONCEIVING CELIBACY

This chapter considers how seminarians and faculty members at St. Mark's thought about celibacy and priesthood. Because their desire to live a life of celibacy cannot be understood apart from their desire to be priests, seminarians' descriptions of their vocations (calls) to the priesthood are presented first. Students' vocation narratives told to me differ but typically share certain features, including ascribing a divine origin and character to their aspirations. This section will also consider how those who see themselves called by God to be priests accept and give meaning to celibacy. It will be shown that students are fashioning a particular kind of "self" in their efforts to become celibate priests. Their reasons for living celibately are strikingly consistent with traditional reasons for the practice; students understood celibacy as a means for living a life purely devoted to "pastoral charity." The chapter concludes by describing how faculty members understood celibacy and how their thinking differed from what the seminarians themselves thought about celibacy.

To those unfamiliar with Catholicism and seminary culture, talk of being called to the vocation of priesthood may seem to be pious jargon and a facile explanation of their choices. However, the language of call and vocation is a powerful symbolic means for seminarians to frame their efforts to make sense of what they will do with their lives and whether they should become priests.

THE CALL TO PRIESTHOOD

When St. Mark's students were asked how they came to be seminarians and how they came to be interested in becoming priests, most spoke of a "vocation" and "call to the priesthood." For Catholics, a vocation is an inclination toward a state or way of life that comes from God (McBrien 1994:1318). All Catholics are said to share a common vocation to love and serve God. *Lumen Gentium* of the Second Vatican Council (1975a: no. 39) taught that all members of the Church are called to holiness. Catholics believe that God calls some people to be priests, sisters, brothers, and deacons. Marriage also is a "vocation" in the Catholic Church (Roman Catholic Church 1997: no. 1603). As described in the documents of the council, no vocation is said to be superior to another. Some Catholics speak of being called to married life and surely believe that their work provides a useful service to others. A particular person may take much time to decide whether to enter law school or medical school. However, it is not a required part of legal or medical training to determine through prayer and the guidance of a spiritual director whether law or medicine is really one's "calling" (though some law and medical students may make use of these practices). Bus drivers may become bus drivers because they hear the bus company is hiring. Greengrocers may enter that line of work because it is a family business. An accountant may choose his profession because of a facility with numbers. A public defender can have a desire to aid the poor and under-privileged. In these and other jobs, typically all that is required for employment is to obtain the necessary training, credentials, and licenses.

It is not enough that there is a demand for priests, that one has relatives who are priests, or that one has certain talents and a desire to use them in a certain way. Priests do not become priests just because they wanted to or had completed the nec-essary training. A seminarian must believe he has received a call to the priesthood. According to the *Program of Priestly Forma-tion*, an essential part of seminary formation is to help students determine if they have a vocation to the priesthood (NCCB 1993: no. 325). Especially, through the use of spiritual direction, Catho-lic seminarians spend much more time explicitly thinking and praying about their vocation, although this was a long process before they entered the seminary, when they began to think they were called to this life.

Catholics (and all Christians, for that matter) understand their particular vocations as an expression of God's will for them. For a vocation to the priesthood to be considered "authentic," a seminarian's calling must be perceived to originate with God. In the culture of St. Mark's, which of course is shared with other seminaries, "calls" and "vocations" were thought to be received from God. The language of vocation implied that a student experienced his calling to priesthood as more than a human preference. As Fr. Dahman, St. Mark's rector put it, seminarians "are responding to the Lord's call to be of service to the community as priests." The *Catechism of the Catholic Church* (used in courses at St. Mark's) is unequivocal in this regard: "No one has a *right* to receive the sacrament of Holy Orders. Indeed no one claims this office for himself; God calls him to it. Anyone who thinks he recognizes signs of God's call to ordained ministry must humbly submit his desire to the authority of the Church..." (Roman Catholic Church 1997: no. 1578; emphasis in the original).

Typically, the first official contact students had with the Middlefield archdiocese and the seminary was with the priest who is aptly titled the diocese's "vocation director." He was a priest of the diocese who publicizes the role of priests, often through talks at Catholic parishes and schools. The vocation director helps determine whether prospective applicants are called to priesthood. Vocation directors are not referred to as recruiters, because when it comes to priests, God does the recruiting. Fr. Moto, the vocation director for the diocese that operated St. Mark's, screened candidates who contacted him. He admitted to using discretion in replying to inquiries. He mentioned occasionally receiving calls from persons inquiring how can they become a bishop or cardinal. Poor candidates for priesthood were likely to receive cool treatment from him because it was his job to recognize "authentic" vocations.

PERSONAL REFLECTIONS ON A CALL

My own thoughts about priesthood and celibacy were first stirred by contact with Catholic priests of the parish I was a member of as a child. They were unassuming men who were kind to me and always interested in my family and were thought of highly by everyone in the parish. As a boy, I admired them as frequently perceptive, compassionate, and happy people who exhibited a tremendous hospitality and capacity to unselfishly be-friend people. Some would eventually resign from the priesthood and give up their promise of celibacy. However, I came to asso-ciate, at least implicitly, their hospitality and generous manner with their public commitment to live celibately. Their celibate lifestyle gave them a special aura and credibility. They helped inspire me to enter the local seminary high school.

At fourteen years old, I had given little conscious thought to what their celibacy or mine would be like. Even as ordination neared, with eyes fixed on priesthood as a prize, I gave little thought to the struggle a celibate life might entail. What drew me to priesthood was the holiness and joy I saw in several out-standing priests at my parish. However, even with the help of my seminary's formation program, I wasn't ready to contemplate the challenges and struggles priests face in living celibately. One might say that this research project is my penance for failure as a youth to grasp what celibacy might mean and entail. From my research I have come to understand and appreciate celibacy in ways not possible in my youth.

Not long before ordination to the priesthood, I was troubled enough to ask my spiritual director what I should do when I felt the urge to masturbate. "Fr. Len" said that he prayed when he had such an urge. Fr. Len went on to become a spiritual director at the well-known North American College in Rome, and then the rector of the seminary I attended. Years later, he resigned as rector and from the active ministry to marry. I believe Fr. Len was probably sincere when he said that he prayed in those situations. In fact, I think his prayers were answered, though not in the way he thought they would be. I hear that he is now happily married. I realize now that my question was a typically adolescent one and that there are better questions and greater challenges to deal with when seeking to live chaste celibacy. I recount this story as a way of highlighting one of the problems and questions of my study concerning the sexual lives of young men preparing for priesthood. I came of age when these issues were virtually ignored or treated as matters of secrecy to be spoken of with a spiritual director. Today, this situation has clearly changed, although it is unclear how much so.

While I tentatively discussed my sexual urges with my spiritual director behind closed doors, I recall little being said about sexuality or celibacy in my years in the seminary. There likely was an annual presentation or two by faculty members; however, these matters were not frequently spoken about among the students themselves. What is most memorable to me are the three occasions when students virtually vanished overnight with no explanation provided to their classmates. This occurred first when a religious order student suddenly ceased to attend classes at my seminary. The scuttlebutt was that he was secretly married and that this was found out by his religious order. In my second year, one of my classmates, "Jack," also suddenly disappeared. It was rumored that Jack left to marry one of the seminary's kitchen staff. That year, two other students abruptly packed and left. Reportedly one of them was found bathing the other in the communal bathrooms. In all these cases, the students departed before I heard what happened, adding to the drama and mystery of their departure. I never saw or heard from any of them again. Perhaps because I was not close to any of these four students, I do not remember discussing these departures much with my friends. One instructor resigned from the faculty over one summer vacation due to an alcohol problem. He sent out a letter of apology obliquely referring to his problems. It was rumored that he had made sexual overtures to at least one student.

Whether I consciously knew it or not, I did learn that failure to "control" my sexual urges surely would have perilous consequences for reaching my goal of ordination. For me sexuality came to be tinged with temptation, failure, and severe, embarrassing sanctions. Failures at celibacy were met with swift action by the administration. Sexuality was to be willfully controlled and people who failed to do so got in big trouble. I thought little about the relational dimensions of sexuality or intimacy. Not much was said about celibacy or why my classmates left, so sexuality also came to be associated with silence. Perhaps this is why I recall sexuality rarely being discussed by my friends. I talked about sexuality only infrequently with my spiritual directors. According to seminary rules, they could share nothing of what students shared with them in confidence. This led me to associate sexuality with secrecy. Especially when the consequences were so grave, being silent about sexuality made sense. Remaining silent helped me distance myself from those who I thought had brought dismissal and ruin on themselves by their actions. In addition, I naively thought that my promise of celibacy and the joys of priesthood would easily keep my sexual urges in check. Why stir up doubts in myself or others by talking about one's own sexuality? If my experience was shared by seminarians in other seminaries, then there was more than a little sexual repression in Catholic seminaries in the 1980s. Thus, while explicit formation for celibacy was only a marginal part of my "official" formation, I believe my own sexual beliefs and thoughts were profoundly shaped by my experiences in seminary. Sexuality was a subject I preferred not to examine too closely, confident that my promise of celibacy would "take care of" that aspect of my life. Nor do I recall faculty members challenging me to think more deeply about my sexual self. If many priests shared my experience, is it any wonder that we sometimes dealt so poorly with the recent sexual abuse crisis, responding with secrecy and silence to the misdeeds of other priests, while expecting those in charge to "police the ranks" as they did in seminary?

STUDENTS' VOCATION NARRATIVES

Students at St. Mark's obviously were accustomed to being asked how they came to be interested in priesthood. In relating their stories, they appeared to have put their call and vocation into a well-rehearsed narrative form. No doubt they had been asked this question by interviewers during the seminary admissions process, as well as by others curious about why they would seek to become priests. However, students' vocation narratives were not wholly of their making. Students were found to appropriate "scripts" shaped by the religious resources they were familiar with as Catholics. This script maintained the unique, divine origin of calls to the priesthood. They were likely to be familiar with stories in the Hebrew and Christian scriptures in which God called people to a particular role or mission. St. Mark's students were required to give occasional talks to young Catholics (prospective vocations) in which they shared the story of how they came to enter the seminary. The repetition of these stories surely had the effect of producing a coherent narrative. In this sense, a vocation was constituted and made subjectively "real" by the articulation of one's vocation story to others. Furthermore, the apprehension of one's storied self is one instance where *conversation* plays the vital role of establishing and maintaining one's personal reality or identity in a world with others (Berger and Luckmann 1966:152ff.).

These stories typically began with the recognition by others that seminarians had a vocation to priesthood. A student sometimes was the last person to know that he had a vocation or, at least, that was the storied claim. It was as if others saw a special quality or aura about them, which the bearers themselves were prevented from seeing. As the former rector of Rome's North American College wrote, a "call is usually filtered through others: parents, grandparents, friends, teachers, priests, sisters, deacons, lay ecclesial ministers" (Dolan 2002:2). Some seminarians even denied that they had a vocation in the face of other people's insistence that they did. Overcoming initial resistance to the call became a part of the narrative and added to the story's drama, as well as to claims about the "authenticity" of the vocation.

In what follows, I have selected characteristic stories from the seminarians I interviewed.

Larry

Prior to entering St. Mark's, Larry participated in a non-residential seminary program for college students considering the possibility of priesthood. Larry was one of the more outgoing and less conventional members of the student body when I met him. Interactions with him were marked by an easygoing informality on his part. While the other students usually greeted me at meals or in the corridors as "Father," Larry alternated between "Father" and "Hey dude" (or a similar colloquialism). He spoke in a rapid-fire manner about his vocation. His first thoughts of priesthood were stirred by other people.

> It first came from other people. It was other priests and brothers saying you should consider priesthood. I remember

going to John Cary [a faculty member], "Can you have a vocation or calling from outside, from other people?" And he laughed and said, "Of course." I think this was my first awareness that other people thought it was something I should consider.

In fact, he insisted that the idea that he was called to priesthood came from other people. Only then, he told me, did he begin to think and pray about whether he indeed had a vocation.

Luke

Luke was a very serious, even humorless young man when I met him. After a period of not practicing his faith, Luke said he was drawn back to the Church through study of its "beauty" and "history." He did not think much about priesthood until the encouragement of friends overcame his resistance to the idea. Like Larry, he stressed that the idea of being a priest did not come to him on his own. For example, when he was in college:

> The more I talked to people, they said, "Have you thought about being a priest?" I thought initially, "No," but thought about it a little bit and figured if other people see some things in me and the Church needs priests, I have an obligation to look into it.

Within a week after his pastor suggested he should be a priest, "three or four people around the campus suggested it." For Luke, this "was one of those odd things" and a sign that he was called to be a priest.

Cyril

Cyril always greeted me warmly and with a wide smile. He recalled a very traditional Catholic upbringing, praying the rosary on his way to high school, where he reported having few friends. In high school he was inspired by Pope John Paul II and impressed with his being named *Time* magazine's "Man of the Year." At this time Cyril began to think about priesthood. He read about the Legionaries of Christ and found the traditional character of the group appealing. He contacted them and two members visited his family for dinner. However, he decided not to join the group: "I was not attracted to their lifestyle. Poverty was not something I wished to undertake." He received an external affirmation of his vocation from the young associate pastor at his parish. A key moment in "discovering" his vocation occurred on a retreat he took with others before receiving the sacrament of confirmation at age sixteen. During the retreat a parish priest told him, "Hmm, I could picture a collar on you someday." Cyril attributed much significance to the admired priest's observation. Commenting on his initial thoughts and interest in priesthood, Cyril said, "So all these thoughts had been going on before and then to have someone outside bring it all together." Eventually, the priest drove Cyril to visit the college seminary residence.

Richard

Richard, a former police officer, had been involved in youth ministry church activities as a young adult. He did not seriously consider priesthood. However, other people told him he would be a good priest and he began to consider the possibility. Finally a bishop told him, "I really want you to be a priest here." As with Larry and Luke, Richard's vocation to priesthood was something he said he resisted. Other people recognized his call before he did. For Richard, this appeared to add authenticity to his call because it suggested that priesthood was not his own idea or choice.

Robert

Similarly, the recognition of priestly traits in him led Robert to consider priesthood. Robert entered the seminary after losing interest in his work as a lawyer and initially considered becoming a missionary priest. A reserved, older student in his late thirties, he had once been engaged to be married.

John

John entered the seminary after several years of being away from the Church. He attended college for a few years and served in the military. However, he found his life "empty" and was "tired of how my life was." He expressed regret that his post–Vatican II religious education classes had taught him little about the Catholic faith. However, he started to pray that God would make his presence known in his life. He went to confession to an elderly priest, who he now reveres and whom he sees as a model for himself. At this time, it was his mother who suggested that he was called to be a priest. He resisted the idea, "wanting to prove my mother wrong" because he wanted to marry and have children someday. At his mother's suggestion, John entered the pre-theology program in a very conservative Catholic college, still thinking he would marry someday. However, John believed God intervened in a dramatic manner to direct him to the priesthood. John said he would confide the story to me, but it was one that he did not readily share with others. One day John "prayed that God would show me that he was there and he did." John could even recall the precise date on which God answered his prayer. A big football fan, John was watching a college football awards show. Two athletes on the show spoke of their faith, especially of their gratitude to God:

> These guys really talked about God a lot and that really struck me. Wow, they really have something there! It didn't affect me until that night when I couldn't sleep at all. I really think this was God calling me.

John believed that through the "witnessing" of the football players, God was sending him a message to dedicate himself to God's service. He used the language of vocation more than any other informant did. His decision on what diocese or order to join also is cast in the language of vocation. Because of his traditional theological leanings, not all dioceses and religious orders were equally attractive. After he graduated from college, he "spent the next two years looking at different dioceses and religious orders and things like that. None of them inspired me to want to be there. I didn't think that I was being called to any of those places." John found that students in those places were not like students in the college he attended. They didn't inspire him and so he was not called to be a part of those seminaries or orders. Eventually he read a book by a bishop, which said that you should study to serve your home diocese and not "shop around." He then decided to attend Middlefield's St. Mark's. He appeared to retain his more traditional preferences. John prayed the rosary regularly and was a great fan of John Paul II. He expressed frustration with faculty members who were critical of official Church teachings.

Frank

Frank recalled events to me that occurred in his native country when he was sixteen years old. He referred to his "vocational moment" as an incident in which people mistakenly thought he was a priest. It led him to think he really should be one. Frank related in broken English (his first language was Spanish) that after several years of seriously delinquent activities and with his life in danger, he was sent to live with an uncle who was a parish priest in another town. While there, his uncle arranged for him to participate in a ten-day parish mission or revival with a charismatic Franciscan sister. With his uncle and the Franciscan sister, Frank visited several towns in his native Latin American country, where they made many home visits and freely engaged villagers, encouraging them to renew their ties to their Church. Frank described how, in one town, children swarmed around him and greeted him, "Missionary! Missionary! Father! Father!" He felt "loved and respected" by the children he met with the Franciscan sister and no longer feared for his life because of his past criminal entanglements. "At that moment I felt peace — like people love me and many other connotations. I discovered this is what I was looking for." However, Frank's delinquent past and poor reputation led others to doubt his sincerity. For Frank, it was problematic that those who knew him better didn't believe he had a vocation. Frank's priest uncle told him to "shut up!" and refused to discuss it for a week. Only after persisting with his idea did his uncle write a recommendation for him to enter a minor seminary.

Frank related the story of the parish mission to me with much relish and emotion. He appeared to enjoy considering himself an unlikely vocation and said that reading Nietzsche had a profound influence on his life. That he saw himself as a "prodigal son" or a less likely candidate for the priesthood, in his eyes, appeared to add to the legitimacy of his call. The parish revival and his calling were very dramatic experiences for him. Until this time he was involved in drugs and criminal activity. However, during the parish mission, his feelings of fear and regret, because of his past, were overcome. Suddenly, he felt approval and respect as a member of a missionary team.

Sam

Sam will be ordained a diocesan priest for the Archdiocese of Middlefield, but he belongs to an international religious association of men and women and will spend some of his ministry doing missionary work outside the United States. For the last two years of attending St. Mark's, he lived in community with members of his religious association. A powerful personal experience led to Sam's call to work with the poor. The event led him to believe that God was personally calling him to be a priest. Sam traveled to Africa with a parish priest and was impressed with the work of priests with the poor there. He was shocked by the poverty he saw there, but believed that the Church surely was very alive and making a difference in people's lives. He related that "to make a long story short, it was as if God was calling me to do something. I just couldn't ignore what I had seen." Sam will spend part of his priesthood serving in the Middlefield archdiocese, but also will work overseas with members of his religious association.

Tobin

Tobin also met a charismatic priest and had a similar experience working with the poor that led him to seek ordination out of a sense of being called to work for social justice and with marginalized people. His call to priesthood was closely tied to a youth group that met to pray over the Gospels and consider their implications for poor people.

Pat

Pat was the only student who never used the language of call or vocation. He was the only seminarian who did not receive encouragement from others that he may have a call to priesthood. As a child, he was an altar boy, assisting parish priests at mass, worked at the parish festival, and was "always involved in church stuff." He reported getting to know and liking a newly ordained priest particularly well. Pat had a fascination with Latin, incense, and elaborate liturgies. He had been active in amateur theater productions. In high school, he took a vocational interest inventory intended to help him identify the professions for which he might have an aptitude. He learned that his interests were similar to those of clergy and brewers of beer. Pat never sought work in a brewery, but by his junior year of high school he began to think that priesthood was something he could do. However, he wasn't sure if he was a good enough student to complete the required training. He talked with some religious order priests and to the priest in charge of his diocese's seminary college program that feeds into the St. Mark's graduate program. Unsure of what he wanted to do and perceiving a lack of interest from his own diocese, he did a brief stint in the military from which he was released because of vision problems. After deciding that "priesthood is something I want to do," he entered the diocese's college seminary program.

Pat expressed much irritation that Fr. Moto showed little interest in his vocation to the priesthood. Originally, Pat was very interested in joining a missionary community that he contacted by mail. However, a very prosaic reason was a contributing factor to entering a diocesan seminary. Pat recalled, "Mom didn't like the idea of me going to St. Louis and leaving." Instead, she contacted Moto at the local seminary, St. Mark's. Pat said that Fr. Moto failed to return phone calls and missed appointments with him. So, he contacted the director of the college seminary program. Regarding Fr. Moto, he said, "To this day, I feel that if it were up to him [Moto], I wouldn't have made it here." Pat obviously remained resentful that the vocation director was not more supportive of his desire to be a priest. Apparently it was a very bad sign if a vocation director didn't concur that God was calling someone to priesthood. As I got to know Pat that semester, it was clear he was very close to his family. However, it was obvious that he was a loner, often eating his meals alone and seldom speaking in group situations. Pat didn't appear to be comfortable with himself or others.

Analysis of Vocation Stories

This cultural framing reinforced students' beliefs that their vocations had a divine origin and were not merely the expression of their own preferences for a career. Their stories also were a powerful tool for structuring their experiences. Applying the insights of Peter Berger illuminates the significance of the language of vocation and call in seminary culture. Berger (1967:89–90) describes religious efforts to explain human action as instances of "alienation" and "mystification." Seminarians are alienated from their call to priesthood in that it is not perceived as a product of their own choice or making. This is not to deny that a divine being may call particular persons to priesthood. The ontological status of a call to priesthood is not open to scientific inquiry. What matters is the authenticity of the call to the recipients. What happens is that a human decision is understood as an expression of divine will. Thus, it is not surprising that some of St. Mark's students first learned of signs of their vocation from other people. Since others "recognized" their vocation before they did, somehow it must have originated "outside" them. This likelihood is heightened by the fact that most reported resisting messages from others that they might have been called to priesthood. Responding to God's call involved surrendering their own will to God's will in the cultural script they employed.

That others attributed a calling to them strengthened a seminarian's claim to what Max Weber called "charismatic authority." Weber understood charisma as a state or quality attributed to someone because he or she is perceived to have received special gifts of grace (Gerth and Mills 1946:245–48). Weber's concern was not that a person actually possessed such a gift, but was rather *perceived* as having the gift. Thus it was important for others to recognize a student's vocation to the priesthood. They did so by attributing special qualities or charismatic gifts to the seminarians and encouraged them to use these gifts as priests. This reaffirmed that their vocation originated with God and explained the lived experience of "receiving" a call.

It is essential that the Church or bishop perceives that a seminarian has received a special calling to priesthood; otherwise he cannot be ordained. Without ordination, the individual is not recognized as legitimately possessing the power to perform efficacious, grace-endowing sacramental rituals. The authority to perform such rituals rests upon receiving a call from God that is recognized by the Church. By his ordination a priest's sacramental powers are recognized as having a divine origin. These powers must have a divine origin since no human being or organization can be the source of the graces of salvation. The language of call and vocation thereby enable a priest to claim a share, in a diluted way, in the charismatic authority of Christianity's original prophet, Jesus Christ. Because he is chosen by God, his call is recognized and affirmed by the Church's ordination; thus priests are seen as configured in an extraordinary way to Christ (John Paul II 1993: no. 21). The recognition by others of his call gives charismatic legitimacy to the authority that priests exercise.

Since the Church must recognize and affirm his call, the language of vocation also reinforces the religious authority of the Church, which provides access to the means of salvation. Only seminarians whose call is affirmed by the Church's ordination are recognized as legitimate religious practitioners and mediators of sacramental graces. The authority of the Church, as providing access to the means of salvation, is preserved in this conceptualization of vocation and religious authority. The language of call and vocation is central to the reproduction of the structuring of the Church and the relationship of laity and clergy.

Students used the cultural frame of call and vocation to understand their entrance into the seminary. In some cases, they related fairly dramatic experiences (especially John and Frank) that led them to seek ordination. In these cases, their dramatic calls appeared to reinforce or confirm the subject's sense that he was a special person. Most reported that other people recognized their vocation before they did. Thus St. Mark's students typically appeared to believe that God called them to priesthood. This appeared to be essential for believing that their vocations were authentic. This belief led them to enter the seminary. However, St. Mark's spiritual director, Fr. Blatsky, said that once in the seminary students engage in a process called "discernment" to determine if they have a "genuine" vocation from God. Some students discern that they are not called to be priests. Others discern that priesthood is their vocation. In other cases, they are told by their directors and teachers that they do (or do not) have a true vocation.

Seminary formators term the process of internalizing the call to priesthood "interiorization." Archbishop Lobble, a former seminary rector, was asked, "What would you see as the greatest challenges or difficulties young men face in making a commitment to live celibately as a priest?" Archbishop Lobble quickly responded that "interiorization of the priestly call" was the greatest challenge to seminarians and seminaries. By this he meant that priests lose their initial interest and the zeal of their early seminary days. As a result they don't truly internalize the values he believes are necessary for priests. In his opinion, many dioceses

> get men into the priesthood who are gung-ho and dramatic, but after a number of years in the priesthood, they just sort of want to move to something else because now we have the TV generation which is trained to think in twelve-minute segments.

Schuth (1999:75–77) reported that many more men than in the past who have had dramatic religious experiences and/or minimal prior contact with the Church are seeking admission to seminaries.[28] This has caused a growing concern regarding men "gliding" through seminary without sufficiently examining the depth of their vocation and internalizing their status as priests in a way that makes a lifelong ministry possible. Their intense religious experiences sometimes end up being a passing phase. For people who have not married or found satisfying work, priesthood, like the military, can be seen as a niche providing security and stability. According to Schuth, formators should help seminarians understand their motivations and desires. Otherwise a permanent commitment to priesthood is not possible (1999:135). Without this commitment, Archbishop Lobble believed the true nature of the priesthood was threatened: "We are talking gospel here. We are talking about a real deep interiorization of every value we hold dear. We have to make sure that that sinks in, that it is cemented within."

From this perspective, successful seminary formation consists of internalizing the roles and values that the Church determines appropriate to the status of priests, an internalization that is meant to be a permanent lifelong commitment. Priests do not sign up for a four- or six-year stint as a soldier or sailor in the military does. Bus drivers retire, but there is a sense in which priests never do. Though they may officially retire, most priests continue to celebrate mass and other sacraments. By virtue of their ordination, they retain the authority to celebrate sacraments. In the words of Psalm 110, an antiphon that is frequently sung at ordinations, a priest is "a priest forever according to the order of Melchizedek." When Lobble says interiorization involves "cementing" values within the seminarian, he is speaking of socialization that shapes the identity of seminarians at a deeper level than other professional training. However, "cementing" conjures up a fixture of significant weight and density: the values weigh one down lest one float away! The metaphor is intentionally harsh and fundamentalist.

The permanence of ordination to priesthood and the depth of the way in which it profoundly shapes the identity of priests are reflected in Catholic teaching on the sacrament of holy orders. Like the sacraments of baptism and confirmation, holy orders "confers an *indelible spiritual character* and cannot be repeated or conferred temporarily" (Roman Catholic Church 1997: no. 1582; emphasis in the original). The *Catechism of the Catholic Church* also states that:

> It is true that someone validly ordained can, for grave reason, be discharged from the obligation and functions linked to ordination, or can be forbidden to exercise them; but he cannot become a layman again in the strict sense, because the character imprinted by ordination is forever. The vocation and mission received on the day of ordination mark him permanently. (Roman Catholic Church 1997: no. 1583)

The failure of socialization to "interiorize" the permanent quality of the status of priesthood is problematic for Catholic theology, which maintains that ordained priests remain priests forever. This failure, one could argue, has made the resignation of priests from active ministry commonplace today.

The language of vocation and call by St. Mark's seminarians also expressed the belief that the scope and depth of socialization is necessarily broader and deeper than in other careers. However, this claim is also an important ingredient of the ideology of training seminarians. That is, there is an overarching rhetoric indispensable to the socialization and transformation of selves in seminaries. This rhetoric, if effective, provides an all encompassing symbolic universe (the Church) within which the priesthood is located and rendered legitimate, purposeful, religiously meaningful, and so forth. In these terms, it certainly makes good sense that priesthood and vocation are understood as profoundly *different from* other life choices, lifestyles, and careers. In fact, without the understanding of priesthood-as-vocation, without a clear sense of the "profound" difference between priests, and, say, medical doctors, priesthood dissolves into other ordinary jobs and careers that are part of the quotidian. Priesthood, by contrast, is part of the sacred, called by the sacred, serving the Church in Christ. Clearly the special nature of priesthood is a central feature of the *ideologizing of priesthood* in seminaries and the Church at large.

Having said this, we can also see how *totalizing* all the features of seminaries (Goffman 1961) are. Seminary formation programs seek to regulate a broad variety of thoughts, attitudes, and behaviors — including sexual activities. What medical or law students do when not in class is largely their "private life" and "their own business." This is not the case with seminarians, because their lives are encompassed by seminary life. In fact, there is a clear sense in which they are not expected to have a life apart from their status and identity as priests. This appeared to be central to the appeal of the priesthood for the students I interviewed. Archbishop Timothy Dolan, former rector of Rome's North American College, emphasized the uniqueness of this priestly identity in a public lecture on vocations:

> The priesthood is a call, not a career; a redefinition of self, not just a new ministry; a way of life, not a job; a state of being, not just a function; a permanent, lifelong commitment, not a temporary style of service; an identity, not just a role. (2002)

Formation and ordination legitimate (and ideologize) the unique authority priests exercise as presiders at sacramental celebrations.

The spiritual formation program at St. Mark's is addressed to what is usually construed as the most intimate or private aspects of a student's life, especially sexuality. Not only is a priest's commitment to his vocation intended to be permanent, it also involves his entire self. In this, it differs from training for other occupations, which is focused upon the performance of specific occupational roles and tasks. One of the seminarians, John, mentioned a book of Dolan's seminary conferences that he finds inspirational. In it, Dolan (2000) said:

> as priests, we totally, exclusively, radically, profoundly, completely — purely — belong to the Lord. He shares us with no one, and thus is able to share us with everyone. Every ounce of our strength, every urge of our affection, every drive of our libido, we freely hand over to Jesus and his Church. We are purely his, from our brain cells to our sperm cells — all belong to him. We are purely his, *totus tuus.* (310)

In the face of this totalizing process of self-change and identity, we can understand the lengthiness, intensity, and scope of seminary training. Such training is seen as necessary to accomplish the transformation in identity and "validation of his charismatic authority" that the ordination ceremony marks. As Dolan told seminarians at the North American College in Rome:

> in our Catholic understanding, priestly ordination is a radical, total reordering of a man in the eyes of man and in the eyes of God and of his Church, bringing about an identity of ontological "reconfiguring" with Christ. This priestly identity is at the very core, the essence of a man, affecting his being and, subsequently, his actions. (229)

The totality of a priest's commitment was particularly appealing to John, who had viewed his life as sinful and empty before he discovered his vocation to priesthood. The structure of seminary, the totality of a commitment to priesthood, and Catholicism's cultural heritage can have appeal to men who are disoriented and disconnected and find secular life a wasteland (Hoge and Wenger

2003:121–22). John found great security in the Catholic faith he discovered as an adult. He said he really admired the elderly priest in his home parish because he doesn't want to retire and doesn't treat the priesthood as a job. John stated, "He takes it as a way of life. He is never not a priest." In the terminology of Peter Berger (1967:94), when socialization is this completely successful, a person's social type and subjective identity are merged in his or her consciousness. Subjective identity becomes fused with the priestly role and expectations he has learned. A person understands himself as nothing except a priest.

In the terms of the social psychology of George Herbert Mead (1934), a vocation to priesthood is interiorized to the extent that the "me" is apprehended as completely incorporating the "I." According to Mead, the self is a social object that cannot be grasped apart from its relationships to others. The self has two parts: the "I" and the "me." The "I" is the part of the person that seeks free expression, to be unique and active. The "me" is the part of self learned through socialization with others, including the roles it assumes. Seminary formation socializes the "me" and leads seminarians to identify with ecclesial culture, its definitions of reality, and the role of priest. According to Berger, such a fusion of identity and role can be a source of great strength to an individual, protect against anomie, and remove uncertainty from someone's life. John wanted his priesthood to be like this too. He seeks something he can give himself to completely and is troubled by those who criticize the Church in which he has found a newfound identity and purpose. John's internalization sometimes sounds complete, finished, unwavering. His identification with the Church, total.

Summary: Significance of Vocation Language

The cultural frame of "call" and "vocation" is used by students to understand their aspirations and entrance into the seminary. The narratives conferred substance and meaning on the events of their lives and made it possible to project a future story of success as a priest. The language of call and vocation gave students' aspirations a mysterious power that transcended the person called to priesthood. In the ordination ceremony, the bishop confers on the priest a share of Christ's charism (a special grace and indelible mark). The language of vocation and ordination sacralizes his identity and authorizes him to exercise his powers in the Church, especially as a mediator of grace, by engaging in sacramental rituals. As Berger asserted, "Socialized identity as a whole can then be apprehended by the individual as something sacred, grounded in the 'nature of things' as created or willed by the gods" (Berger 1967:95).

Middlefield's Archbishop Lobble called this internalization of the vocation "interiorization." He maintained that it was at the heart of the seminary formation process. Sociologically, a priest's identity is grounded in a suprahuman reality outside of himself, a reality that is introjected into himself and sealed at his ordination. In the culture of St. Mark's, a vocation to priesthood is viewed as much more than a human preference. God is seen as the source of both the vocation and the authority that priests exercise over laity in the Church. The "indelible character" imprinted on the priest's soul at ordination, according to Catholic theology, mystifies and symbolizes the permanence, completeness, and profundity of a priest's call that necessarily came from God.

STUDENTS' DESCRIPTIONS OF CELIBACY AND PRIESTHOOD

Students were asked how they would explain the practice of celibacy to others who didn't know much about it. Because it became clear that how they conceived of celibacy was closely linked to how they thought about diocesan priesthood, students were asked what they looked forward to in the priesthood and helped them to live celibately now. They described what St. Mark's has done or failed to do to help them live celibately. Students also were asked if any part of celibate practice made them uneasy or was difficult for them. In answering these questions, informants described not only the practice of celibacy and the role of the diocesan priest, but their perceptions of sexuality, romantic relationships, and marriage. Luke is considered first because he named the largest number of reasons to undertake the practice of celibacy. All of the other students stated one or more of the reasons that Luke articulated.

Luke: Learning the Lingo

Though only in his second year in seminary, Luke wanted me know he knew *all* about celibacy. If having reasons to live celibately constituted a form of religious capital, then Luke was well on his way to becoming the richest man at St. Mark's. He also was the most adamant in defending the practice of celibacy and held the fewest doubts or fears of all the students. Luke said that the most appealing part of priesthood was this:

> an opportunity to really connect people to God. That great Catholic understanding of sacramentality — that God makes each of us instruments and you [priests] get to be an instrument in a real sound sense both on behalf of God in general but also on behalf of the entire Church in an institutional kind of way. My faith in God is important and I hopefully will take that sense of faith and help other people connect to God. A priest is in a unique position to be able to do that.

When asked about celibacy, Luke began by describing it as forgoing an intimate relationship and a family in order to establish a different relationship to the Church. He stated that:

> we give up a committed relationship with a particular person and a family in the traditional sense so that we can make the entire Church our family, the entire people our family.

Luke strongly supported the policy of mandatory celibacy, arguing that "I like the fact that I can be there with people more than I would otherwise be able to be." He added, "I like being able to go out and tell people this is a valid lifestyle. This is an important lifestyle because I think people need to hear that. I would be upset if the Church changed the discipline." Luke observed that when he was growing up:

> there was something very unique and powerful about the knowledge that they [priests] were not married. The parish

was their family. They were always there. I like that sense of priesthood and the kinds of ministry that I have been able to do so far and the schedule I keep. . . . I don't know how I would be able to do all those things if I were in a committed relationship with a person.

For Luke, celibacy enabled him to be more available to work longer hours, thus focusing a priest's life in a singular way on his relationship to those in his parish.

Luke said that this way of living involves sacrifice, but it relates him to Christ in a significant way. "So there is a sacrifice that joins you to Christ. It is the lifestyle of Christ you follow and that sense of evangelical poverty of not owning or wanting a person. You are just committed to people non-exclusively." Luke went on to speak awkwardly of celibacy in nuptial terms, with the priest identifying with Jesus, who is the groom taking the Church for his bride. He also used eschatological imagery, saying celibacy symbolizes "the love of heaven" where "we are not committed to each other, but to everyone."

Luke perceived celibacy as a "sign" and "countercultural alternative" especially for a "culture [that] says that people can be used and sex is something that can be manipulated. It can be 'for sale.' It is anything but an intimate bond between two people." He said the clergy abuse scandals "have almost made me recommit [to celibacy] to try to do as well as I can. This is the time we really need priests to try to be as healthy a model as possible." He said that celibacy is "a kind of countercultural alternative [that] should be offered to people in terms of the way to live your sexuality and to love people."

Luke was "pretty confident" that he would be able to live celibately. He was among St. Mark's youngest students, and he had not dated much. On that subject he revealed that:

the only real girlfriend I had was a Southern Baptist and we dated for about a year when I was a freshman in college. But she was in another college, so we saw each other about four times that year. It was tough. But in any case, after we broke up, there was never any relationship after that.

Luke felt that staying connected with family and friends helped him live celibately. He especially gained strength from associating with others, including friends in religious orders who are "on the same journey, committing to a chaste celibate lifestyle." He also found prayer helpful. Luke turned to the saints for help. "I pray to St. Augustine and St. Maria Goretti, asking them to give me a hand." He said he monitored his relationships and carefully established boundaries (a word used by several students) to remain celibate. To fix a boundary, he would ask himself, "How are you feeling about this person, are you treating them differently because of that, are you trying to be more exclusive with them because of that, are you making them into some sort of object?" Other students also mentioned that exclusivity in relationships was to be avoided. Just as previous generations avoided "particular friendships," "exclusive relationships" were seen to be a threat to celibate chastity at St. Mark's.[29]

Luke was critical of the formation program at St. Mark's. He lamented what he saw as an overuse of psychology, stating, "Some of us had a phrase after all our formation nights last year, 'more saints and less psychology.'" He felt students were led to believe that "if you keep studying psychological studies, you will be fine. . . . Sometimes I find myself saying 'Where is God in all this and not Dr. Rossetti.'"[30] Luke also said he doesn't "always sense a very supportive attitude in this place on the Church's policy on celibacy. If I am going to be inspired, to strive for that lifestyle, that detracts from that."

In the interview, Luke alluded to a number of reasons for celibacy: the pastoral (serving with undiluted attention); the christological (from Christ's example); the ecclesial (a configuration to the nuptial relationship of Christ to his Church); and the eschatological (the unmarried state of all in heaven, implying a world beyond earth's attachments). Most students referred affirmatively or negatively to the reasons for celibacy that Luke identified. Luke was very serious throughout our conversation. He was "heady" and he talked in abstract terms. He appeared to want me to know how edifying he believed celibacy really was, and how familiar he was with various advantages of celibacy. However, Luke was very awkward in conveying these reasons for celibacy. He sounded as if he was using a script and lingo that he was still working on making his own. The wooden ways in which Luke described celibacy contrasted with his ability to smoothly glide about the chapel sanctuary with much refinement.

John: Married to the Church

John, it may be recalled, believed God called him to priesthood while he was watching a football awards program. He now saw priesthood as a heroic way of life that demanded complete devotion. He entered St. Mark's after military service and graduation from a Catholic college well known for its traditionalist leanings. The elderly pastor in the town where he grew up was a continuing inspiration and model for him. In expressing his own understanding of priesthood, he claimed that:

> the thing that is most important is being there for the people, being a minister of the sacraments. . . . Not only that but just to be there when people are in need, in their happy times, in their sad times, being really a part of their lives.

Besides celebrating sacraments and "being with people in need," he looked forward to having time alone: "I am an introvert and I like to have some time by myself, praying for others and myself too, of course. I really enjoy prayer time for myself."

Like Luke, John conceived of celibacy in a nuptial manner, saying that he liked the idea of "being married to the Church." However, he was ten years Luke's senior. He has not always been a student, having served in the armed forces. John differed from Luke in expressing a fair amount of anxiety about promising to live celibately. Once engaged to be married, John admitted struggling to treat "people as people rather than objects." He was straightforward about his difficulties with what he called "chastity." He stated that his associations

> with women were very physical and sexual relationships. It is hard for me to control that. I think back about that and try to leave those in the past, but they just keep coming up. What scares me is that I am not going to be able to control that in the future.

Although he was remorseful about his sexual past, John did not believe priests should be allowed to marry. He made a point of assuring me that he "doesn't have a problem" with any of the Church's teachings, specifically mentioning the bans on artificial contraception, homosexuality, and the ordination of women. However, if the Church would allow priests to marry, "I would be fine with that." His willingness to accept a change in the policy didn't seem to indicate a desire for change as much as a willingness to accept whatever policy the Church establishes. He seemed to eschew thinking for himself since he believed the Church authorities already had everything figured out.

During the semester he was interviewed, John candidly admitted that he was thinking a great deal about celibacy because "there is a woman who is going to one of our classes that I am really attracted to." Even if he married, John worried that he would still struggle with chastity. "I would have to deal with the same things because I am committed to this other woman. Either way there has to be a purity of intention there on giving yourself fully." He said he had gotten help in his struggle from reading Aristotle, St. Augustine, St. Thomas Aquinas, St. Thérèse of Lisieux, and Pope John Paul II's theological writings on the human body. Of John Paul's II's *Love and Responsibility*, he observed that the pope's book "really helped me in not looking or using people, women for my own gratification, but putting others first and looking at them as people created by God and not just as body parts."

Among all the students, John was toughest on himself regarding his own sexual urges. He set high standards for himself and expressed disappointment in those members of the faculty whom he believes do not encourage students to aim as high. Regarding a weekend workshop on celibacy that was held the previous year, John stated:

> They have opened me up to some new angles to look at things I think and the psychological view, I would have to say. But it seems like everything is psychological. They don't really talk about the spiritual parts. They don't talk about the virtue of chastity, which I think they should try to. . . . I can

say that I have been told by a faculty member that it's okay if you masturbate. God doesn't care. I guess I don't agree with that. I haven't talked to him since then about this because I want to be challenged.... Mediocrity doesn't inspire me. I want to be challenged to something greater.

Another example was that a faculty member once told John that if you are going to look at pornography, "Don't look at it on the Internet. Look at it in magazines." In answer to my question regarding what the faculty member saw as the difference between the two sources, John replied that the archdiocese was St. Mark's Internet provider:

> ... if you get caught with that you get kicked out. I really think that [pornography] is not good to do either way. I think it is another thing of telling people to get away with what you can in terms of celibacy. I think that is what led to this crisis in the first place.

John indicated that he has been helped by the spiritual formation program at St. Mark's because it is another perspective than the spirituality that he learned at his very traditional Catholic university. At the same time, he said that he would like things to be more inspiring. Regarding the formation program he observed:

> I really like Fr. Blatsky. He is a great guy but it seems that if there is something they want us to deal with they throw it on spiritual formation.... Last year one of our spiritual renewal days was twelve hours about racism. I didn't really feel like that was spiritual or renewing because it was a spiritual renewal day and I was dead tired at the end of that day. It was an important topic to talk about, but I didn't feel it was appropriate on the spiritual renewal day. That is what they seem to do — throw a lot of psychological things on us on the spiritual renewal days.

John was not alone in complaining that there was an overuse of psychology and not enough emphasis on living virtuously at St. Mark's. Luke and John appeared to believe that spiritual formation was supposed to be edifying and reaffirm the specialness of their calling. Inspiration for celibacy for Luke and John was gained by seeing it as the practice of a virtue. John said he commiserates with a friend about this: "We talk about using the 'V' word here. You can't use the 'V' [virtue] word." John's and Luke's reasons for celibacy are the most explicitly spiritual ones used by students, as opposed to more pragmatic ones, such as pastoral availability.

Robert: Celibacy as "a Part of the Package"

Robert, the former lawyer, was born in Latin America and was active in politics there. When asked what he looked forward to in the priesthood, Robert said he wanted to work with Middlefield's growing Hispanic communities. He mentioned social ministry and improving the working conditions of migrant workers. His understanding of ministry appeared to be less cultic than that of his classmates, and he saw celibacy in more practical and less spiritual terms.

Robert struggled to put into words what being celibate meant to him. He said celibacy was something he has come to accept because he wanted to be a priest. Of his past, he stated, "I was close to marriage, but I was too selfish. I was too engaged in my profession, my preoccupations, my thoughts and ideas." He said marriage was an "equally good option for people" and that priests should be allowed to marry. However, he doubted that he would seek to marry if he were allowed to and is content with his decision to live celibately. For Robert, celibacy "is something that comes with the package of being a Catholic priest. So you take it or leave it." Thus it struck me that Robert was not so much called to celibacy, as he was to diocesan priesthood. He struggled to find benefits to celibacy for himself. Of celibacy, he noted:

> One of the positive things is maybe that you are not committed to just one person and you try to commit your whole self to the community, which gives you a wider frame of time in your life because you don't have a family to take care of.

Robert understood celibacy in instrumental terms as a way to be more available to people. To help him live celibately he said it is important for him to stay in contact with friends, with people he met in his internship year, and his family, whom he visits two or three times a year. Robert related that people in Middlefield have warmly received him. He mentioned a good relationship with his spiritual director. They became friends, and he has shared his concerns about celibacy with him. He admitted doubts about living celibately, but feels he is making progress in accepting the practice.

Richard: Celibacy as Requirement

Richard, who was encouraged by his bishop to enter the seminary, came from a very religious family and was always involved in the Church, except during his teenage years. He said he always knew many priests and played basketball with them as an adolescent. Like Robert, Richard also accepted celibacy as a requirement for his ordination, but believed celibacy should not be required of all priests. Also recruited from Latin America to study at St. Mark's, he found life lonely when he first arrived. He regretted that early at St. Mark's he made "many mistakes" about celibacy because of his loneliness. However, "If you are able to put the pieces together again as soon as possible and to follow your choice [celibacy], it is a normal process of growing. . . . It is not the end of life." He admitted mistakes but did not want to provide details about what happened. He believed he had learned from his mistakes. He said he has come to develop "good friends" in Middlefield to help him deal with his struggles. "I really want to be a celibate man. It [celibacy] has helped me deal with many things." Richard said that through prayer and the support of others, he has come to accept it because of his desire to be a priest. He appeared upbeat and optimistic about his future, saying that he had grown in his acceptance and appreciation of celibacy in his years at St. Mark's. His spiritual director and other faculty had been helpful. He said, "I really think the seminary has done everything possible and they have done a very good job on me."

When asked how he understands celibacy, he observed that "a celibate person is a little bit different. Which way, I don't know." Richard was tentative in his responses and sounded as though he was still looking for a way to make sense of the practice: "I haven't found a book that has given me specific ways to be [celibate]." At the same time he defined celibacy behaviorally as "a choice for not having a sexual relationship with another person."

He said the practice helped him to see God through his friends. Celibacy "has been a help in relationships with people and also with God." Celibacy rejected what he called "the capitalistic mentality" where people focus on pleasure and getting "what you want from others." Celibacy revealed what is at the basis of a relationship: "self-giving." He mentioned that celibacy has also made his prayer different, making him aware of "a need to pray for justice or pray for peace in the world." Additionally, he stressed it is important for there to an alternative to married life:

> I think it is a good way to show to people that we have another option. You can become married. You can be single. You can be celibate. I think it is a good option, in a healthy way. I think it is something possible.

Although he was nearing ordination, it was clear that Richard was having a hard time articulating what celibacy meant to him.

Cyril: Breadth Instead of Depth

Cyril and Larry also spoke of celibacy in terms of pastoral availability. Cyril was hesitant at first to be interviewed, but eventually agreed after repeated phone calls. Cyril, who prayed the rosary every day on his way to high school, had only dated

> a little bit in high school, but not in [seminary] college and certainly not here. It is enjoyable, but I don't know that is what I want out of life, trying to date. I know there are beautiful outcomes of that, you know, for more committed loving relationships, but I don't know that I want to get involved with that. I think that part of the reason that celibacy isn't driving me nuts right now is because I don't want a personal ad. I don't want to go through personal ads-type relationships. I don't want to do that. So right now it isn't much of an interest. It wasn't a big interest then.

Initially, Cyril was drawn to the priesthood as an opportunity for prayer and study. He also saw it as an avenue to defend the faith that he loved. Cyril said that he was raised "with a sense that Catholicism is the way to go. The right way. The only way. I wanted to defend it against a world that was going astray and to bring that to others, to be a defender of the faith in some sense." At one time he had been in contact with the Legionaries of Christ and seriously considered joining the very traditional religious order.

Cyril said that these initial ideas had changed. He now appeared to think of priesthood in more relational terms. He described what he saw as a priest's "ability to enter into relationships with people; they bring me God, so to speak, and I can bring them God. It is the chance, the opportunity to take my love of God and my love of Church and to bring it to someone else who desperately wants it.... It is about bringing joy to people's lives."

He said he looked forward to leading people in prayer: "I think myself and a large number of my generation are interested in that more than the administrative side of parish life. It is being a person of prayer... and praying with the community and for the community."

Regarding celibacy, Cyril began by saying he doesn't think of celibacy as a kind of marriage to the Church. Instead, he contrasted celibacy with marriage. Cyril recalled a priest who once told him that "marriage shows the depth of God's love. Celibacy shows the breadth of God's love":

> That really struck me. It is a way of being able to serve others in a very special way and a very committed way toward others. Celibacy is much more than not having sex or not getting married. Celibacy is so much more than that. Really it is almost sacramental. It reveals something and for me it reveals God's love, how God's love works. It's not exclusive. It is not jealous. It is a gift of one's self for others. Marriage shows a different way God's love works.

Cyril also spoke of celibacy in terms of pastoral availability, saying that a priest "can be of service, anytime, anyplace, anywhere, for any amount of time for the people of God." Yet he was quick to limit what he will do as a priest: "Meetings, I won't do that." Cyril had no interest in parish administration, saying that, "There are laypeople who are much better trained" to do that. He believed, rather, that "the seminary is training me to be a leader of prayer, someone who brings prayer to others."

When asked if anything about celibacy makes him uneasy, Cyril responded emphatically, "Loneliness, fear of loneliness, fear of wanting to talk to somebody on a deep level, on an intimate level, and not having someone there." While doing his parish internship, loneliness was something that he battled:

> I realize that if I just hung around the rectory, even with the pastor there, I would go nuts. I would be terribly lonely. Friday nights I would go home [to his parents' house]. Saturday night I usually try to go with a friend or clean my room. I may sound a little silly but I know that those are vulnerable points for me, those weekends. So I try to say I am not going to sit here and stare at the wall and be depressed about myself and celibacy. I will try to do something about it. That is the bonus of celibacy. Celibacy allows me to go and to cultivate these relationships with friends where a married life would not allow that.

While Cyril said that celibacy revealed something positive about God's love and made the priest more available, he believed celibacy takes a toll on those who practice it. His understanding of celibacy lacked the spiritual veneer of Luke and John's descriptions. Besides cultivating friendships and support from his parents, how will he manage to live celibately as a priest?

> The grace of God. I think maybe I am being naïve, but I try not to look ten years when I will be thirty-four, saying if this is the way things are going now I probably would be getting to be a pastor, associate pastor. But I try to take it day by day and realizing that's sufficient for today. If God is calling me to this, I do believe that His grace is there. I have to accept it and commit and be open to it. Not to be fatalistic, but I may not be here in fifteen years, so I am not going to spend time worrying about it now. I will cross the bridge when I come to it.

Cyril talked like someone who has never been in a serious relationship or felt a need to seek one. He had shown little interest in ever dating. He appeared to realize that his commitment to celibacy was untested and therefore tentative. "I am trying hard to see the value in it, to recognize the graces of it. Sometimes I wonder if I am fooling myself." However, with the support of family and friends, he appeared to believe he could live celibately as a priest. I wondered if Cyril didn't sense he was delaying facing something, perhaps some aspect of himself or his sexuality. Instead, he seemed resigned to dealing with it when he was thirty-four and already ordained several years.

Larry: Struggling to Maintain Boundaries

Several months after my interview with Larry, a faculty member revealed that the seminarian was dismissed from the seminary for discussing sexual matters too frankly on a youth retreat and for viewing Internet pornography at his internship parish. Larry had spoken enthusiastically about the priesthood, but expressed reservations about his ability to live a life of celibacy.

When asked what he looked forward to in ministry, Larry singled out "celebrating liturgy with people who you can tell are enlivened by it. It really means something for those people." He expanded on this, saying that "interaction is probably what it comes down to. Because that might happen in a counseling session too." When asked how he would explain celibacy to someone, the extroverted seminarian said that "I have never been really strong with the Church's definition in saying you're giving something now for the Kingdom or it is a taste of the Kingdom and things like that." He elaborated:

> It has been hard for me even understanding it as a gift. So I usually say celibacy is also the ability to be fully available to those people that you serve, whether it be 11 p.m., 2 a.m., or 6 a.m. Yes, with a family you can do that, but without a family it might be easier.

Larry continued by saying that his understanding of celibacy was changing and that he was "realizing that it can be seen as a gift." He believed that there is no way he could live celibacy alone. However, with community support, God, and prayer, celibacy enabled a priest to be "fully available." It does this by enabling what Larry calls "breadth instead of depth" in his relationships:

> I have learned it is more than just no sex, no marriage, and being fully available. . . . It is giving up one singular in-depth relationship and instead having many relationships that still have meaning but aren't as deep. Not to say they are superficial in any way because they obviously have meaning, so they are more than superficial, but it is not the full intimacy you can have on a physical, emotional, intellectual level with many people. You are forgoing the physical aspect and that allows you to engage with so many people.

Like most other seminarians interviewed, he appeared to accept celibacy as a basis for greater pastoral availability. Celibacy, he said, "enables you to devote more time and energy" to serving a parish. At the same time, when Larry talked about celibacy as enabling him to have "breadth instead of depth" in relationships, he sounded somewhat like he was describing celibacy as a means for "playing the field" rather than "going steady" with anyone in particular.

Larry acknowledged that celibacy "is still so hard." He described himself as a "flirt," and said he realized that in the future "I know I will be with people I find attractive. What is difficult is how do I channel sexual energy." He said masturbation is "one topic nobody talks about formally. . . . That is definitely a no-no to talk about. Yeah, everyone might say they have done it or not, but that is about it." To deal with celibacy, he said:

> I have got to know what tools I need. This is the hard thing. I don't know if there is any easy way, any certain behaviors I can learn or tools that would really help me in being perceived correctly and in dealing with my own sexual energies, to be effective and to still be a great personable person who can develop relationships and just not go in a direction that would not be allowed.

Unlike Luke and John, Larry talked about managing celibacy in psychological rather than spiritual terms. He is looking for psychological tools to help him live celibately because he believes it makes a parish priest more available. He wants to curb his tendency to flirt. He praised the work Fr. Schrieter has done with the students on sexuality and human development. He mentioned maintaining "boundaries" in his relationships with others several times in the interview. By "boundaries" he said he meant "verbally not making sexual innuendoes toward specific persons":

> I know I shouldn't make them in general but at my age I still do. Definitely no sexual genital contact. This is just how I would describe boundaries. It is hard because a kiss on the cheek can be okay in an appropriate context, so it is taking I guess the context and the environment and who I am with and putting what can you do physically and can't do, and in general even kissing whether that be French kissing or kissing on the lips or whatever, even that isn't allowed where kissing on the cheek might be with a friend. For me, that is at least an easier boundary.

Larry dated in college. He emphasized that he had to work at observing boundaries in his relationships now. This appeared to be a struggle for him. He made a point of assuring me that "I have been a virgin":

> A lot of people say, "Don't you think you should have it [sex] so you know what you are missing?" . . . I don't want to know what I am missing. Because I have no doubt that it would be great, so it is better without it because your body doesn't have the memory.

Larry admitted some trepidation. If celibacy were optional, he would feel more confident of his vocation. Key to managing celibacy for him is the way the seminary formation program has built his own "self-awareness." He enjoyed the support he received from the seminary student community. He was "becoming more comfortable" in celibacy and he described his progress saying, "I have a sense of control over myself." Perhaps it was not surprising that Larry talked so much about "boundaries" since it was boundary violations that led to Larry's departure from St. Mark's. His "control" and ability to respect "boundaries" was not as great as he had told me it was.

Pat: Isolated and Lonely

Active in theater productions in college, Pat hoped to bring a dramatic flair to the liturgies he would preside over. He said he loved the symbols, icons, rituals, incense, and processions of Eastern Rite liturgies. Pat also talked about priesthood as a means of serving others. In his parish growing up, and later in the military, "Everything I did volunteering or whatever it was always kind of helping out, helping others, working for the greater good." For Pat not only did celibacy mean not having sex; it meant not treating people differently because of their personal appearance. Pat related that he hadn't dated much because he said he was always busy working and never had the time, even in high school and in the military. (Pat and Cyril are the only St. Mark's students that I interviewed who reported dating very little. They made a point of mentioning that they will likely not miss having children.) Pat doesn't regret not dating. In high school he found:

> knowing you could date you would always be kind of aware of other people, and you would tend to look toward people not just as equal, but you see people you are attracted to or something like that, and you look at them differently. But then being in seminary you drop that. As a result, when you meet a person, you look toward their good qualities right away. You don't look toward their physical qualities as much.

Pat appeared to see physical beauty and attractiveness not as a blessing and dimension of some relationships, but as a threat to treating all people equally well. Like John, Pat believes that celibacy helps value people beyond their physical attributes. However, Pat admitted little of the sexual temptation and none of the failure that John confessed in his interview.

Celibacy, Pat contended, made him more available to love those who otherwise might not seem lovable. In seminary college, a man in the neighborhood would come looking for him. Pat recalled "this drunk guy following me because I was the only person who would talk with him. If I had a family, that would be a conflict. Just the ability for me to be able to be kind I think is extremely important." Pat added that he believes a priest's lack of sexual interest in those being served makes priests "safe" and "non-threatening." He found that in high school friends would approach him with their problems because he wasn't seeking anything for himself. For Pat, celibacy was about being "in service of people. We need to be for the people, so we need our time freed to be giving to the community." Pat combined the ideas of having more time and caring for those who are less desirable in some way:

> As a practice we give that up for the sake of seeing the good in all people and for having the time for all people and for having the time to be in prayer and to focus all our intention on our relationship with God and our people that we serve.

Pat saw himself as particularly sensitive to caring for those who are perceived as less desirable because "I tended to always be on the outskirts. I was never part of the in-group. I was always part of the out-groups. I think I would be more open and look toward the outer people and try to look for their needs and stuff." This experience colored how Pat saw priesthood and himself ministering within it. On campus, he appeared to be something of a loner. In ministry, he saw himself reaching out to people on the margins.

Regarding his future as a celibate priest, Pat mentioned loneliness as a real fear. Even at St. Mark's he felt "isolated and lonely." "I wish there were more community. You get very lonely here because you are living in community and have so much expectation," he said. But instead of building relationships, "you kind of lock yourself in your room and try to get your stuff [coursework] done." He had few friends outside the seminary, but looked to his family for emotional support.

How he will manage in the future worried him. Unlike the case for most students, spiritual direction hadn't been much help because "I haven't hooked up with the right person." Nor did he feel free to talk to other students about sexuality and celibacy. He stated that "sometimes they will joke about things, but never honest struggles or what they are going through." During my observation periods on campus and during the human development workshop, Pat kept his distance from the other seminarians and appeared to want to avoid talking with me. It was not surprising that he confessed that he felt "lonely and isolated" as a seminarian and feared loneliness as a priest.

Tobin: Made More Available and Approachable by Celibacy

Like Pat, Tobin (and Sam) saw priests as ministering to people on the margins of society. For Tobin, this has been brought home to him by his experience working as a missionary overseas. Tobin expressed disappointment that some students eagerly met to pray the rosary, but they were hesitant to be involved in social ministry. He said that celibacy made people recognize priests as more approachable and available without expecting something in return. He said that "it gives you a freedom sometimes, hopefully always, so people know why you are taking care of them." Celibacy means "you are not looking for possessing someone in sex. . . . It is giving up on the will to possess people."

Tobin related that he disagreed with people who said that "priests don't know about married life." Living in community taught him about what it meant to be committed to people. He confidently stated that "I do need to commit to people in a direct way and I think I am committed to people at the same level as marriage." Except for sexual intimacy and having children, "celibacy is like marrying another person, except that you're marrying a good number of persons." He clearly felt supported by the community in which he lives.

Sam: Freed to Minister

According to Sam, a priest was "a combination of two things: a prophet and servant." As servant he was called to "the people most in need." He was a prophet in that "you have to stand up in the culture as opposed to the culture, to the place that you find yourself often times. I think it is a very important role for the Church to play and obviously for the priests to play, to stand up for those people and things and attitudes that aren't always given voice. I feel very strongly on that." Sam looked forward to two things in priesthood. First, "working with the poorest people who don't have housing, food, or whatever." In addition, he will "try to give people meaning, but not just in the sense of who they are in the light of God and Jesus Christ."

Sam, like Luke and John, emphasized celibacy as a counter-cultural practice, but without their disdain for American culture. Sam insisted he was not originally a likely candidate for celibacy, saying, "I was a little bit wayward when I was a teenager; I had long hair and went to raves and stuff like that." At first, the thought of celibacy was difficult:

> In the beginning it was scary because I thought as though I was losing something and missing the opportunity to have sex. I come from a very early twenties, late teens mentality that I was somehow losing out on an opportunity to have a girlfriend and why would I want to do that. But then I came to the conclusion very quickly that I wasn't willing to be so egotistical in the sense that you can't be having sex every day anyway. You don't have thousands of women breaking down the door. It became the idea of how I wanted to commit myself. I was afraid, but then I decided what it was I was afraid of — because what I was losing was a theory. It's actually a practice. So it wasn't that I was going to lose. I was losing a myth in my head.... Society creates for us that sexuality or the sexual is so important, and I don't think that that is necessarily the truth.

For Sam, celibacy involved rejecting the notion that every person needs an exclusive, intimate, genital sexual relationship.

Sam, like Pat, believed that celibacy helped orient him beyond considering only a person's physical attributes. However, he was less harsh regarding human attraction to physical beauty:

> The more I approach that person, the more I get to know them, the more that person grows and becomes more layers of the sea, to use the metaphor, and that is very, very beautiful, but it is also something that I have to have respect for. It is hard. I wish sometimes it wouldn't happen because you could just remain feeling sexually attracted to somebody and then keep it there. I find myself being forced into the position that once I get to know, then all the other stuff that

comes with the personality of a person appears, then I have to deal with it.

His experiences helped him get beyond responding only to a person's physical appearance. He was not fearful anymore that he would treat people as objects, as John clearly still was.

Sam, like Pat and Tobin, stressed that people perceive celibates differently. A priest's celibacy "makes it more possible for people to come to you," he said. He went on:

> People see you as a person who somehow made a commitment to you and God and that they too can have confidence in that.... It allows you to go to places with people they otherwise wouldn't be able to go to. People trust you with their information. Maybe you could say, "Well they would trust you anyway," but I don't know. I think it opens up that possibility.... Celibacy allows you to do that with many, many people. It brings you into a great contact with lots of people on a very intimate level that probably otherwise wouldn't have the time or possibility to do. It makes you free. It is a sacrifice but it makes you free.

This freedom to be more available was at the heart of celibacy as Sam and several other students described it. Students presumed that they would be more trusted and approachable because of their celibate commitment. I asked Sam what helps him live celibately. He responded:

> Two things: one is theoretical and one is very practical. The first one I will say because I don't mind saying it is that you have to masturbate. I think to release the tension that sometimes it causes. I believe biologically that is what happens to a man and therefore there has to be some kind of release of that tension. As long as it remains in a healthy context, it is not necessarily a bad thing to do.

The other thing that helped Sam was:

> my family of my brothers in my community and sisters and I see that they are somehow trying to do the same. At the

same time, I am able to go to them with all the difficulties that I have in life. I can basically dump on them.

Like Tobin, Sam believed that his religious community was a great support to him and made it possible for him to live a good life without marrying.

Frank: It's Economic

Frank, whose call to priesthood came while assisting with a parish mission, began his interview by telling me that he was going to take a year from seminary to decide whether or not he can live celibately. Frank said he had been taught that celibacy is a gift, but that this had not been his experience. However, he maintained that the Church's real reasons for requiring celibacy today were financial. Without wives and children, priests could be paid lower salaries. He made vague references to Church history and said that the Church sought to prevent children of priests from inheriting Church property. He told me this almost as if he had uncovered a conspiracy. Whatever the Church taught, these remained the real reasons for mandatory celibacy.

The only worthy reason for celibacy that Frank could see was the eschatological one mentioned by Luke. Frank referred to a story Jesus told of seven brothers who marry the same woman (Matt. 22:23–33). Jesus is asked whom will the woman be married to in heaven. Frank recalled that Jesus said, "in heaven they were as angels." He believed that people who do not have sexual relations are a sign of heaven. "In the heavens, we don't reproduce. There are people who don't reproduce. They are examples." He believed that celibacy was an authentic sign of the way life is lived in heaven. However, Frank wrestled with whether or not he was capable of living such a life on earth. He reported having girlfriends all through minor seminary. He didn't express the remorse that John did for past sexual experiences. His experiences showed him that it is important "to feel and know that someone is next to me and that that person loves me." If it weren't for the requirement of celibacy, Frank was emphatic that he would have no questions regarding whether he should be a priest.

Frank appeared embittered by his experiences at St. Mark's. He said he loved his classes and talked easily with his spiritual director. However, his relationships with other students were "very bad" because of his temper. He did not feel free to talk with other students about sexuality because they wear "masks." He said, "I cannot speak with them. I can only speak sincerely right now with my spiritual director and my supervisor [formation advisor]." He feared seminarians who might want to have him expelled from the seminary. If a faculty member finds out that a "seminarian has a relationship with a woman, [or] with a man, it's immediate dismissal. It's that simple."

Frank found community life at St. Mark's with its regular schedule of prayer and masses restrictive, saying it's "almost a prison." Frank, the former delinquent and Nietzsche fan, resented having to write an apology to the rector for being late for mass. (A priest who sometimes visits the campus suggested to me that the faculty might have imposed Frank's "leave of absence." He said that Frank frequently did not show up for activities because he "was always watching TV.") Frank said he looked forward to going on leave and working for a year while living in a parish. He appeared to have many difficulties with the structured routines and expectations of St. Mark's.

Summary of Students' Conceptions of Celibacy and Priesthood

All the seminarians interviewed spoke of celibacy as a practice that they were undertaking because of a desire to be ordained priests. In other words, none said they would be striving to live celibately if they did not want to be priests. This does not mean that the requirement of celibacy was not part of what attracted them to the priesthood, but that is not how they explained their efforts to live celibately in the interviews. It was not surprising, then, that the way in which students gave meaning to the practice and accepted it as worthwhile for themselves was bound up with two factors: the call they experienced to be ordained priests and how they thought about what a priest is.

Both in interviews and during formation sessions, all informants described celibacy as a permanent, lifelong practice that included two elements: not marrying and forgoing genital sexual intimacy with others. In my interviews with the students, all mentioned these two elements. Most students began by mentioning these elements when they were asked how they would explain the practice of celibacy to someone who didn't know much about it. For students, this appeared to express a behavioral norm, a boundary, or a minimum requirement for celibate practice. After describing celibate practice this way, students very quickly and without coaxing went on to elaborate on celibacy in a variety of ways. Their tone suggested that celibacy was a practice that needed explaining, even defending. Its value was not self-evident, and it was assumed to be a practice that was misunderstood or was not highly esteemed by most people.

Students varied in the number of reasons they gave for seeking to live celibately. Luke and John stated the largest number of reasons, and offered more highly "spiritual" explanations for undertaking the practice. Robert and Richard spoke of celibacy in more instrumental terms. Their reasons for celibacy were closely tied to how they perceived the role of diocesan clergy, especially parish clergy. This was not surprising, as diocesan priests do not live a community life as do religious priests, sisters, and brothers. Celibacy was not perceived as having the same usefulness that it might have to vowed religious who live in community. St. Mark's students explained celibacy as a practice that enhanced priesthood generally or their own priestly ministry in some way.

The most common way the practice was explained was that it made possible greater availability for pastoral service. Students reported that they believed celibacy was appropriate for parish priests because of the large variety of tasks priests perform, and the need for them to be "on call" at all times. Celibacy enabled priests to devote themselves in a more singular way to ministry, keeping the focus of their lives on those they would be serving. Generally, students believed (with Larry) that not marrying enabled priests to have "more time and energy availability to serving the parish community." In this sense, celibacy was understood in the instrumental manner of enabling priests to work more hours or to be available at odd hours.

It was clear that most students saw celibacy as fitting for priests for reasons greater than just allowing a priest to work more hours. Among the things that celibacy meant for Cyril was that a priest would be "of service any time, anyplace, anywhere, for any amount of time to the people of God." Cyril said this with such emphasis that his statement connotes more than simply working more hours or at odd hours. Cyril went on to say that celibacy is a way of "being available to serve others in a very special way and a very committed way." For all the students except Frank, celibacy was more than commitment that expressed itself in working longer hours, but a way of living that holds priesthood as a singular commitment and identity that excludes other exclusive relationships. It is not just that one's time was seen as less divided, but that one's loyalties also were less divided. Students believed that celibacy not only enabled priests to work more hours, but that it brings an intensity of focus to the ministry. Celibacy added to what they saw as the heroic quality of a priest's calling.

Even though Pat confessed some anxiety about loneliness in celibacy, it was a practice that he willingly undertook and went to some lengths to defend. He was typical in relating celibacy to the way he defined the role of the priest. When asked what is most appealing or important about priesthood to him, Pat responded, "Serving others is the most important thing." He viewed priesthood as a life in which you can "give yourself for others." The priest was seen as the servant par excellence, and therefore priesthood excludes the possibility of marriage.

Celibacy was conceived as giving up genital intimacy and exclusive relationships that some students construed as selfish. For most students, celibacy appeared to be a strategy for transcending "selfish relationships" for a "selfless" life of service to others. Students also commonly reported that celibacy enhanced ministry by making priests more approachable; people perceive their celibacy as making them less self-involved. Their service was more selfless because priests seek no sexual gratification or an exclusive relationship with the person to whom they are ministering. Only Frank, whose attitudes significantly diverged from the other seminarians in a number of ways, said he would agree to celibacy simply because it is required and did not believe celibacy would enhance his ministry as a priest. It was also significant that Frank's critical attitude toward celibacy made him distinctive: he was the only one who viewed the requirement suspiciously as a practice rooted in the Church's need to pay priests relatively low wages; if priests were married, the costs would be much greater. For Frank this was not a sufficient reason to live celibately. As a result, he said that he was taking a leave from the seminary the following semester.

Apart from its appropriateness because of the ministerial demands of parish priests, students specified other ways of understanding the practice. These reasons included seeing celibacy as an eschatological sign and a means of imitating and identifying with the life of Jesus. Several students also spoke of celibacy as a countercultural practice. It appeared that celibacy was a response to a highly sexualized culture in which sexual experience is valorized as a *sine qua non* for human fulfillment. Though celibacy is routinely referred to as a "gift" or "charism" in the official documents and by some spiritual writers, only one student explicitly used this language. Two students saw celibacy as mystical sharing in Christ's spousal relationship to the Church.

The majority of students had a highly cultic understanding of priesthood. They primarily conceived of priests as people who pray and who lead others in prayer in the sacraments. Sam, Tobin, and Robert on the other hand, saw the priest as a person who is heavily involved in social justice work and engaged extensively in ministry to the poor.

Most students mentioned loneliness as a real fear and potential drawback of celibacy. Relationships with family and friends were seen as current and future antidotes to loneliness and as aids in helping them live celibately. All students except Frank spoke positively of "the seminary community" as a source of much support for living celibately now. Seminary community appeared to especially refer to two elements: affective ties to other students and faculty and to the seminary's daily communal prayer life. (The term "community" is explored more fully in chapter 6.)

Should celibacy be required of diocesan priests? Student responses ran the spectrum. Luke and John did not see a reason to change the current policy of mandatory celibacy. Cyril wasn't sure. The rest all agreed that celibacy should be optional. Some mentioned that a change in policy would make their vocational discernment easier. Only Frank would marry if given the opportunity.

Analysis of Students' Conceptions of Celibacy and Priesthood

Students at St. Mark's are well rooted in a Christian tradition that sees the renunciation of romantic and erotic relationships as freeing believers for single-hearted devotion to God and the Church. While some students said that celibacy should be optional, all except Frank believed that celibacy was the most appropriate practice for organizing their interpersonal and sexual lives. There was a strong consensus that celibacy would enhance their ministerial service. This attitude surely has the effect of reducing the amount of dissonance they may have experienced if the practice were seen as an imposition without value. Without this conviction they would face their vocation divided, wanting to be priests, but not wanting to be celibate. If this is so, then St. Mark's Seminary is successful in this respect, since students are unlikely to live celibately if it is not a practice they esteem. All informants expressed a strong desire to serve others. Generally, the students interviewed described celibacy as a practice undertaken to live their lives in a way that transcends narrow self-interest, making them more available for service to others. While some students were concerned about loneliness, students did not primarily see celibacy as a privation. Rather, they saw the practice as productive of a certain kind of self and especially the virtue of charity. Of those interviewed, only Frank did not describe celibacy in this fashion.

In his own words, Pat conveyed St. Paul's sense that an unmarried person's loyalties are less likely to be divided than are a married person's (1 Cor. 7:32–33):

> In the service of people, we need to be for the people, so we
> need our time freed to be giving to the community and to be
> giving to God, and it would be hard for us to do both.

Such pastoral availability in the minds of students was not simply
a matter of a greater number of hours of work but also the intensity of focus. It also generally implied a greater freedom to serve.
Students also saw celibacy as making a person freer to love those
perceived as less highly esteemed or less lovable by others. Pat
reflected these students' sentiments when he said that celibacy
meant the willingness to "take the time to be kind to people nobody else will be kind to." Most students would likely agree with
the view expressed by Paul VI's *Sacerdotalis Caelibatus* (1967)
that celibacy provides

> the maximum efficiency and the best disposition of mind,
> psychologically and affectively, for the continuous exercise of
> perfect charity. This charity will permit him to spend himself
> wholly for the welfare of all, in a fuller and more concrete way
> (2 Cor. 12:15). It also guarantees him obviously a greater
> freedom and flexibility in the pastoral ministry. (no. 32)

St. Mark's appeared very successful in acquainting students with
this official rationale for celibacy.[31]

A central feature of celibacy, as St. Mark's students saw it, was
that celibates avoided particular, exclusive relationships. Because
a celibate priesthood functioned as a symbol of complete dedication to ministry, exclusive relationships such as marriage were
seen as incompatible with priesthood. While no students said
anything to explicitly devalue marriage, there was a tendency
to view relationships involving sexual attraction as selfish because they were a "particular attachment." Within the culture
of St. Mark's Seminary, charity or a disinterested love of neighbor
was more highly esteemed than romantic and erotic (or sexual)
love. Charity (*agape*) is used in the New Testament to refer to
the boundless love of God (John 3:16) and the love that distinguished the early Christian community (1 Cor. 12–13). Students
dualistically tended to see erotic love as undermining the practice
of *agape*.

Among St. Mark's seminarians, Pat most clearly exhibited this judgment. Celibates "don't look at people's physical qualities as much" and are able to treat people "equally." Pat has never dated and believes that dating leads to making evaluations regarding whether one is "attracted" to another person and treating people "differently." Romantic love and sexual desire were devalued because attention to them led to the preferential treatment of some people over others. On the other hand, Pat said celibacy means "being able to love everyone, no matter who they are, regardless of size or shape." I found Pat's rationale for never dating daffy to say the least. I also doubted if it was possible to humanly not favor some people over others.

While it is unlikely that any student at St. Mark's would evaluate sexual desire and sexual intercourse as sinful, there was clearly a tendency to see them as "selfish" because they were particular. That such activity was out of place in the seminary recalls the assertion by Mary Douglas (1966) that dirt is "matter that is out of place" (36). Douglas maintains that attitudes regarding pollution and bodily function reflect concerns regarding boundaries and group survival. By not engaging in genital sexual relationships, seminarians see themselves as more available and focused in their devotion to the Church and God. Sexual activity is out of place for people who want to devote themselves to *agape* — the loving service of neighbor. It is a polluting activity, explicitly proscribed in the seminary rule, that detracts from the purity or single-heartedness of their commitment to Christ and the Church. No student mentioned ritual purity or a need to avoid contact with women as a reason for celibacy. However, Archbishop Lobble described celibacy as "belonging *purely* to Christ and no one else" (emphasis added). For a more traditional seminarian like John, who struggled with sexual temptation, chaste celibacy was seen in terms of virtuously maintaining what he called his "purity."

Within the culture of St. Mark's Seminary, students were remarkably traditional in the way they understood celibacy. Their thinking was generally consistent with official Church teachings. Celibacy was seen to allow for an undivided commitment to God and ministry. At St. Mark's, formation for celibacy was a means for students to create a self-surrender to *agape*. By overcoming the imperfect self that sought exclusive relationships, romantic love, and erotic love, a more perfect self was created. This detached self sought to realize itself through the practice of charity, the selfless love of neighbor. It was precisely because they were celibate that students believed that they would be seen as more approachable and wanting nothing in return. Romantic and erotic relationships are seen as distractions or impairments in the practice of charity rather than as sacred places where the divinity is found. Sexual desire and pleasure (*eros*) were not evaluated as having the spiritual potential of charity (*agape*).

Several students saw rejection of sexual activity as a form of countercultural witness. Perhaps because American culture was seen by seminarians as so cheaply sexualized, sexuality was interpreted as lust or unbridled sensuality rather than a form of relatedness, mutuality, and intimate communion. The virtues of romantic and erotic attachments and their ability to foster mutuality, communication, and collaboration in ministry were not grasped by seminarians. Because *eros* and *agape* were seen as dualistically opposed, people who had such attachments were not seen as capable of being as available or single-hearted in their service to God and the Church. They could not "belong to the Lord" in the exclusive way that those who preserved their boundaries and purity of intention could.

The self that celibate practice produces is a detached self that avoids particular commitments in favor of a more abstract or universal commitment to all people. It is more abstract than a marriage promise to love a particular person for the rest of one's life. This detached self is a *providing* self, not a *receiving* self. By abstaining from genital sexual activity, the celibate self *preserves its physical boundaries and is not dissipated in sexual activity*. Most students mentioned that maintaining "boundaries" was important for "guarding" their celibate commitment. Luke said that he monitors himself closely to see if he is treating people differently or "trying to be more exclusive with them, because if you are," this led to "making them into some sort of object." Relationships were a perilous area that Luke said required observing "boundaries" so that they did not become exclusive. Larry struggled with what he perceived as his own flirtatiousness but appreciated the emotional, social, and physical boundaries that he said seminary formation stressed. Like other students, he mentioned guarding against "exclusivity" in relationships.

St. Mark's students saw the celibate priest as providing for the well-being of others, but since he must be selfless, he was seen as receiving nothing in return. What this celibate self preserved for itself as a providing self was its own power to confer on others what they needed. Cyril quite simply described wanting to be a priest so that, "I can be bring God to people." There was more than a little grandiosity in Luke describing the priest as an "instrument" who acts "on behalf of God and the entire institutional Church." Students believed priests helped people in a variety of ways; however it was the cultic role that was seen as the most important element in most students' conception of priesthood. Thus, their most essential work involved providing access to the means of salvation by virtue of their sacramental powers. This celibate self who provided believers with access to salvific graces appeared to reflect the image of a divinity that is powerful, inviolable, and receives nothing from those who worship and depend on the divine self. Students did not speak of ministry in terms of mutuality or what they might receive from those to whom and with whom they minister.

Students tended to view celibacy as consistent with the altruism that they associated with the priesthood. Such altruism justified the sacrifice they were making. Frank was the only exception. His contention that the real reason for the policy of mandatory celibacy as to allow the Church to pay priests lower salaries constitutes what has been called "cynical knowledge" (Goldner, Ritti, and Ference 1977). Although it may also be designated, more neutrally, as "critical knowledge" or debunking knowledge, the term refers to "knowledge that presumably altruistic actions or procedures of the organization actually serve the purpose of maintaining the legitimacy of existing authority or preserving the institutional structure" (Goldner et al. 1977:540). Cynical knowledge poses a threat to an organization's authority relationships and the commitment of professionals to the organization. Frank's assertion undermined the various altruistic and sincere motivations for celibacy articulated by the other students.

FACULTY MEMBERS' APPRAISAL OF CELIBACY

Faculty members are important to the reproduction of celibacy at St. Mark's because they are both teachers of theology and behavioral models for seminarians. Their beliefs regarding celibacy are likely to be important in shaping student attitudes and behaviors. For people to remain committed to a belief system it must be validated. It could be expected that faculty would be influential in shaping a culture that seeks to validate celibate practice. They shaped student attitudes in the spiritual formation program, in the classes they taught, and in their daily interactions. John Paul II (1993) insisted that seminary faculties present celibacy "clearly, without any ambiguities and in a positive fashion" (no. 50). Faculty members were asked how St. Mark's Seminary articulated the value and importance of celibacy.

There clearly was a gap between the way faculty members spoke about celibacy and the way that it was described in the official documents that seminarians read during the month-long Intensive. No faculty members spoke of celibacy as "a priceless gift of God for the Church" as Paul VI (1967: no. 42) and John Paul II (1993: no. 29) did. Only Archbishop Lobble spoke in such glowing terms about celibacy.

Fr. Dahman and Fr. Schrieter

Fr. Dahman, the rector, was succinct in stating what he believed St. Mark's conveyed to students regarding celibacy: "It enables the person to be completely committed to a life of service in Jesus Christ for the community." Dahman was pleased with what he called the "comprehensiveness" of St. Mark's formation for celibacy, saying that it is "a part of every facet of the formation program." He was confident that the seminary provided "the kinds of contexts and relationships that will allow people to grow and develop."

Fr. Schrieter, the dean of resident students and pastoral counseling professor, offered a similar rationale for celibacy. He stated
that the value of celibacy was "that it allows us to engage in
ministry with a depth of focus that might not be possible in
the context of another lifestyle." By "depth of focus" Schrieter
said he meant that celibacy "brought a greater freedom to be able
to engage solely or primarily in the lives of the people we are
called to minister to." He strongly believed that celibacy allows
greater "emotional and spiritual availability." By this he meant a
priest could say, "My primary responsibility is to prayer. My primary responsibility is ministry. My primary responsibility is to
be engaged in a relationship with Christ Jesus."

Fr. Blatsky

Fr. Blatsky saw the practice less as a "charism" and more as "an
ecclesial discipline." The soft-spoken spiritual director for priestly
formation was more tentative than Dahman and Schrieter. He
said he was not really drawn to some of the "traditional theology
that is coming out right now" that views the priest as having
a spousal relationship to the Church. Blatsky said that celibacy
could be "rather advantageous for ministry if lived out well." He
believed the "exclusive" nature of the celibate commitment could
free a priest for "greater availability in parish work and perhaps
a greater chance of focusing in prayer." Blatsky said that married
men could be effective priests too, but this simply was not the
discipline of the Church at this time and that seminarians must
adjust to this fact. He thought students needed to realistically
assess whether they can be happy living celibately and deal with
the loneliness that he said was inevitably experienced by those
who practice it. Blatsky saw celibacy largely in practical terms and
said he did not find all of the theological explanations promoted
by John Paul II compelling.

Fr. Wisher

Fr. Wisher, a moral theology professor and former rector, held
a position similar to Blatsky's. He believed celibacy "may be
an assistance to those who have given their lives in ordained

ministry to the Church." Wisher was at odds with some recent interpretations of celibacy:

> I would challenge at times the traditional manner of presentation as a gift. It wasn't a gift for me and I don't think it is a gift for most of us. I think it is a discipline and there is even a question about the wisdom of the discipline, but rather than get into all that, simply say, "Look, this is the way it is."

Wisher said his visits with retired priests have made him wonder about the long-term effects of celibacy on some men. He said, "We don't want to become burnt-out old men." He wondered if "damage" was done to men who "closed out the possibility of having an intimate lifelong companion." Wisher worried about men who looked like they were "neutered." He recalled the monsignors he said he saw in the Vatican offices when he was a young student in Rome and wondered what they really knew about sexuality:

> When they give some new enunciation about celibate life or celibate formation, I always just wince and I think, "What do they know? What is their experience? What do they draw from?"

Wisher believed that attempts to give meaning to celibacy by attaching it to devotional practices was unsatisfactory:

> This piety, this strange piety, this devotion to the Sacred Heart or the Blessed Mother, I find that really empty, not very meaningful at all. I think we better get down to earth about some of these things because it is a strange kind of a pious practice. . . . It is a bodiless spirituality that I find not real and not helpful.

Regarding priests he has known, he said that some are able "to capitalize on the discipline and make the best of a life of service." However, he believed that most priests "just struggle with it." Wisher, who was nearing retirement, spoke as if he was a "survivor" who had made his peace with celibacy. Regarding his own life, he said,

I know of no other way to manage all this than to maintain a rather healthy schedule of personal prayer and honesty and in conjunction with that, friends.

Wisher clearly believed that celibacy could have value, but he avoided some traditional theological rationales that are used to legitimate the practice. For him celibacy was not a gift, but a way of living fraught with peril that must be carefully "managed." To live celibacy well, "You really have to be on the ball most of the time."

Fr. Green

Fr. Green, a moral theology professor, said it was unclear what it meant to be celibate "for the sake of the Kingdom" and clearly believed celibacy should be optional for diocesan priests. Green didn't think St. Mark's had effectively conveyed "a valid, intrinsic motivation for celibacy" to students. He blamed the Church for this:

> The rationales that are given for celibacy by the external entire Church are not compelling and it makes your job as a seminary institution that much harder, because then you have to present as best you can the official teaching on it, but it is not very helpful.

Green believed that St. Mark's "has done a pretty good job of training people who have accommodated themselves to celibacy in a relatively responsible way." For him, training for celibacy appeared to be a matter of living maturely with an unfortunate imposition. He believed that there were "institutional restrictions" on how St. Mark's could publicly address some issues related to human sexuality and maturity. He highlighted that the seminary was especially ill-equipped to aid homosexual students whose sexuality was "devalued" by the Church. He said the seminary was limited by a "Don't ask, don't tell" policy regarding sensitive matters such as sexual orientation. He was concerned that homosexual students received the message "that the only safe place to talk about who I am really as a sexual being is in a forum where it cannot be revealed publicly. Doesn't that very dynamic set up the conditions for shame or guilt?" No students ever identified themselves as homosexuals to me, though several spoke of themselves as having dated or having been sexually active with women. From Green's perspective, St. Mark's formation program was hampered by an inability to deal openly with homosexuality or students who identified themselves as homosexuals.[32]

Fr. Coughlin

Fr. Coughlin, a homiletics professor, felt that St. Mark's was dishonest and unrealistic in how it dealt with homosexuality:

> I think there are two secrets that we don't say out loud as part of the formation process. The first one is that more than half of the priests ordained twenty years ago or fewer are gay. We never say that publicly. The second thing is that many priests are sexually active in one way or another. To me that is relevant data that somehow needs to be part of the formation process. The fact is that there seems to be this code that disallows us talking about those things.

He found that the failure to openly acknowledge the number of homosexual priests had harmed heterosexual priests, whom he believed were more likely to resign from the priesthood. Coughlin said that heterosexual priests often felt "isolated" and like "they just don't fit in" because "there were so many bonds among the gay priests." He also said it was dishonest "to form somebody to make a commitment to celibacy without helping them to realize that ultimately different priests figure out different ways of living that life and to be totally honest, whatever decisions are made don't correlate with their effectiveness as priestly ministers."

Coughlin said he very much regretted not being able to be an openly gay priest: "I feel that this is a role model that is completely missing, both for gay and straight seminarians." He was troubled that the only public models of homosexual priests that students had were those who were removed in the clergy abuse scandals. Coughlin believed that there was a role for an openly gay priest on the faculty that would allow students to say, "Yeah, we really like him. He is a great priest." This public representation would "take away the mysteries, the demonizing, but I never thought that was possible."

Coughlin was alone in contending that many St. Mark's students were not convinced of celibacy's value. He said that students promised to live celibately because it was required, but that they did not necessarily feel bound by it. Coughlin was not at all supportive of mandatory celibacy. He said, "I think it is the rare individual who can live a full human life apart from some kind of intimate relationship that would include sexual expression. The unitive drive is a very strong one."

When his sabbatical was to end in the summer of 2003, Coughlin said that he would not be returning to St. Mark's and would likely be resigning from the priesthood. Archbishop Lobble had become aware of his sexual orientation. Coughlin said that Lobble did not want him to return to the seminary after his sabbatical, adding that Lobble told Coughlin that he had received letters stating that St. Mark's was "a hotbed of homosexuality and he [Lobble] did not want to appear to be contributing to that."

Archbishop Lobble

There were similarities and differences in how Archbishop Lobble and St. Mark's faculty members spoke about and legitimated the practice of celibacy. While most faculty members believed that celibacy enabled more "focus" and "undivided service," they did not speak of celibacy in nuptial terms in the way Lobble did. He gave the lengthiest and most elaborate justifications for celibacy by referring to the official documents issued since the Second Vatican Council. More than the faculty members, he believed the Church's official teachings offered a convincing rationale for celibacy. Lobble noted that seminaries for three decades had stressed the practical reason of pastoral availability. He believed that in addition to this, seminaries also should stress the more theological and mystical rationales for celibacy. For Lobble, Pope John Paul II's *Pastores Dabo Vobis* has usefully done this. His comments were peppered with references to the document.

Lobble described celibacy as "a beautiful charism that has been treasured by the Church from the beginning that was modeled especially by Jesus himself, of total complete giving to God and his Church." Celibacy enables "a complete radical intimate configurement with Jesus." In the ordained priesthood, Jesus "shares his bride," the Church, with the priest. Lobble said that "the intention and the care and the intimacy and the love that usually a male would give to a spouse and children, the priest would give to his people." More than the faculty, Lobble spoke of prayer and a relationship to Christ for strengthening celibate commitment.

Lobble's rapid-fire, nearly automatic responses to questions suggested a facility with the "lingo" of Church documents that eluded students like Luke. Faculty members were more likely placing an emphasis on supportive friendships as a means to living celibately. Unlike faculty members, Lobble made no reference to his own experiences or those of priests. They were more frank than Lobble in speaking about difficulties priests encounter in trying to live celibately. Lobble showed little familiarity with the ways in which parish priests lived their promise of celibacy.

Comparison of Faculty and Seminarians

Faculty expressed more reservations than students did about celibacy and requiring celibacy of diocesan priests. The argument that celibacy enabled greater focus and availability was the most popular positive rationale for the practice among faculty and students. But even this was challenged by some. Students tended to talk in more abstract, theoretical terms and make more references to official documents. In this they were more similar to Archbishop Lobble. Faculty members were able to talk more in terms of priests' and seminarians' actual experiences of living celibately, both good and bad.

Most students appeared to believe they could choose among the various reasons for celibacy and the strategies for living it out. For students, this appeared to be a matter of finding the rationale and means to living celibately that was the best "fit" or worked for them. Larry settled on the formula "breadth instead of depth" to celibate relationships and his rationale for celibacy. Luke believed praying to St. Maria Goretti "worked" for him. Larry and Luke appeared unconcerned if these formulas and practices didn't "work" for others.

For the faculty, choosing a rationale and means for living celibacy were more matters of discerning between good and bad theology and mature and immature ways of living. Professors were much more likely to be critical of some of the rationales for celibacy and the means for living celibately. For instance, Fr. Wisher was troubled by what he saw as the "bodiless spirituality" of some recent writings on celibacy. He was worried that sometimes celibacy contributed to some priests becoming "burnt-out old men." The reservations of some faculty regarding celibacy did not appear to keep students from finding ways to make the practice meaningful for themselves.

There are several obvious interpretations for why the faculty and students differed on these issues. One explanation would be "social desirability bias," in that faculty members felt freer to be honest than students did in the interviews. In other words, students may have offered responses that they believed appropriate for seminarians seeking ordination. If this were the case, it may have been indicative that seminarians also feared the consequences of frankly sharing experiences and feelings in formation activities because they might be evaluated negatively by the faculty or peers. This could be a problem for seminary training because it would be advantageous to have an environment where students can speak openly about their questions and struggles. Students might fear that sexual "mistakes" would be held against them. If students are reticent to state reservations or difficulties regarding celibacy, then they are learning even before ordination how to keep "secrets," to "closet" their sexualities, and "manage" their public identities to please their superiors.

Another explanation is that differing attitudes were the result of life-cycle differences. If this were the case, then students' attitudes would become similar to those of faculty as they grew older. Because they have "lived" more, one would expect their attitudes to be less theoretical and more based on actual experiences. Faculty members' experiences have taught them that celibacy is often difficult and life is more complex than ecclesiological documents on sexual matters suggest. However, differences may also have resulted from faculty and students being of different generational cohorts and their divergent answers reflect a "generation gap." Most students were raised entirely within a post–Vatican II Church. They appeared more open to the traditional rationales for celibacy and reflected the theological conservatism that Hoge and Wenger have argued exists among younger priests (2003:61–69).

A final reflection: I identify more with the views expressed by the faculty than I do with those of the students. There surely appeared to be a greater degree of honesty and humanity among the faculty, in contrast with the almost rote, sometimes defensive, accounts of the seminarians for whom I sensed something both remote and closed. I will return to these reflections in chapter 6.

Six

COMMITMENT PRODUCTION AT ST. MARK'S SEMINARY

St. Mark's as a social institution is structured to produce commitment to the seminary, the Church, and the role of celibate priest. The term "commitment" is adopted in this study as Rosabeth Moss Kanter (1968:500) defined it in her study of utopian communities: it is used to mean the process through which seminarians' interests are joined to the carrying out of socially organized behaviors or practices deemed appropriate for seminarians and priests living lives of celibacy. As seminarians engage in these practices, they are shaping an identity for themselves as future priests. From this perspective, as commitment increases, these practices come to be seen by seminarians as fulfilling their interests and as fulfilling the mission of the Roman Catholic Church. Seminary administrators develop commitment to celibacy and priesthood by engaging in practices called for in the *Program of Priestly Formation* (NCCB 1993).

The *Program of Priestly Formation* states that its guidelines are based on the documents of the Second Vatican Council, as well as on subsequent documents on priestly formation, such as *Pastores Dabo Vobis* by John Paul II (NCCB 1993: no. 1, 8). According to the *Program,* the conciliar documents provide the "normative understanding of presbyteral office in light of conciliar reforms" (NCCB 1993: no. 1). Seminaries are required to follow its guidelines, and faculty members at St. Mark's sometimes referred to the *Program* when describing formation at St. Mark's. It would be expected that the practices prescribed by the *Program of Priestly Formation* are intended to form priests according to a model and set of role expectations that Rome and the American bishops hold. Life at St. Mark's clearly was structured to meet the requirements of the *Program* in many ways. However, the faculty members and students who were part of the seminary when this research was conducted produced the day-to-day life and culture of St. Mark's. Faculty members and students together engaged in commitment-building practices even when their ideas about celibacy and priesthood differed.

While expressing differences in how they understood celibacy, most faculty members and students appeared to be intent on succeeding at living celibately, and willingly engaged in the practices called for by the *Program*. While recognizing that these practices may have had varying meanings and significance for different members of the faculty and student body, this chapter reports the commitment-building practices in which faculty and students engaged. All of the practices described were either mentioned by faculty members and students, or observed by the researcher. How faculty and students understood these practices is also reported when it arose in the interviews. While many of these commitment practices did not appear to relate directly to celibacy and sexuality, they did develop commitment to the role of priest and to the social system of the Church. Central to this commitment process at St. Mark's were practices through which seminarians were encouraged to identify with Jesus Christ, as they understood him.

A preliminary to the reader: when a commitment practice is referred to in the documents utilized in this case study, the practice is introduced by reference to this document. Thus, I usually cite relevant passages from the *Program of Priestly Formation* of the NCCB (1993), St. Mark's student handbook, or seminary rule of life when introducing a commitment practice. When it is appropriate, some historical background regarding a practice is provided. Then the commitment practice is described, and impressions and evaluations of the practice are provided when this practice arose in the research interviews. Analysis is then made by reference to sociological studies of commitment, especially to Kanter (1968), Borhek and Curtis (1972), and Goffman (1961). Also referred to in this chapter are two unsolicited letters to the seminary administration written in the semester after interviews were conducted. One letter was written by a group of five native-born seminarians from the first and second years of formation. Six international students from four different years wrote the other letter. The letters suggested changes to the spiritual formation program at St. Mark's and are useful for revealing student attitudes about the priesthood and the formation program.

CELIBACY AS A COMMITMENT PRACTICE

The *Program of Priestly Formation* views celibacy as "configuring" priests to Christ in a special way and providing an ideal disposition for complete commitment to Christ and to those whom they serve in pastoral ministry (NCCB 1993: no. 65). According to Fr. Moto, Middlefield archdiocese's vocation director, applicants for admission must be celibate for a minimum of three years prior to application to St. Mark's. Some students acknowledged in their interviews that they had been sexually active prior to admission. However, only one student acknowledged sexual activity while at St. Mark's. In considering applicants' life histories, Moto said he looked at applicants' relationships over the years and their ability to demonstrate fidelity in those relationships as an indicator of whether they would be likely to follow through on a commitment to live a life of celibacy. Once enrolled at St. Mark's, students were bound by its rule, which explicitly proscribed "exclusive" relationships and relationships involving sexual intimacy. Fr. Blatsky said this allowed seminarians to "test" whether or not they could happily live lives of celibacy.

Fr. Schrieter, the vice-rector and dean of resident (priesthood) students, maintained that celibacy enabled priests to be completely focused on discipleship and to undertake ministry as their primary responsibility in life. From this point of view, exclusive, intimate relationships interfered with their commitment to the Church. Likewise, these relationships could also interfere with seminarians' commitment to their training. The celibacy of seminarians made possible a much more intensive formation program than is possible for Protestant ministers who frequently are married. Other seminarians and priest faculty members provided the largest part of a student's daily, face-to-face interactions. The result was that students' primary relationships were most likely to be with people who were priests or preparing to be priests. Requiring seminarians to live as celibates made it more likely that they would develop affective ties with other seminarians. I found strong evidence of such affective ties at St. Mark's. These ties are explored below under the topic of "community."

Celibacy is a form of what Kanter (1968) terms "dyadic renunciation," a practice that structurally decreases the intensity of ties between any two individuals to emphasize ties to the entire group. It is a cohesion commitment practice, in that it binds the affective ties of an individual to the group and reduces competing loyalties. Cohesion commitment practices emphasize group participation. Besides increasing cohesion, celibacy was a means for producing commitment by providing consensual validation of Catholic beliefs and practices, and celibacy in particular. Relinquishing exclusive relationships meant that more of a student's time was spent with people who shared his Catholic beliefs and values, including celibacy. Theoretically, this made consensual validation of Catholic beliefs and practices more likely. Living together as celibates was a means of social support for reinforcing the validity of a practice that is no longer widely esteemed even by many Catholics. Seminarians prayed, studied, ate, and recreated with others who viewed celibacy in the positive ways described in the previous chapter.

SPATIAL SEGREGATION
AS A COMMITMENT PRACTICE

The *Program of Priestly Formation* assumes that candidates for diocesan priesthood will reside together with priest faculty either on the campus of a free-standing, self-contained seminary or in a house of formation if candidates are studying theology at a university. It is worth recalling that today's practice of requiring students to live with priests apart from the laity they will one day serve is due at least in part to the Council of Trent's call over four hundred years ago for free-standing diocesan seminaries.

Diocesan seminaries developed to consciously separate priesthood candidates from the negatively evaluated "secular world." This ecological separation was a physical insulation from secular influences and laypeople. Post-Tridentine spiritual formation programs taught seminarians to engage in spiritual exercises, practice

supernatural virtue, and ready themselves for elevation by ordination to the dignity of Jesus Christ, the high priest (White
1989b:11–13).

Most U.S. diocesan seminaries have been self-contained institutions conducting both intellectual and spiritual formation
programs at one site. Combined with the school's homosocial environment and shared timetable of activities (especially prayer),
their spatial isolation gave diocesan seminaries a monastic quality. Students were closely supervised and required to reside with
faculty members on campus. Their location on large pieces of
property in remote areas away from population centers heightened their exclusiveness (White 1989a: 222). Before the Second
Vatican Council, most candidates began their training in seminary high schools. They were removed at an early age from
other formative influences including family and friends, as well
as the larger culture. Formation for priesthood (including celibacy) occurred through complete immersion in an ecclesiastically
regulated seminary subculture. Seminaries approximated what
Goffman (1961) called a "total institution" because all daily
activities occurred in the same confined, regulated space.

Like that of most other diocesan seminaries, St. Mark's spiritual formation program took a residential community as a
starting point, with academic and spiritual formation occurring
on the same site. Such a community was made possible by the
fact that neither seminarians nor resident faculty were married.
Indeed, formation programs had as one of their goals preserving the unmarried status of their students. By making seminaries
residential schools, they were overwhelmingly male, homosocial
environments. An elderly alumnus of St. Mark's encountered during the research period said that students were rarely allowed to
leave campus before the 1960s. Students seldom interacted with
laypeople, with the result that they had little contact with women
during their twelve years of schooling except for the vowed religious who prepared their meals, did their laundry, and cleaned
the seminary. Prior to the 1970s, summers were spent at a lake
villa, thereby reducing possible contact with women and enforcing
separation from their families.

St. Mark's (and to my knowledge, all other diocesan seminaries) required all priesthood candidates to reside on campus. St. Mark's Seminary is located on a spacious, wooded campus in a suburb of Middlefield. When the seminary moved to its current location in the nineteenth century, it was a remote area. Residential neighborhoods now surround the sprawling seminary grounds. The main building contains a chapel, classrooms, administration and faculty offices, living quarters for resident priests and priesthood students, several lounges, and a cafeteria. An adjacent building contains additional staff offices and a large parking garage. The seminary library, gymnasium, and a facilities/operations building also are located nearby. Statues and paintings of saints are found throughout its well-maintained buildings. Because enrollment has significantly declined since the 1960s, some buildings on the grounds have been converted by the Archdiocese of Middlefield to non-seminary uses.

The spatial insulation of seminarians was not nearly as strict as before the Second Vatican Council. When I conducted this study in 2002, students were free to come and go as they pleased. There was no curfew. Some students owned cars. Seminary-owned cars were available to other students for travel to field education sites and ministerial experiences. Prior to the 1960s, the safeguarding of seminarians from "worldly influences" in spatially segregated seminaries was reinforced by limiting the flow of uncontrolled information. According to an alumnus I spoke with, students at St. Mark's previously were not permitted to own televisions, stereos, or radios, and could read only periodicals and newspapers selected by the administration. Telephone calls provided an infrequent privilege. This is no longer the case: many students own televisions and stereos, cable television is available in student lounges, each student room has its own telephone, Internet access is widely available throughout the campus. St. Mark's students had access to varieties of media comparable to that of other U.S. adults. How to appropriately use these media was a concern for some students. The letter to the administration by five native students specifically requested that the spiritual formation program at St. Mark's provide more moral guidance to students regarding prudent use of media.

Fr. Blatsky said that if he suspects a seminarian "is not around a lot," it might mean the seminarian was not "actually living celibately." Requiring seminarians to live together on campus was intended to reinforce their commitment to celibacy. Interestingly, being off campus too much did not elicit the assumption by Blatsky that students were busying themselves in apostolic or parish activities. Though students were preparing for the active ministry as parish priests, the normative culture of St. Mark's appeared to encourage students to spend a lot of time on campus.

While St. Mark's students are free to leave campus without permission, requiring students to live on campus continued to produce a degree of physical and social isolation from non-seminarians and unbelievers. As a boundary marker, celibacy enabled priesthood students to develop a close "community" that excluded the lay students who did not live on campus and were permitted only in certain parts of the building. I once remarked to a faculty member that visits to the campus left the impression that the seminary "belonged" to the priesthood students, and that lay ministry candidates are more like visitors or guests on campus. He said that this perception was an accurate one. Though both priesthood and lay ministry students were attending the seminary, only priesthood students were referred to as "seminarians." Compared to priesthood students, lay students spent only a fraction of the time that priesthood students spent on campus. Because they lived on campus for five years, the seminary became their home more than for the lay students, who spent only a few hours a week on campus. This may have given seminarians a sense that the seminary "belonged to them," and may have also contributed to a sense that they were more a part of the Church than lay students, who did not make their home in an ecclesiastically operated institution. Living in a Church-owned building clearly was a means for encouraging seminarians' identification with their occupational role.

Spatial segregation of students, like celibacy, worked to build cohesion among students. Requiring seminarians to live on campus helped assure that other seminarians would be a student's primary group, providing the largest part of his daily face-to-face interactions. Because they lived together, the cohesiveness of the priesthood students as a group was more likely to be built up through the deepening of affective ties. For the roughly 40 percent of the student body who came to St. Mark's from foreign countries, entrance to St. Mark's resulted in a significant rupture of relationships with family and past friends. Living in close physical proximity in a dormitory, they were more likely to turn to one another for support and friendship. Affective ties among students contributed to a "we-sentiment" that was observed among students and is described below in my account of students' descriptions of "community" and community life.

Like celibacy, spatial segregation of students also worked to build commitment to Catholic beliefs, values, and practices by consensual validation of the group. Because they were part of a residential community, contact was reduced with those who did not share their convictions. While Catholics, including seminarians, surely differ among themselves in their beliefs and practices, attending the seminary likely narrowed the range of beliefs and practices students would encounter. Students were obviously unlikely to have atheists or advocates of free love as their dormitory mates in seminary. Most of their conversations throughout the day were with priests and other students who likely shared similar Catholic definitions of reality. "One must be rather careful to huddle closely and continuously with one's fellow believers" in order to maintain a deviant definition of reality (that celibacy is praiseworthy) (Berger 1967:164). Requiring students to live together provided many more opportunities to "huddle together" and enhance consensual validation of celibacy's value. It encouraged more frequent face-to-face interaction and conversation with people who had similar convictions and were seeking similar definitions or knowledge of the way things were.

In *Discipline and Punish* (1977:170–76), Michel Foucault commented on the consequences of spatial enclosure in disciplinary institutions such as prisons, factories, hospitals, and schools. Foucault argued that enclosure of populations widened the possibility of surveillance. In schools, students are subject to the gaze of their teachers, as well as to their judgments. Requiring seminarians to live on campus increased the amount of time that they were observed by St. Mark's faculty members and meant that their personal habits were more readily subject to the faculty's scrutiny. Seminarians could more easily be evaluated against the norms found in the school's rule of life.

SHARED DAILY SCHEDULE

The requirement to live on campus had significant ramifications for the way in which the seminary's formation program was structured. A residential community of faculty and students facilitated a structured timetable of activities from rising in the morning until bedtime. A seminary's daily schedule is the means by which the school community orders itself, establishes a rhythm, and determines where and when people interact.

The *Program of Priestly Formation* calls for seminaries to establish a schedule for students "with community prayer at its center" (NCCB 1993: no. 327). This schedule allows the community to gather to symbolize itself and sacralize particular times and places. On weekdays, St. Mark's seminarians were required to attend Morning Prayer (before breakfast), Eucharist (usually before lunch), and Evening Prayer (before supper). Night Prayer was celebrated twice weekly. Communal recitation of the Liturgy of the Hours was intended to prepare students for their obligation after ordination to pray the Office daily. In addition, scheduling prayer near meal times meant that students were more likely to eat their meals with one another. The sheer amount of time required for attending classes, formation conferences, prayer services, and Eucharistic celebrations substantially reduced the amount of time available for contact with people outside the seminary. The requirement to attend prayer throughout the day meant that it was difficult for students to be away from the campus for extended periods of time.

The shared daily schedule organized students' daily lives and made possible an immersion in an ecclesiastically monitored version of Catholic culture. Like the requirement to live on campus, a shared schedule of activities limited contact with those who might generally challenge that culture and the value of celibacy in particular. The daily schedule increased the intensity of the formation program and meant it was able to regulate more aspects of candidates' lives, including their human maturity, character, and moral development. The schedule also encouraged regular seminarian interaction and involvement with one another in a prescribed set of activities.

LAY FORMATION PROGRAMS

In the *Program of Priestly Formation,* non-romantic relationships with women are said to "contribute to the overall development of seminarians" (NCCB 1993: no. 305). However, since St. Mark's priesthood students were required to live on campus, in many respects students lived in a largely male environment. At St. Mark's, lay ministry students were not permitted to live on campus. However, seminarians interacted with women much more than they did before the Second Vatican Council, when no women or lay ministry students were enrolled. Before the 1970s, the only daily interaction students had with women was with the vowed religious nuns who cooked and cleaned for them. This menial labor was consistent with their lower social status as females and women religious. When this research was conducted, all cooking and cleaning was performed by lay workers, almost all of whom were women. Women also served on the faculty and staff, as well as in clerical positions.

Unlike in the past, seminarians and female students attended classes together. Roughly 80 percent of the lay ministry students were women. No students in the lay formation program were vowed religious. According to the director of the lay formation program, Jason Fox, most lay students were married and had children. Though lay students outnumbered priesthood students by a ratio of more than 2:1, only 10 percent of the lay students studied at St. Mark's full-time. All priesthood candidates were required to study full-time, and they were much more visible during periods of observation in the semester during which this research was conducted. The largest number of lay students observed at any mass or evening prayer was four. During the "sacred" activities of the day (when students were at prayer) lay students were always a distinct minority, if any were present at all. A few lay students ate lunch or supper in the seminary cafeteria if they had class near meal times. Their part-time student schedules did not require them to be on campus for long periods of time. Since most classes were held during the day, lay students were absent from the campus in the evenings and during weekends. St. Mark's homosocial environment contrasted significantly with American parish life where women are heavily involved in parish activities. (This is a point I will take up in the final chapter.)

Lay ministry students were not required to attend communal prayer or weekly formation nights. Even though they did have spiritual directors, they were required to participate in far fewer formation activities. They were invited to participate in some activities, such as days of recollection, which were held for students in both the priesthood and lay formation programs. According to Fox, students in both programs were called "to grow in holiness." He pointed out that the spiritual lives of lay students were more likely to be centered in the parishes to which they belonged. It wasn't that seminarians had stronger vocations than lay ministry candidates. Rather, the spatial locus and organization of the lives of the two groups of students differed immensely. It would be expected that lay ministry candidates' lives remained enmeshed with their spouses, children, co-workers, non-seminary friends, and parishioners. While both priesthood students and lay ministry students would likely work together in parishes, lay students lived much more in "the world," away from the seminary campus. Lay students' lives were not structured by the seminary administration to the same degree as those of the priesthood students.

Lay students presumably were immersed in Catholic culture too; however, it was more likely to be the Catholic culture of their homes and parishes, which may have varied from the "official" Catholic culture cultivated at the seminary.[33] Most lay students lived in the greater Middlefield area before enrollment. They did not change their residence to attend St. Mark's, nor were they obliged to follow the St. Mark's rule of life. Fox described the experience of someone in the lay formation program as being one of "integration."

Usually in their late thirties or forties, lay students were older by a decade or more than most priesthood students. According to Fox, lay students strove to integrate what they learned and experienced in seminary while maintaining their prior marriage and family relationships. Lay students were striving to "forge a new identity for themselves" as lay ministers through a process of integration. He suggested that priesthood students were more likely to identify with the features of a predetermined identity or set of role expectations associated with the diocesan priesthood. These expectations also left me with the impression that much more care and resources went into the formation of priesthood students than lay ministry students.

THE ROLE OF "COMMUNITY" IN COMMITMENT PRODUCTION

The *Program of Priestly Formation* says that community life is meant to help students mature in their ability to relate to others (NCCB 1993: nos. 304–5). All the seminarians interviewed, except Frank, spoke positively of the community life they experienced at St. Mark's. In students' usage, "community" referred to several different realities which are described below. However, community most often appeared to refer to a positive "we-sentiment" among priesthood students that reflected a cohesiveness that students experienced. It was sometimes used to include faculty, other school employees, and lay ministry students. The cohesiveness that resulted from the affective ties observed among the student body can be understood as a benefit or reward that offset at least some of the sacrifices involved in the requirements to live as celibates and reside at a confined campus.

Community as Communal Living Arrangements for Organic Necessities

Students sometimes spoke of living "in community" to refer to the communal living arrangements of residing in the same dormitory, sharing bathroom and lounge areas and "house chores," and eating meals together in the same dining room. All students resided together in the dormitory wings of the seminary.

Each student had a single room and shared a bathroom with a neighboring room. In this sense, "community" was a utilitarian arrangement for sharing the same physical space and some cooperative arrangements of the organic necessities of daily life.

Community as Camaraderie and Friendship

"Community" also referred to a satisfying level of interpersonal relationships experienced at the seminary. These relationships varied in their levels of intimacy and depth, but together constituted an important dimension of students' experiences of community at St. Mark's. At one level, community meant an easy sociability and camaraderie among students in comfortable though undemanding relationships. Students routinely mentioned this aspect of community as one of the most appealing parts of seminary life and as an aid in celibacy. Larry's remark was typical: "Community is of the utmost importance to me." Regarding his dormitory floor he said, "We are very social and have developed a community. Our lounge is so active." In response to what he liked best about the seminary, the jovial Cyril quickly responded, "First and foremost is the camaraderie in the community. Camaraderie with other seminarians has especially been important." In this usage, community implied a positively evaluated "we-sentiment" or cohesiveness that was an antidote to loneliness. Living in community meant that students were never without company at meals and there was someone to talk with, or watch television with, during study breaks. Community living was observed to facilitate the informal organization of social outings, such as trips to bars, restaurants, and movie theaters. In the letter written by five native students, they asked that occasional "social outings" be formally scheduled and organized after Compline (Night Prayer).

Living in community created expectations that were not met for all students. For Pat, who had fewer off-campus friends, community was particularly important as a social support: "I wish there were more community. You get very lonely here because you are living in community but you have so much expectation. . . . You [can] get very isolated." Because of the pressure to study, "you kind of lock yourself in your room and try to get stuff done. I don't think that is good." Pat said there should be more "balance" between coursework and community relationships:

> Unless we build these relationships here, when we are out on our own, we will have nothing to fall back on, and I think that will be problematic later. So I wish that we could strengthen those bonds here more — have it more fraternal, so that when we do leave [seminary] celibacy will not be as much of a concern because we do feel part of a greater group and we will still have friendships of some kind.

Pat liked "a seminary situation where you are with a lot of people," people whom he said he knew and trusted. Regarding his future, Pat was concerned that after ordination "I would get very lonely, that I wouldn't have anyone to actually be able to talk to all the time" or "someone to come home to." Pat's statements about what should happen at St. Mark's were inconsistent with his behavior. He frequently sat alone at meals and appeared to seldom interact with others in social settings. Given the lack of support he already reported, Pat seemed to have especially good reasons to fear loneliness as a priest.

The enthusiastic way in which seminarians spoke about community life indicated that it was one of the greatest rewards they reaped for the "sacrifice" of living together as celibates. The anxieties that students reported regarding being lonely as priests appeared to indicate that students were aware that the emotional support found in the seminary community would disappear after ordination. Rather than living in small groups, most priests in the Middlefield diocese lived alone. Nor would the diocese be able to require priests to gather for prayer and socials, as the letter of five native students asked the administration to do while they lived at the seminary. The letter from six foreign-born students to the seminary administration lamented that "despite our willingness to be 'good friends,' St. Mark's Seminary does not provide a way for us to develop growing relationships." This may indicate that these foreign students felt more isolated than native students do and perceived more difficulty forming relationships in an American social context. At the same time, since some were already thirty or forty years old, it might be wondered how adaptable and likely they were to change their relational styles when already approaching middle age.

Generally, students spoke much more about enjoying "community" at St. Mark's than about forming friendships with particular students. For some students, living in a supportive community with other seminarians appeared to be a substitute for forming more emotionally intimate relationships. Some students said that they developed closer relationships with other students in whom they confided. For example, Luke and John both said they shared their complaints about the formation program only with small groups whom they felt shared their sentiments. Neither mentioned one another by name, as students appeared to feel it was inappropriate to talk about other students by name in the interviews conducted for this study.

The importance of supportive interpersonal relationships in building attachment to Catholic culture should not be underestimated. Borhek and Curtis (1974:97) asserted that satisfaction with interpersonal relationships could be more important for successful recruitment to an organization than the content of its beliefs. This case study cannot specifically determine if this is true for St. Mark's students. However, given the high cost of celibacy, the importance of cultivating satisfying interpersonal relationships as expressed in the term "community" would theoretically be important for students' continuance in the seminary. Frank is an example. He stated that it was hard for him to live at St. Mark's and that his temper had alienated him from the other students. He spoke with bitterness, maintaining that students wore "masks" in their relations with one another. He acknowledged that "my relations with the other students are very bad. I have few friends here. . . . Most of my friends are outside." Frank, who had girlfriends all through minor seminary, was the only student who reported a high level of dissatisfaction with his interpersonal relationships at the seminary. The affective bonds created at St. Mark's represented an investment by students and meant that leaving the seminary would be more costly, since students would lose the "profit" accrued by investing themselves in these relationships. Frank apparently had fewer friends to lose by leaving the seminary.

Community in a Religious Association

Tobin and Sam, who were drawn to priesthood because of a desire to serve the poor, spoke of "community" as something that would persist beyond the years spent together in seminary. "Community" referred to the positive affective ties they enjoyed with those with whom they lived, as well as their ties to other members of their religious association. Members of their religious association lived at St. Mark's their first two years in seminary, at their parish internship their third year, and with members of their religious association during their fourth and fifth years in seminary. They spoke especially passionately of the "brothers" who were also members of their religious association. In their usage, "community" suggested a relationship beyond those persons with whom they currently resided. Community also referred to the positive affective ties they experienced with other members of their religious association. Speaking of those in his religious community, Sam stated:

> It helps a great deal to be able to go home to somebody and to say it was a terrible day. I just need to talk to somebody, and you can just sit down and chat. It relieves a lot of tension, like I know I can hold hands with them, hug them, I can be with them. That is very important. I know that those relationships are people who love me no matter what. They don't want anything from me. They don't need anything from me either. They just want to be able to love me and can help me grow, and that reassures me a lot.

Tobin said that being a member of his religious community involved being "committed to one another at the same level as marriage." Tobin said he couldn't understand how diocesan priests manage to live celibacy happily without the support of a religious community. The other students who were not members of Sam and Tobin's religious association did not indicate they felt supported or joined by fraternal bonds to the other priests of Middlefield with whom they hoped to minister.

Prayer and Community Life

"Community" was also used in reference to the communal prayer life students and faculty engaged in at St. Mark's. The *Program of Priestly Formation* states that "the seminary is first a community of prayer" (NCCB 1993: no. 191). As noted earlier, students are required to gather three times daily for communal prayer. Most students spoke positively of communally praying the Liturgy of the Hours and celebrating Eucharist. Luke stated, "I love the chance to pray as we do in the community. We have mass everyday and I live for the [Liturgy of the] Hours." A group of students organized independently to pray the rosary together three evenings a week.

Prayer appeared to contribute to the cohesion and affective bonds referred to as "community." The schedule of communal prayer contributed to the monastic rhythm of daily life at St. Mark's. Once they were living alone in parishes, it is unlikely that they would be able to re-create this experience. The most common type of communal prayer they would celebrate in a parish is the Eucharist. If they prayed the Liturgy of the Hours, they would probably have to pray it alone.

A Shared Moral Order for Like-Minded Individuals

Students experienced a sense of community by being a part of a group of like-minded individuals, in which similar cultural values were shared and behaviors rewarded. Pat said he liked life at St. Mark's because "you meet people who are thinking about the same things you are." Everyone is interested in priesthood even "if they don't understand why. . . . Still, everyone is here together and struggling through it." When asked what he liked about St. Mark's, Luke said he enjoyed being "around people who are committed to ministry and faith and ways they want to share, i.e., staff, lay students, seminarians," and

> just to have a life where you think about God and be in a faith context all the time. Being able to study theology and ministry. [These are] opportunities that this place connects me with and allows me to have.

At St. Mark's, students found others with similar values and interests. Growing up, Cyril prayed the rosary as he walked to high school. He perceived entering the seminary as an opportunity to nurture his faith: "I enjoyed prayer. I enjoyed the possibility of deepening that relationship with God." John also said he loved his time in seminary because it offered the chance to pray often. At St. Mark's, seminarians found other people who esteemed prayer and were willing to spend a fair amount of time in daily private and communal prayer. Now Cyril was free to join with a group of students who regularly prayed the rosary together. For him, seminary was a place where Catholic beliefs and practices could be studied and elements of Catholic culture were validated as worthwhile.

Therapeutic Community

Presbyterorum Ordinis reaffirmed that priests "are bound together by an intimate sacramental brotherhood" and "in a special way form one priestly body" in which priests "cooperate in the same work" (Second Vatican Council 1975b: no. 8). Priests, united with their bishop, "are joined to the rest of the members of the priestly body by special ties of apostolic charity of ministry and of brotherhood" (Second Vatican Council 1975b: no. 8). Their shared apostolic work was viewed as essential for the bonds they seek.

Community as experienced by St. Mark's students appeared to be primarily rooted in the ties they experienced and the emotional support they received from one another. "Cathetic ties" result from affective relationships and promote group solidarity (Kanter 1968:499–500). All students but Frank stated that their experience of community (with the varied referents described above) was a source of satisfaction. These bonds of community had a largely therapeutic function; that is, they were evaluated positively for their ability to meet individual psychic needs. The seminary community was particularly important for providing social support, as well as being a group with whom to engage in a favored activity (e.g., praying). The experience of community contributed to students' sense of well-being, but was usually not spoken of in reference to any ministerial or apostolic activities in which students were engaged. In other words, students did not speak of experiencing community because they were engaged in work related to the Church's apostolic mission. Most students were involved as volunteers in parish ministries or did required field work in a variety of placements. However, these experiences did not provide students with the basis for seeing themselves as a part of a community engaged in, and preparing to serve in, the Church's mission. Their experience of community did not appear to prepare them to view themselves after ordination as sharers in a unified presbyteral order dedicated to the Church's work.

The personal and supportive bonds that grew out of their spatially segregated living arrangements would likely decline when students left the seminary and were living distant from one another. Because it was oriented toward meeting personal and psychological needs, their community life at St. Mark's did not appear to provide the basis for a post-ordination identity as members of a presbyteral order engaged in cooperative apostolic work. Community living provided many satisfactions to students including camaraderie, a protective shell of supportive (though undemanding) relationships, frequent opportunities for prayer, and support for their vocation from like-minded people. However these rewards would no longer be available to them after ordination when they were living in parishes. Given this, one could question how well community living prepared seminarians for life after ordination where supports would come from their own efforts and relationships.

PRAYER AS A COMMITMENT PRACTICE

According to the *Program of Priestly Formation*, it is essential that presbyteral candidates develop a habit of personal prayer (NCCB 1993: no. 553). The Liturgy of the Hours and Eucharist are said to be central elements in daily seminary life, and attendance was mandatory for St. Mark's seminarians (NCCB 1993: no. 273). St. Mark's students generally appeared to be enthusiastic about engaging in private and communal prayer forms. The letter written by five native-born first- and second-year students was noteworthy for requesting more occasions for individual and communal prayer. The letter did not criticize the existing program but asked that several activities be added to the seminary's spiritual regimen. The letter was dated "April 17, 2003, Holy Thursday" and was tellingly titled, "Be Perfect, Just as Your Heavenly Father Is Perfect: Conforming Ourselves to Christ." The letter stated that prayer is central to what it called "self-formation" for priestly identity. It rejected "giving in to mediocrity and settling for something less than our best." To accept mediocrity, they said, meant they would be " 'no longer good for anything but to be thrown out and trampled underfoot (Matthew 5:13).' " Despite preparing for an active apostolate, these students appeared to view spiritual perfection as primarily achievable through intense prayer and asceticism.

The students' letter evinced their traditional orientation. They saw themselves raised in a post–Second Vatican Council Church with "no experience of what could be considered a Catholic culture." They lamented growing up after the Second Vatican Council because they believed this resulted in their lack of familiarity with certain doctrinal, devotional, and spiritual practices. The students called for Exposition of the Blessed Sacrament for adoration for one hour on the first Friday of every month. They also suggested more frequent communal recitation of Compline in small groups organized by Fr. Blatsky. The letter also asked that their formation include more attention to the liturgical seasons and calendar, the Eucharistic fast, and days of fasting; they asked that Fridays ordinarily be observed as a day of penance. Fr. Blatsky, who showed me the letter, said that no official response to the letter was made. However, he said the students' suggestions would be kept in mind when planning the following year's formation activities.

Because students gathered at least three or four times daily for prayer, it appeared that prayer was very important at St. Mark's for developing commitment to priesthood by cultivating a relationship to God through both private and communal prayer. That seminary formators anecdotally associated personal prayer with commitment to priesthood was reflected in a statement in a conference for seminarians by the former rector of Rome's North American College. He recounted that "a priest who is well known for his work with priests told me, 'The first thing to go when a priest is heading for trouble is his daily Office' " (Dolan 2000:164). Empirically, it is not clear if priests' failure to pray the daily Office proceeded or followed the events referred to as "heading for trouble."

As noted earlier, many opportunities for communal prayer was one of the "rewards" or satisfactions several students mentioned. Besides developing cohesiveness among students, prayer also builds commitment in other ways. In addition to deepening their devotion to the Eucharist, attending mass also served to validate the high status of priests in the social system of the Church. Leading people in prayer, especially the Eucharist, was the most important work that students identified as the priest's. In doing so, they were singling out a form of ministry that the Church reserves exclusively for priests. Requiring students to attend daily Eucharist underlined the importance and sacredness of the role of the priest as a vehicle of grace through his power to engage in sacramental activity. Attendance at Eucharist daily presented to the students the high status of the role they would someday hold, since only priests are allowed to preside at Eucharist.

The seminary's liturgical rituals also served to separate and stratify seminarians over lay students. Seminarians usually led prayer and ministered as acolytes, readers, and sacristans. As seminarians they began to share in the power they would be authorized to exercise in the liturgical sphere as priests. Prayer became an important way for seminarians to use the ritual capital of the Church to reinforce its traditional authority.

Theoretically, this high status of the priest within Catholicism can provide a reward for the cost of celibacy. Attendance at the Eucharist may also have served to reinforce students' identification with Christ, the "high priest" from the Letter to the Hebrews, who is said to have initiated the ritual of Eucharist and to whom a priest is "configured at ordination." As a commitment practice, prayer calls for the collective participation of group members in symbolic rituals and raises membership in the group beyond the mundane to a transcendent level. In addition, the celebration of the Eucharist recalled events of great symbolic import to Christians. These rituals were important in shaping the worldview of seminarians.

SPIRITUAL FORMATION NIGHTS AND RETREATS

While the *Program of Priestly Formation* holds that prayer should establish the rhythm of daily life in the seminary, it calls for conferences, days of recollection, retreats, and workshops to specifically address topics of human and spiritual growth (NCCB 1993: no. 277).

Wednesday evening was referred to as "Spiritual Formation Night" at St. Mark's. Occasionally there was a joint formation evening for students in both the lay ministry and priesthood formation programs. Lay students were invited to attend these joint evenings, while priesthood students were required to attend. However, most formation evenings for the two formation programs were conducted separately. In the fall of 2002, the rector, Fr. Dahman, gave a conference to the priesthood students, as he did each semester. The vice-rector, Fr. Schrieter, and the spiritual director, Fr. Blatsky, gave a joint conference at the beginning of the semester. During four evenings that fall, "class formation nights" were held, and topics appropriate for that year of formation were addressed. For the priesthood candidates, an issue related to celibacy was addressed one evening per year. Each year another evening was dedicated to a topic related to human development. Presentations were developmental and thematic. Guest speakers on specialized topics often were featured on these evenings. The letter from the Latin American students requested that a day of recollection be held once or twice a year in Spanish.

I observed a formation evening for the two fourth-year students. Fr. Schrieter talked with the students about celibacy and priestly life. Schrieter described self-knowledge, supportive relationships, and mental and physical health as essential for celibacy. During the second semester of the 2002–3 school year, priesthood students attended a week-long retreat. Students who were ordained deacons also attended another retreat in August 2002, a month before their ordination to the deaconate.

THE MONTH-LONG "INTENSIVE"
AS A COMMITMENT PRACTICE

New priesthood candidates are required to participate in St. Mark's "month-long Intensive," an introduction to seminary life led by Fr. Blatsky, the spiritual director. Four weeks prior to the beginning of the 2002–3 academic school year, three priesthood students began the Intensive. The month's activities immersed new students in the culture of the seminary by exposure to its official central values and practices. Fr. Blatsky stated that the weeks were intended to familiarize the students with four of the elements that he said were integral to a priestly way of life: prayer, celibacy, obedience, and simplicity. Cultivating these four elements in the lives of students was central to the entire spiritual formation program at St. Mark's. They are thought to have been essential practices in Christ's life, which was taken as a model for seminarians' and priests' lives. Each week of the Intensive focused on one of these four key elements and served as a much-truncated version of the traditional year-long novitiate that novices in religious communities undergo. These four elements were dealt with in presentations and discussions. Students prepared for sessions by reading Church documents, articles and books by spiritual writers, and the code of ethics for all employees of the Archdiocese of Middlefield.

In the first week, the three new students were introduced to Morning and Evening Prayer from the Liturgy of the Hours, the Eucharist, and silent meditation. Mastery of these prayer forms built the "religious capital" of seminarians and their attachment to Catholic culture. These activities were mandatory parts of the daily schedule during the Intensive and the school year. The second week was devoted to study and discussion of priestly celibacy and "appropriate relationships." The official Church documents read by students included *Presbyterorum Ordinis* of the Second Vatican Council (1975b), *Sacerdotalis Caelibatus* by Paul VI (1967), *Pastores Dabo Vobis* by John Paul II (1993), and *Program of Priestly Formation* of the National Conference of Catholic Bishops (1993).

I attended most of the sessions during the week on celibacy, including an afternoon session in which *Presbyterorum Ordinis* was discussed. Students challenged some of what was said in *Sacerdotalis Caelibatus*. One said "the document is beautiful," but he didn't feel it acknowledged how difficult celibacy was. He said that when he was close to a woman, it was hard for him to maintain boundaries. Another said he felt the document really doesn't speak directly to how celibacy was to be lived. Another said that in the Latin American town where he lived as a child, the people did not seem to mind that the village priest lived with a woman and had several children by her. During a discussion of an article on ways people deal with sexual energy, one student wondered if masturbation "broke" one's celibacy. Fr. Blatsky replied that masturbation is more than a response to physical urges. He said it is not condoned by the Church and is "not helpful for growth in the celibate lifestyle." Other times, the sessions tended to be very abstract and theoretical regarding celibacy and human relationships. The fact that Blatsky simply read aloud sections of documents and articles, without comment, did not encourage student dialogue.

The third week of the Intensive dealt with the virtue of obedience to the will of God. In particular, Blatsky said the week stressed obedience to religious authorities, especially the ordinary of the archdiocese. The last week focused on how to live a simple, non-acquisitive life. Students also wrote a "spiritual autobiography" during the Intensive that included significant events in their lives that they believed illustrated how God was calling them. In writing the autobiography, students began to form a new narrative of their lives and to make sense of their emerging identity as men preparing to be priests. Frank spoke enthusiastically about writing his autobiography. Social activities such as a visit to an art museum, attendance at a baseball game, and dinner with the resident priests also were a part of the week. Sociologically, the month's activities immersed new students in the culture of the seminary by initiating them into the practices that were held to be integral to priestly life. Normative documents, including the seminary rule and *Program of Priestly Formation*, were studied. The month conveyed the school's expectations for them as candidates for priesthood. Fr. Blatsky said the transition into the seminary is not easy for all students and that it is not uncommon for a new student to decide during the Intensive that he does not want to attend the seminary. However, this did not occur during the time I conducted this research.

HUMAN DEVELOPMENT WORKSHOP
AND COMMITMENT

One weekend in the fall semester, Fr. Blatsky, Fr. Schrieter, and sixteen seminarians traveled to a retreat house for the biannual human development workshop. It was a new addition to the priestly formation program at St. Mark's. The human development workshop and the celibacy workshop were conducted in alternating years. Fr. Blatsky and Fr. Schrieter worked cooperatively to organize both weekends. The two weekends were developed in response to the call for greater attention to human formation and formation for celibacy by John Paul II in *Pastores Dabo Vobis* (1993: no. 44). The human development weekend was intended to develop students' "affective maturity," according to Fr. Schrieter.

During the weekend Schrieter administered the Myers-Briggs Inventory to the students and gave several lectures. All Schrieter's presentations that weekend were packed (perhaps too packed) with psychological theories, recent empirical findings, lists of "helpful hints," and self-help jargon. It was not clear whether students had assimilated the material presented or whether they would then process what they had heard with their spiritual directors. The sessions appeared to me to be easy for students to passively sit through. There was no clear indication that students comprehended their content or were prepared to integrate what they heard into their daily lives. There was little interpersonal sharing and no attempt to break down into smaller groups for discussion. As with many of the formation sessions observed, seminarians appeared passive and unengaged.

SPIRITUAL DIRECTION, PSYCHOLOGY, AND THE
SACRAMENT OF PENANCE AND COMMITMENT

Spiritual Direction

All students at St. Mark's were required by the *Program of Priestly Formation* to have a priest as their personal spiritual director

(NCCB 1993: no. 323). Seminarians chose from a list of priests selected by Fr. Blatsky and approved by Fr. Dahman and Archbishop Lobble. Spiritual directors were faculty members or parish priests in Middlefield whom students met with once or twice a month. Conversations with spiritual directors were considered privileged and confidential; what was discussed could not be shared with faculty members. In addition, spiritual directors abstained from participating in the formal evaluation of students they directed. A seminarian's spiritual director is intended to be someone a seminarian can talk to about anything without fear of negative sanctions.

The *Program of Priestly Formation* specifies that the content of direction sessions should include a seminarian's "personal relationships, prayer experiences, and other significant topics" (NCCB 1993: no. 324). Spiritual direction also is supposed to play a key part in "vocational discernment" (NCCB 1993: no. 325). Directors should aid students in determining if their call to the priesthood is authentic or if "signs indicate another mission in the Church" is appropriate for the seminarian (NCCB 1993: no. 325).

The *Program of Priestly Formation* is careful to specify the kind of advice the spiritual director should offer:

> It is especially important that all spiritual directors share the same understanding of an integral celibate commitment and the kinds of behaviors that are counterindicators of growth. It is also essential that advice given in spiritual direction accord with the public presentation of its value, its importance for the priesthood and the common understanding of its practice in the seminary community and the Church. (NCCB 1993: no. 293)

Fr. Blatsky said he was working more closely with spiritual directors and gathering them to meet periodically because he was not sure all of them were sufficiently addressing matters related to sexuality. He stated:

> Last year I really made an effort to emphasize to the spiritual directors the need to talk directly about those issues to

the students, sexuality, celibacy, sexual orientation, and relationship intimacy, and those kinds of things. In the past I just assumed it, but this past year I really hit on that to make sure that that be articulated to sexuality and celibacy.

Asked if he knew if students were talking about these matters with their spiritual directors, Fr. Blatsky replied, "I don't know and there is no way to really control that. I don't know to what extent that happens." He does meet with each seminarian once a semester and encourages them to talk to their spiritual directors about sexuality and celibacy. Blatsky said spiritual direction also was important for helping students to clarify their own motivations and to discern if they are called and capable of a permanent commitment to a celibate priesthood that would last their entire lives.

In interviews for this study, students were asked about the degree to which they felt they could be open with their spiritual directors regarding celibacy, sexuality, and their relationships. Students were evenly divided. Pat, Cyril, and Larry tended to blame being paired with the wrong spiritual director, even though they chose their own directors. Pat said, "Spiritual direction hasn't been helpful for me because I haven't hooked up with the right person." Cyril said that it is "not that I don't trust him, but simply because he is not someone I particularly want to talk about that kind of stuff with." He reported that he talked about those things more with other seminarians. After not feeling he could share in depth with his first spiritual director, Larry said he now has found one he can be open with. Foreign students like Robert, Richard, Sam, and Tobin appeared to utilize their spiritual director extensively and he had clearly become a mentor. Judging from their comments, other students were more guarded in their relationships with spiritual directors to protect their sexual lives. Blatsky clearly was ambivalent about how successful spiritual directors were in encouraging students to talk with them about sexual matters.

Psychological Services

At St. Mark's, psychologists assist with testing and consultation during the admissions process. Seminarians at St. Mark's were able to seek psychological counseling at the school's expense. Fr. Schrieter, the vice-rector, who was trained in pastoral counseling, made referrals to consulting psychologists. Blatsky said that he had seen anxious and depressed students benefit from counseling. Faculty indicated that the use of psychological counseling was more exceptional than routine. Unless problems surfaced in their years at St. Mark's, students did not meet with a psychologist after they had undergone screening in the admissions process. However, Schrieter was working on a plan that would require new students to meet periodically after admission with a psychologist. Students would meet with the testing psychologist during the Intensive to develop human formation goals that would be shared with the student's spiritual director and formation advisor. Second, Schrieter would like to give students the option of meeting with a psychologist to do a "psychosexual history," which would be shared with the student's spiritual director and formation advisor. Third, Schrieter definitely wanted all students to undergo a psychological review with the testing psychologist before the end of their second year, "so that we know that after two years here they are relatively psychologically stable to go into C.P.E. and inflict them on a parish. Because some of our guys aren't."[34] Schrieter would like another psychological interview and screening to occur prior to the "Rite of Admission to Candidacy for Orders." Schrieter said the purpose of the increased use of psychological interviews and testing was to provide more information for both students and faculty. These plans appeared to indicate a significantly increased use of psychological tools and knowledge at St. Mark's in the coming years.

The Sacrament of Penance

The *Program of Priestly Formation* encouraged the frequent reception of the sacrament of penance by seminarians "as a means of conversion" (NCCB 1993: no. 276). Communal celebrations (Rite II) for the entire school occur during the liturgical seasons of Advent and Lent at St. Mark's. Twice a semester, external confessors are available for individual confession (Rite I). Students also were free to arrange to go to confession with the spiritual director or other priests at any time, as well. The seminary's Advent reconciliation service was observed during the semester this research was conducted. Fr. Green preached in a dynamic manner on scripture readings that emphasized that students should be "light in the darkness of the world." Two external confessors and two faculty members were available for individual confessions at the service. Less than half the student body made an individual confession.

The letter by five native students to the resident priest faculty members referred to earlier requests that individual confession still be available on a monthly basis. The students asked the faculty to consider offering students more instruction on the sacrament, as well as on the importance of asceticism. The group of students also asked that the relationship of the sacrament of reconciliation to simplicity, obedience, and apostolic work be more clearly addressed and that this instruction be integrated into retreats, formation nights, days of reflection, coursework, and daily homilies. The students also requested more reflections on chaste celibacy, the moral teachings of the Church, and "our daily interactions with varying societal media."

These students said they regretted their own shortcomings in becoming men of prayer, simplicity, obedience, and chastity. As they saw it, instruction in the moral life could help them overcome their mediocrity and address "the need to 'Live Jesus.'" In doing so, students said "the seminary will help us address these weaknesses, and continue to raise before us the important question: 'Would a *good* priest act in this manner?'" (emphasis added). For the writers of the letter, imitating Christ (as they understood him) was the only acceptable normative behavior for seminarians. This group of students, along with the rest, did not shy away from claiming to aspire to what they saw as the highest ideals. Expressing and striving after the realization of these ideals, including celibate chastity, was expected in the culture of St. Mark's. At St. Mark's, celebration of the sacrament provided students with an opportunity to evaluate themselves according to their own ideals and the Church's moral teachings and then submit themselves to the guidance of confessors. The practice reinforced the role of the cleric as the one who provides access to forgiveness and the supply of grace.

At St. Mark's, spiritual direction and psychological services are increasingly being called upon to address students' psycho-sexual development. Along with the sacrament of reconciliation, they could be described as "social control" commitment practices because they sought commitment and obedience to norms and values faculty and students generally shared (Kanter 1968:501). However, from another perspective they could be viewed more therapeutically, as tools by which students discern their own future and fashion an identity for themselves as priests.

INTELLECTUAL FORMATION AND RELIGIOUS CAPITAL

This research project primarily focused on the spiritual formation program of St. Mark's, apart from intellectual (academic coursework) and pastoral formation (internships). However, a brief mention should be made of St. Mark's program of intellectual formation since students likely spent more time in studying than anything else. The *Program of Priestly Formation* states that the goal of a seminarian's theological studies is "the conversion of the mind and heart" (NCCB: no. 335). Their coursework was intended to prepare them to become "part of the tradition of authorized teachers and living witnesses by which the Gospel of Jesus is handed down from one generation to the next" (NCCB 1993: no. 333). Theological studies were intended to deepen their own faith and prepare them for ministry as priests. At St. Mark's, priesthood candidates usually earned a master of divinity degree after five years of study, including an internship year.[35]

The curriculum at St. Mark's closely observed the norms outlined in the *Program* (NCCB 1993: nos. 364–96). Students took courses in biblical, systematic, moral, spiritual, historical, pastoral, and sacramental theology. Only three class sessions were observed during the semester this research was conducted. All of these appeared to mix lectures and class discussion of required reading. Required courses at St. Mark's generally had eight to ten students. Elective classes often are smaller. According to the seminary academic bulletin, courses are pastoral in orientation since the students were likely to spend most of their ministry working in parishes after graduation. Priestly celibacy received modest attention in the courses on holy orders and moral theology. Otherwise, faculty members said that celibacy was not addressed significantly in the curriculum.

It is beyond the scope of this project to gauge and assess how the experiences of attending class, preparing reading assignments, writing papers, and taking tests contributed to St. Mark's formation for celibacy. However, coursework appeared to be students' most time-consuming activity. Several students mentioned that being able to study theology was one of the things they really liked about being at St. Mark's. As might be expected, there was some grumbling about long reading assignments and having too many papers to write for courses. Only Pat expressed fear that he would not be able to handle all of the schoolwork required of him. He candidly stated, "I am not a very intelligent person. I am not a good speaker." He worried about how he would manage to teach and preach in a parish. Yet, later, when asked what he enjoyed most about the seminary, he said, "The fact that I am learning about my faith, about the Catholic Church." This was a common sentiment among students.

The six international students criticized the school's curriculum in a letter to the administration. All recruited from Latin America, they asked for more emphasis on training for Hispanic ministry at St. Mark's and they encouraged more dialogue on multicultural matters. The letter requested that a Hispanic priest be appointed to the faculty as a mentor for them. The students also expressed regret that native students showed little interest in Hispanic ministry.

Though they were supposed to be engaged in the study of theology at the graduate level, I was struck by the lack of theological sophistication of students during the research interviews. In terms of their preparedness to study theology, Dr. Litkowiak, the academic dean, characterized students as representing a "pretty broad spectrum." Some students entered without ever having studied theology and were required to take philosophy and basic theology courses in St. Mark's pre-theology program. Students appeared to spend several hours each day studying in their rooms or in the school's library.

From a sociological perspective, by studying Catholic beliefs, rituals, and practices, students were offered a symbolic framework for their lives and gained religious capital through their mastery of Catholic faith and culture. While spiritual formation developed commitment to Catholic culture, classes provided distinctive expertise that few Catholics attained. The development of religious capital through coursework would distinguish them from most laypeople and enhance their status as priests.

THE SEMINARY RULE OF LIFE AS COMMITMENT PRACTICE

The *Program of Priestly Formation* (NCCB 1993) required that major seminaries publish a rule of life for their priesthood students. According to the *Program,* the rule should "establish the basic patterns and expectations of community living" (NCCB 1993: no. 202). The rule should "foster an atmosphere that balances freedom, responsibility, and accountability" and elaborate "all important points of discipline that affect student conduct and behavior" (NCCB 1993: no. 203). No rule of life is required for lay ministry students, and St. Mark's has nothing comparable to it for them. Fr. Dahman said that the rule was written to help students live in a Christian community. It was also meant to help students "grow in holiness" and to practice Christian virtue. The rule stated particular expectations and their relationship to values found in the New Testament.

The St. Mark's rule of life was exhaustive in regulating student conduct and providing a schedule of daily activities. It challenged students to make good use of their time according to the schedule that the rule outlined. It specified appropriate behavior both on and off campus and encouraged students to engage in "fraternal correction" with classmates who deviated from the rule. The first section dealt with time and called for punctuality. It specified what community activities are mandatory (the Liturgy of the Hours, the Eucharist, and all other aspects of the formation program). The second section regulated relationships inside and outside the seminary. They were to be marked by "mutual respect,

192 _____ *Commitment Production at St. Mark's Seminary*

charity, and fraternal correction." It mandated that interpersonal conflicts among students be resolved through fraternal discussion and correction. Regarding celibacy, the rule proscribed permanent exclusive relationships, with or without physical intimacy. Viewing pornography on computers or engaging in "inappropriate online relationships" on personal or school computers on campus also was not allowed and could result in probation or dismissal. Lewd, sexist, or racist jokes and stories were forbidden. The rule outlined what parts of the building guests were allowed in and during what hours. Non-seminarians, other than family members, were not allowed in student rooms. A detailed dress code specified four levels of formality in attire. Students at St. Mark's did not wear clerical clothing, except for deacons, who were expected to wear a clergy shirt at formal occasions. Generally students wore slacks and dress or sport shirts throughout the school day.

Violations of rules that came to the attention of the vice-rector or other administrators were, according to the rule, dealt with by an initial conversation with the vice-rector and dean of resident students, Fr. Schrieter. Subsequent violations were dealt with by disciplinary letters and meetings, then by probation, and finally by dismissal if there was no progress. Students at St. Mark's are encouraged to call one another to task when they do not behave appropriately. The rule states that men who are preparing should engage in "fraternal correction" when they observe infractions of the rule. It is characteristic of members of a profession to monitor one another according to the norms and code of ethics of that profession. Students were encouraged to do that monitoring even before ordination.

Some students chafed at always having their behavior monitored and being subject to disciplinary sanctions. Frank, who was going on a leave from the seminary, was the only student who told me he was formally disciplined for his behavior. He said reprimands were "a big part of his life" at St. Mark's and compared it to living in a prison. Frank was not alone in being sensitive to the "gaze" of faculty members. After supper one evening, Pat commented to Fr. Schrieter and me that "the only time faculty talked to him was when he did something wrong." Fr. Schrieter took issue with Pat and said he was exaggerating. Pat also said that he would fear for his physical safety if he candidly filled out a peer evaluation form on another student whom he considered mentally unbalanced.

Richard reported having a number of "run-ins" with Fr. Schrieter, the dean of resident students, though he felt things were going better during the semester when the research was conducted. He felt hemmed in by the seminary's rules and expectations that cover every conceivable detail and stated that he thought the faculty was inflexible. He stated, "If you have three memos [in your file], you are out. It is so mechanical." Increasingly, he felt "it is more like if you break a rule, you are out. It is like 'zero tolerance' but in a small seminary." Larry complained of "rigidity," and Cyril was upset that students were too frequently reprimanded for matters that were insignificant. Referring to reprimands for moving lounge furniture and parking in the wrong parking lot, Cyril said, "Those kinds of issues end up getting people angry and suck up their energy. . . . These petty little issues drain us and suck us dry." On the other hand, when asked what he liked about St. Mark's, Robert said "they [the faculty] treat you as a mature person, so there is the opportunity to have a good time to organize yourself, your time."

That students bristled at having to comply with school rules need not be seen as a problematic feature of life at St. Mark's. Rather, such grumbling can also be understood as evidence of students' efforts to assert their own autonomy. The desire of subordinates to assert themselves within complex organization has been seen as a natural property of organizational life (Becker et al. 1961). This desire arises from the peculiarity of the seminarians' living situation and the problems that arise from never being far from the critical gaze of faculty members who examine all areas of seminarians' lives to determine whether they will reach their goal of ordination.

The particular rules of the seminary rule were articulated with reference to values that were found in the New Testament. By linking its rules and values to scripture quotations, the administration provided a divine basis and legitimation for the norms. They were viewed not only as authorized by the seminary administration, but as rooted in a moral order (*nomos*) established by God and revealed in the scriptures. Deviant behaviors not only were violations of the school's rules but were imputed to be opposed to the will of God. As Kanter has pointed out, to gain commitment to norms, "An individual whose personality system is attached to norms of a social system should see himself as carrying out the dictates of a higher-order system, a system which orders and gives meaning to life" (1968:510). Thus compliance with its norms is sought, according to the rule, "for your own good, for the good of ministerial priesthood, and for the good of the Gospel."

St. Mark's rule of life was a clear statement of the administration's prescribed norms of behavior for students. The St. Mark's rule of life stated it was intended to help students "grow in holiness." Establishing a rule of life compelled students to subordinate themselves to the seminary and purposes of the social system of the Church, especially in the area of sexuality. Compliance with norms is necessary for any organization to meet its purposes. Commitment to norms, according to Kanter (1968), "involves securing a person's positive *evaluative* orientations, redefining his symbolic environment so that the system's demands are considered right in terms of his self-identity, and obedience to authority becomes a moral necessity" (510; emphasis in the original). According to the rule of life, obedience to the rule resulted in holiness, becoming more Christlike, and in the seminarian's behavior becoming more like that of a priest. This was a high level of authority, as well as a reward. Failure to live according to the rule was not only failure as a Christian, but also a failure to live like a priest. Failure to live by the rule also could lead to probation, dismissal from the seminary, and failure to be ordained a priest.

That all areas of seminarians' lives were addressed by the rule indicated the breadth of the socialization process and the depth of commitment that together transformed seminarians into ordained priests. In her study of commitment in utopian communities, Kanter (1968) asserted, "In order to be totally committed to the group, an individual may reserve no private areas of himself, no domains not subject to the group's awareness, at the very

least, if not its jurisdiction" (512). The rule of life and the formation program at St. Mark's addressed nearly every significant area
of a seminarian's life (including sexuality). This is not surprising
since the life and work of priests goes beyond simply providing
services for clients. Priestly formation seeks to shape what are
usually thought of as personal or private matters in other professional schools. Perhaps in no other occupation (including the
military) are so many aspects of life subject to social control.
Areas addressed in the rule included sexuality, friendships, use of
one's own material possessions, how leisure time is spent, how
often one prays, and the manner of prayer. The requirement that
deacons wear clergy attire at formal occasions functioned as a
boundary marker distinguishing them as clerics, thus set apart in
their status from the laity.

The St. Mark's rule of life sought to address all of these matters
and prepare seminarians for subordination to the organization's
purposes and demands as priests. Compliance with the princi-
ples on which the rule was based was a basis for each student's
evaluation by faculty and by other students. The detailed written
rule seminarians were to observe, and the scrutiny they received
in their annual evaluations, contrasted with the relative autonomy and lack of supervision that seminarians would enjoy after
ordination.

Living on campus with their peers and resident priest faculty,
they were constantly in the presence of people who would be
writing formal evaluations on them. Since seminarians lived on
campus, they ate, prayed, and interacted with faculty throughout
the day and evening. The small number of students made the activities of any one student more visible. It was easy to count the
number of students in class, at prayer, or at a meal and know if
any were missing. Students were infrequently absent at the meals
attended by the researcher. These absences were usually observed
and verbally noted by other students. Students appeared to keep
track of one another's whereabouts in this way. Seminarians were
subject to what Giddens has termed "surveillance," by which he
means "the supervisory control of subject populations" (1992:15).
That some students had conflicts with Fr. Schrieter and were subject to annual evaluations suggested that surveillance appeared

to be an important part of life at St. Mark's. Such surveillance was a means of social control that enforced behaviors deemed appropriate for future priests.

EVALUATIONS OF STUDENT SEMINARIANS

The *Program of Priestly Formation* requires an annual evaluation of seminarians. The goal of the assessment process was said to be "the internal appropriation of priestly values by seminarians" (NCCB 1993: no. 311). Assessment must include an estimation by faculty members of a student's capacity to live chaste celibacy (NCCB1993: nos. 529–541).[36] St. Mark's faculty evaluated students in each of their five years before ordination. Seminarians also wrote a self-evaluation and some years were evaluated by peers. The evaluation form at St. Mark's also included a question regarding students' ability to work respectfully with women.

Not surprisingly, annual student evaluations were a source of anxiety to some students. Larry acknowledged that he limited those with whom he would talk to about celibacy: "It all depends on who it is because I really don't like the idea of evaluations." However, faculty evaluations covered nearly all areas of students' lives. Faculty members were asked in their interviews how they evaluated students' capacity for celibacy and what would be indicators of such a capacity. Most said that when gauging students' capacity for celibacy they considered their interpersonal skills. Fr. Green's response was typical of the faculty members:

> I look for someone who is comfortable when relating to members of their own sex and members of the opposite sex. By comfortable I mean able to relate in tender, respectful, mutual ways.

Green also considered whether a student had any close, supportive friendships. Fr. Dahman added that in evaluating students' capacity for celibacy, he considered whether they were able to relate positively to people in authority. Green and Blatsky both said they looked for students who exhibited "joy in their lives." How faculty could objectively make these judgments was not made clear.

Archbishop Lobble said that when he was a faculty member in another seminary, he listened attentively to students practicing to preach. He considered a sense of conviction regarding what they were preaching as an indicator that they would live a life of celibacy. How Lobble could ascertain a particular student's conviction by this method was left unspoken. He also said he looked for students to demonstrate a "sense of self-mastery" and "the ability to be responsible, disciplined, and in control" in other areas of their lives. If they carried through with other commitments, he believed they could effectively commit themselves to celibacy.

Fr. Schrieter, in evaluating potential for celibacy, looked for four other indicators: self-knowledge, freedom, conviction in one's vocation, and a student's prayer life. These criteria struck me as difficult to assess unless the faculty member knew the student well.

When asked how he could know about all the things he mentioned in order to evaluate a student, he did not answer directly but said that the faculty never agreed upon the criteria for evaluating students' capacities for celibacy. Similarly Fr. Green said:

> We have never come to any consensus on what we as individuals look for. What the institution primarily relies upon is the absence of evidence to the contrary. So we presume that you are living celibately and by that we mean we presume you are living a life with sexual abstinence until you prove you are not.

He added that he believed that many students "don't want to engage in a sexual maturation process," but that this was unlikely to lead to their getting "kicked out" as long as they don't act out sexually. According to the faculty interviewed, few (if any) students were negatively evaluated on the evaluation form question regarding capacity for celibacy. Dr. Litkowiak, the longtime academic dean and professor, did not recall ever negatively evaluating a student's capacity for celibacy. "Unless I have some strong evidence to the contrary, I don't pay much attention to that question," the dean said.

Even though students were seldom negatively evaluated regarding their aptness for celibacy, disciplinary action has been taken in recent years when students were believed to provide evidence to the contrary. Four faculty members mentioned that a student was dismissed two years ago for impregnating a woman. Fr. Coughlin also related:

> We threw someone out of the seminary for organizing a trip to a gay bar. It was after a Halloween party, so people had a little bit to drink, and he got a bunch of guys and some of the kitchen ladies to go.

He was unsure if there were other issues related to the student's dismissal. Though some students were negatively evaluated in the past and dismissed outright, these were exceptional cases. More typically when a student left the seminary, it was a voluntary decision. Four students who began the 2002–3 school year withdrew from the school by the following fall, including two who participated in this study.[37] At least three of the four left the seminary by taking leaves of absence. In these cases, the many ways in which the formation program sought to build student self-awareness appeared to result in students' initiating the decision to leave the seminary.

While some students understandably exhibited anxiety about the evaluation process, faculty expressed skepticism and frustration with its effectiveness. Green, Blatsky, Schrieter, and Coughlin generally found it difficult to address problems with students' behavior. They sensed that students who want to be ordained learn to "jump through hoops" without internalizing the desired norms or values. Fr. Blatsky framed it this way:

> As it is, as long as a person is kind of obeying the rules and not getting into huge trouble here and is effective in pastoral ministry and getting good grades and everything else, they will be ordained because they were accepted into the system. Yet there have been some who really have held their cards very closely and some who once they have been ordained have gotten into trouble.

Fr. Schrieter echoed the concern in strong terms:

What we have found and what my experience has been telling me both here and at St. Joseph's [another seminary Fr. Schrieter worked at] is that when you try and try to do everything to get them to be who you want them to be, they will figure out a way of jumping through the hoops. But they haven't changed. They have just figured out how to jump through the hoops.

Schrieter said he frequently clashed with the former rector over whether candidates should be allowed to return the following year. He believed that the current rector, Fr. Dahman, also was uncomfortable with conflict and did not challenge students as much as he should. Schrieter, clearly frustrated with some students, said:

We will talk to them and talk to them and talk to them until we are blue in the face and they are blue in the face, and then something serious happens, and we are forced to dismiss a student or forced to help them move on out of here.

When asked if there was a tendency to bend over backward to retain students because of the shortage of priests in the Middlefield archdiocese, he responded, "I will be honest, Paul. That is my fear here. I think we do that with some of the guys." Fr. Wisher, the former rector, admitted with regret, "We have ordained too many mistakes."

Faculty members' consternation with the effectiveness of the mandatory evaluation process was not mere handwringing. In a highly publicized case the semester before interviews were conducted, a recently ordained graduate of St. Mark's was removed from his parish because of more than one alleged relationship with an adult parishioner. Regarding the priest, Fr. Coughlin commented, "That is a particularly interesting case because this was a man who prided himself on his orthodoxy."

In conclusion, in evaluating students' capacity for celibacy, faculty members were attentive to students' relational abilities. This practice was consistent with John Paul II (1993) in *Pastores Dabo Vobis*, in which he contended that "of special importance is the capacity to relate to others. This is truly fundamental for a person who is called to be responsible for a community and to be a 'man of communion'" (no. 43). However, among the faculty interviewed, there was considerable dissatisfaction with the effectiveness of students' evaluations.

In her study of American seminaries, Schuth (1999:86) reported that faculty believed they lacked adequate tools to evaluate a student's progress in developing positive human qualities. In addition, Schuth reported that there has not been enough research to understand how seminaries can cultivate the human qualities the faculty desires in seminarians. St. Mark's faculty appeared to believe it was difficult to change the behavior of students. Faculty members acknowledged that some students showed external compliance with expected behaviors without internalizing a commitment to maintaining those behaviors after ordination. Faculty admitted to positively evaluating candidates' potential for celibacy only because they showed no evidence to the contrary. Some stated that there was pressure to advance students because of Middlefield's shortage of priests. Fr. Schrieter blamed the two rectors he worked under for advancing weak candidates. A tendency to "wave" students on toward ordination appeared to be a problem at St. Mark's. A failure to produce any new priests for Middlefield would have threatened the continued existence of St. Mark's Seminary. It was in the seminary's institutional interest to produce priests in order to justify the large financial subsidy it received from the Archdiocese of Middlefield.

The annual evaluations subjected all areas of a student's life to the scrutiny of the faculty and his classmates. The evaluations also showed that the seminary sought to influence all areas of a candidate's life and that in order to progress toward ordination, a seminarian was dependent on the approval of his peers and the faculty. For some students "jumping through the hoops" to meet faculty expectations was a dimension of the culture absorbed at St. Mark's.

OATHS AND LITURGIES
MARKING COMMITMENT

Extended training, the mastery of esoteric knowledge and skills, and living by a prescribed set of norms elaborated in the seminary's rule of life all prepared St. Mark's students to live as celibates and become legitimate practitioners in the religious profession. Of course a seminarian does not become a priest simply by successfully completing a series of classes, exams, or licensing requirements; he must first be ordained a priest by a bishop. However, prior to ordination to the priesthood, canon law requires a series of public rituals that signal a seminarian's progress toward ordination and progressive commitment to the priesthood. Students had to be approved by faculty evaluations to celebrate the particular rites.

Reader, Acolyte, Candidate, and Deaconate Ceremonies

At St. Mark's, a student's progress was marked by institution into the ministry of reader (during a student's first year), ministry of acolyte (second year), and the Rite of Admission to Candidacy for Sacred Orders (fourth year).[38] Admission to candidacy occurs only "when candidates have reached a maturity of purpose and are shown to have necessary qualifications" (Roman Catholic Church 1976: no. 1). At St. Mark's students are admitted as candidates for ordination only if they have successfully completed a nine-month parish internship. Evidence of students' ability to relate maturely with others, and to live chaste celibacy, is required for admission to candidacy. At St. Mark's, ordination to the deaconate occurred at the beginning of the fifth year. The archbishop or an auxiliary bishop of Middlefield presided at all these liturgical celebrations during the 2002–3 school year. A formal dinner for the entire school followed the liturgies.

The ceremonies were joyous, central moments in the school year that assured students that they were making progress toward their goal of priesthood. The celebrations also provided social approval and reward for accepting the group's belief system and norms of behavior. Students invited family and friends to the ceremonies. Their attendance provided further confirmation of the student's changing identity, role, and status as he prepared for the priesthood. Thus, it is not surprising that these initiation rituals were intentionally celebrated with such prominence, solemnity, and festivity at St. Mark's.

Oaths and Professions

It is not until their fifth year of formation, prior to ordination to the deaconate, that candidates at St. Mark's take a public oath of celibacy, as required by Canon 1037 of Church law. At this time, students also made a formal public profession of faith (the Nicene Creed) and an oath of fidelity to the Apostolic See. At their ordination to the deaconate, candidates again publicly promise celibacy. All these oaths are repeated again before ordination to the priesthood. I attended the ceremony at which two fifth-year students took the oath roughly two weeks before ordination to the priesthood. Each student promised to "fulfill the obligation of celibacy . . . in its entirety to the last day of my life, with the help of God." The seminary rector, Fr. Dahman, administered the oaths in a solemn manner after the celebration of the Eucharist one weekday morning.

Students were initiated into the role expectations of Catholic priests and membership in the presbyteral order by the oath. It required seminarians to commit themselves publicly to celibacy and to upholding the teachings of the Catholic Church. The oath was intended to publicly recognize and deepen commitment to the Church's mission and structure. Oaths can be an opportunity to state dearly held convictions, as well as a means of social control. The ritual also supported the new social identity the seminarian was taking on as a priest. The public nature of the oaths emphasized that the seminary community accepted and supported the students' acceptance of their new status, as evidenced by the warm greetings and congratulations that the two students were offered after taking the oaths. Taking the oaths publicly implied that non-conforming behavior would not go unnoticed. Cynically observed, the oath may have been another "hoop" that students were required to jump through to be ordained.

Ordination to the Priesthood

The Church teaches that the sacramental rites forever alter the identity of the person ordained to the priesthood. A priest is said to be joined in a unique way to Christ, whose powers he now shares. According to the Church's official teaching, in the ordination ritual "priests by the anointing of the Holy Spirit are signed with a special character and so are configured to Christ the priest in such a way that they are able to act in the person of Christ the head" (Second Vatican Council 1975b: 2). They are authorized to celebrate sacramental rituals and are recognized to share in the powers of the priesthood given by Christ to the apostles and handed on through the centuries by the bishops of the Church.

The ordination celebration appeared to be the high point of the school year at St. Mark's. I talked with one of the students a week before his ordination at the conclusion of the 2003 school year. He said he was anxiously looking forward to the day and the arrival of his family, who were traveling to Middlefield from out of town.

A detailed account of the liturgy of ordination to the priesthood of St. Mark's two 2003 seminarian graduates will not be provided. However, their ordination was the occasion for one of the most solemn, elaborate, and lengthy liturgies held annually at Middlefield's cathedral. The cathedral was packed for the celebration, featuring two large choirs and presided over by Archbishop Lobble. Many students assisted Archbishop Lobble as acolytes and deacons. In their participation, perhaps they anticipated their own ordination. The special prayers and solemnly performed rituals that were part of the ordination ceremony, along with the singing, chanting, colorful vestments, processions, incense, and presence of many vested priests appeared to have an awe-arousing effect on those in attendance.

Both students began the service seated in the cathedral's pews with their families. During the service they were called into the sanctuary for the ordination rituals, which included kneeling before the archbishop, to whom they promised obedience. Afterward, for the first time, the two new priests were able to stand at the altar table clothed in priestly vestments and join in leading the prayer that is said to transform bread and wine into the body and blood of Jesus Christ. No longer would they stand, sit, or kneel in the pews at mass; instead they would now daily preach and lead congregations in prayer, wearing vestments in the sanctuary.

After the ordination celebration, a reception was held for the two new priests in the cathedral's reception hall, at which the new priests appeared overwhelmed but pleased with the attention. Well-wishers gathered around the new priests. Many people offered gifts, and several people knelt down in front of the new priests and asked for their blessing. Masses of thanksgiving, at which the new priests presided, were held in their home parishes and in parishes where they had served internships.

The collective effervescence and awe-inspiring effect the liturgy had on those assembled were intended to imbue not only the new priests but also the entire Church organization with power and meaning. The ceremonies situated the entire Church organization and its members in relationship to the sacred. The words of the hymns sung during the service suggested that all those assembled were blessed and made holy by God. The hymns encouraged all participants to see themselves as sharers in a sacred cosmic order. The liturgy appeared highly effective in generating sentiments of solidarity among the participants.

Public recognition of the new identity acquired by the new priest is celebrated in the ordination ceremonies. The rituals externalize the internal transformation of a seminarian's identity into that of a priest. The presence of family, friends, and classmates, enforces this new identity. The newly ordained is now said to be configured in a special way to Christ, a status that can be bestowed only by a bishop, who is said to be a successor of the twelve apostles chosen by Christ. Through their bishops they are thought to share in Christ's power. Indicative of their new status and authority is the fact that people come and kneel before the new priests and, addressing them as "Father," ask for their blessing.

The festivity, elaborateness, intensity, and well-wishing of the priest's ordination day and his masses of thanksgiving parallel the experience of newly married couples at their weddings. Both events have immense consequence for the actors and celebrate a transformed identity and public status. The rite of ordination confers upon the seminarian the clerical power to make grace available to the laity through the sacraments. The ordination celebration enhances the mystery surrounding the social system of the Church, particularly the bishop's authority, and the system's authority to command the loyalty, obedience, and moral convictions of both priests and laity. As with their oaths, the public celebration of their ordination makes it more likely that behavior incongruent with the priest's role will be scrutinized and negatively sanctioned.

THREATS TO BELIEF
AND COMMITMENT PRODUCTION

The reports of the clergy sexual abuse that swept the Middlefield archdiocese and the rest of the nation did not appear to lessen students' belief in celibacy's value and usefulness. While these reports called into question whether priests were truly living lives of celibacy and, for some Catholics, challenged the legitimacy of the policy of mandatory celibacy, student support for the ideals of celibacy appeared to increase. Several students mentioned the clergy sexual abuse scandals in their interviews, but none said that this had negatively affected their commitment to celibacy or the practice's validity. In fact, as Borhek and Curtis wrote, their commitment to the Church and celibacy was strengthened. Luke was typical in this regard:

> I think in a certain sense the scandals have almost made me kind of recommit [to celibacy] to try to do as well as I can. [At] this time we really, really need priests to try to be as healthy a model as possible, now more than ever with the credibility at stake.

It is important to note that Luke did not blame the scandals on the Church organization or its policy of mandatory celibacy. Rather, the problem, in his view, originated outside the Church, in the larger society that he saw rejecting the Church's sexual ethic. Luke maintained that American culture had made sex something that is "for sale," and he saw celibacy as a protest against this sentiment.

During the height of the media's coverage of the scandal in the spring of 2002, a special meeting was held in which St. Mark's priest faculty members and seminarians assembled to discuss the scandals. Several students characterized the meeting as memorable because they believed the faculty shared, with great candor, their thoughts regarding celibacy, priesthood, and the events reported in the media. They said the meeting was exceptional in that it eased some of the distance students reported between themselves and the faculty. Students said the meeting gave them a sense of solidarity with the faculty and a feeling that they were "all in this together." Students appreciated knowing that faculty were deeply troubled by the scandal.

Rather than undermining their commitment to the organization or its ideals, the clergy sexual abuse crisis appeared to deepen in-group solidarity. In addition, whenever the topic came up in interviews, students affirmed that the scandals had actually strengthened their commitment to celibacy. Archbishop Lobble, commenting on the impact of the scandals on vocations recruitment, said that he believed that the effect had actually been to attract men to the seminary who believed in celibacy's value and were more eager to embrace the practice. Throughout his interviews, Lobble consistently colored the events in terms so positive that it was difficult to accept that these were the same revelations the public and press viewed so negatively.

The dynamic observed at St. Mark's is consistent with the assertion by Borhek and Curtis (1974:114) that a serious threat to belief could work to build commitment within an organization. Festinger (1956) found that the failure of UFOs to appear on predicted dates led to only a few marginal members leaving UFO cult groups. Remaining members increased commitment to their beliefs regarding UFOs and increased their support for one another. The missing UFOs were reinterpreted in a way that bolstered the group's beliefs and cohesion. Threats to community brought from outside can provide an effective means for strengthening loyalty and identity within.

Seven

REPRODUCING FATHER

As we have seen from a historical perspective, Christians significantly differed from pagans in the potential that they envisioned
in the disciplining of the body for a spiritual transformation of
the world (Brown 1988). Sexual asceticism was a central feature
of the alternative moral and social order that Christians proposed.
In the subsequent centuries, celibacy and then continence came
to be expected of diocesan clergy. By the twelfth century, secular
interference in ecclesiastical affairs and the need to protect the
Church's property from married priests' heirs contributed to the
development of mandatory celibacy in the Western Church. As
it did in Christianity's early centuries, sexual asceticism served
to mark a boundary between the world and the Church. By the
Middle Ages, celibacy also increasingly served to distinguish the
clergy from the laity. Not only does celibacy continue to mark this
boundary today, but also my research suggests that seminarians
use celibacy to internalize their differences from laypeople.

Seminary formation is a unique and particularly intense form
of professional socialization because of the role expectations of
the Catholic priesthood, especially the requirement of celibacy.
Through interviews and on-site observations, I examined the
daily lives of seminarians at St. Mark's Seminary through the
lens of cultural practices — collective ways of acting and thinking — through which groups and individuals situate and orient
themselves in the world. Within the structures of St. Mark's
Seminary, seminarians exercised agency by emphasizing certain
practices over others and interpreting them in ways that varied
from how faculty members understood them. For instance, regarding their conceptions of celibacy, students were more likely
to imbue the practice with elaborate theological meanings and
see it as an enhancement of priestly ministry. Faculty members

were more ambivalent regarding the practice and sometimes saw it as something that should be maturely endured. Even within the highly structured life of the seminary, where students are subject to faculty surveillance throughout the day, seminarians did not passively receive the cultural meanings that were imposed on them. Instead, St. Mark's program of human, spiritual, academic, and pastoral formation provided a repertoire of skills, habits, and ideas to fashion a particular kind of self, a priestly, celibate self distinguished from the laity with whom they attended classes and to whom they would one day minister in parishes.

What most characterized priestly formation at St. Mark's was that seminarians learned what they were *not.* Their training continuously involved them in activities that told them they were part of a group that was different from others, especially the lay students at the seminary. In fact, the seminarians at St. Mark's preferred those activities that set them apart, such as gathering for prayer and living together "in community" on campus. While they did not all embrace it in the same way, celibacy was another means by which students learned to see themselves as distinct, asserting a higher status for themselves as future priests.

By far the most important structural feature of seminarians' training was the administration's requirement that they live on campus. This spatial segregation of seminarians meant that their lives could be organized and managed in ways that contrasted starkly with lives of their lay ministry classmates, whose daily activities were distributed over many more places. In this chapter, I will discuss the effects of the spatial segregation of priesthood students at St. Mark's, namely, that it enabled them to use prayer, community living, and celibacy to identify with and internalize the role of priest.

A SCHOOL AND CULTURE ORGANIZED TO PRODUCE COMMITMENT

Already understanding themselves as distinctive from most people because they were called to the priesthood by God, St. Mark's seminarians' sense of specialness was heightened by their training, which provided many opportunities for the development of religious capital (the mastery of and attachment to Catholic culture). Mastery of Catholic culture was developed through the study of beliefs, rituals, and practices in their classes. Students' emotional attachment to Catholicism was deepened though the seminary's prayer life and other spiritual formation activities. Through study and prayer, students imbued daily life and their world with meaning. While not nearly as restrictive as in the past, seminaries like St. Mark's still functioned to separate students from the "world" and their former status as laypersons. The requirement to live on campus meant the daily routine of students could be organized to facilitate commitment to a celibate clerical identity and the Catholic Church through a host of "formation" activities. It is unlikely that anyone who was not drawn to an environment saturated with religious culture would be comfortable at St. Mark's.

Christian Smith (1998) has called the faith sustaining worlds that believers construct "sacred umbrellas" (106).[39] Under the "sacred umbrella" of Catholicism, St. Mark's provided a shelter of meaning and belonging under which seminarians came to see themselves as "set apart" by identifying with a celibate priesthood. The daily schedule of prayer worked to "sanctify" everyday life at the seminary within a symbolic universe. In the strong boundaries of the seminary subculture, seminarians developed distinctive norms and social networks. "Formation" activities produced a cohesiveness, camaraderie, and "we-sentiment" that was cited by students as one of the most desirable features of their lives. Shared prayer, meals, and recreation in a shared moral order, with men of similar aspirations, all contributed to this experience of "community" at St. Mark's.

PRAYER: A SOURCE OF IDENTITY, STATUS, AND RELIGIOUS CAPITAL

While engaged in their five-year program of human, spiritual, and academic formation, students made choices about which forms of Catholic knowledge and culture they would develop most intensely and enthusiastically. Students readily gave themselves to a daily schedule organized around occasions for communal prayer.

Not only did they celebrate the Eucharist and the Liturgy of the Hours daily, some students arrived well before services began and appeared to linger in chapel after services concluded.[40] They did not appear to view communal prayer as an imposition, and some seminarians even organized on their own to pray the rosary regularly. Some students wrote a letter requesting that the administration incorporate more prayer into the daily schedule. While students felt free to voice complaints to me about other facets of seminary life (such as too much homework and being disciplined for minor rule infractions), none complained about the requirement to gather for prayer at least three times a day or that they could not be away from campus for very long because of the schedule of prayer. Seminarians were not as enthusiastic about their classwork, formation conferences, or field education placements, while prayer was frequently mentioned as an appealing part of seminary life. Students did not ask for more demanding classes or to spend more time in field education placements, but some did want the administration to establish more occasions for prayer. They looked forward to having time for personal prayer and for leading others in prayer as priests.

By being required to gather for prayer at least three times daily, seminarians received the message that praying and leading others in prayer are among a priest's most important roles. Students amplified this message by eagerly giving themselves to the daily schedule of prayer. Their coursework did not provide the same opportunity for them to mark themselves as different from the lay ministry students. Though the services were open to them, lay ministry students seldom attended the Eucharist or prayed the Liturgy of the Hours with the priesthood candidates. That lay ministry students were not required to attend and infrequently attended liturgies reinforced the message that praying is a role expectation for priests. Of course, lay ministry students also prayed, but priesthood students did not routinely see them praying. Instead, seminarians mostly saw themselves and priest faculty members praying. Sometimes a few lay ministry students attended the Eucharist, and on one occasion a lay ministry candidate read the scriptures at the Eucharist. Seminarians led the communal praying of the Liturgy of the Hours and almost always performed the liturgical ministries of reader, cantor, acolyte, and sacristan for the celebration of the Eucharist.

By praying, seminarians develop religious capital as spiritual virtuosi and master elements of Catholic culture that they believe have valuable practical usefulness to parish priests, namely, leading prayer. Teaching a religion class or running a food pantry also are activities that priests engage in, but these weren't St. Mark's seminarians' favorite activities, and they did not identify these activities with holiness or priesthood to the same degree. Tobin and Sam, who were members of a religious association that worked in poor parishes in the United States and the Third World, are exceptions to this generalization. They spoke with zeal about their experiences working on development projects that improved the economic status of poor people. Besides celebrating sacraments, they looked forward to continuing to work with the poor, while the other students looked forward primarily to presiding at sacramental celebrations. Thus, there was a "good fit" between students' favorite formation activities and their priestly aspirations.

Public prayer also provided St. Mark's students opportunities to *display* their quest for holiness and mastery of prayer forms when leading the Liturgy of the Hours and assisting as reader, cantor, acolyte, and sacristan for the Eucharist. At liturgies, students subjectively internalized the role of priest, "acting" and "being seen acting" like priests by peers and the faculty. These also were occasions to demonstrate that they could fulfill the office of priest and were worthy recipients of the authority to preside at sacraments. Since only clergy can preside at sacramental celebrations, mastering liturgical rituals is an especially valuable form of religious capital.

Doing coursework did not allow seminarians to display their "priestliness" or identify with the role of priest to the same degree. Lay ministry students and seminarians enrolled in the St. Mark's master of divinity degree program took similar courses. Enrolled together in the same classes, lay ministry and priesthood candidates faced the same expectations from professors. However, a seminarian who earned only modest grades in his coursework could still display his spiritual virtuosity and "priestly difference" simply by fulfilling the requirement of attending mass and prayer services. Since lay students participate to only a very limited degree in the liturgical life of seminaries, liturgy is reinforced as the preserve of the clergy.

SET APART FOR SERVICE:
EFFECTS OF THE RESIDENTIAL AND
SEXUAL SEGREGATION OF SEMINARIANS

As was the case with the requirement to gather frequently for prayer, St. Mark's students did not appear to resent the requirement to live on campus. Students generally spoke very favorably of the "community" developed from praying, dining, and recreating with those who shared their aspirations. Most of the formal elements of the formation program (prayer, classes, formation conferences) as well as eating, recreating, and sleeping occurred under one roof. Students performed even the most mundane activities such as brushing their teeth and washing their clothes in the seminary's main building. The distance from any student's bathroom to a place in chapel could be traveled in under a minute.

Students and priests living together on campus meant that most of the formal elements of the program of human, spiritual, and academic formation were fused with the other activities of daily life. Being a seminarian became a twenty-four-hour endeavor and not something students did only a few hours each day in classes. The administration's requirement that priesthood candidates live on campus supported the expectation, which students expressed in their interviews, that priesthood was not only a career, but rather an entire way of life characterized by undivided service to God and the Church. Priesthood was not a job that they would be able to "go home" from. By contrast, lay students, except for their coursework, had far fewer formation activities that required them to be on campus. Lay ministry candidates frequently had full- or part-time jobs, marriages, and children, and parishes that they tended to. Though seminarians sometimes had friends and families off campus, their lives were more focused and seamlessly given over to preparation for ministry than were the lives of lay students.

Not only did seminarians live, work, and make their homes under one roof, they lived under an ecclesiastical roof. The presence of religious pictures, statues, and crucifixes, not only in the chapel but also throughout the hallways, classrooms, library, lounges, dining rooms, offices, and student dormitory rooms, added a sacred "gloss" to the environment that students inhabited. The absence of secular artwork and the profusion of holy images everywhere except in bathrooms marked seminary space as "holy" and "churchly" space.

More significant than the gaze of the saints and generations of ordination classes, whose pictures filled hallways, were the eyes of faculty members and classmates with whom seminarians lived. Students always were subject to the gaze of their peers and faculty members, both of whom evaluated their fitness for ordination. Seminarians couldn't "escape" from the expectations of the faculty and their classmates in the way that lay students did. Like students everywhere, seminarians sometimes bristled at the scrutiny they received from faculty members. They did not experience the gaze of their classmates as coercive to the same degree. However, the fact that the seminary rule called for students to engage in "fraternal correction" and that students did evaluate one another, surely provided more incentive to manage their behavior and identities with care.

The tendency to manage their identities in light of their priestly aspirations was evident in many different ways. For instance, faculty members reported that, in formation conferences and retreats, seminarians felt free to admit to sexual liaisons with women before entering seminary. However, none reported in these formation contexts that they engaged in sexual activities with men. While students may have privately confided such activities to one another and faculty members, an unwritten norm operated to prevent these disclosures in public. Faculty members divulged in interviews that St. Mark's enrolled homosexual students, but that none have ever "come out" in public formation contexts.

Part of all programs of professional training involves students learning to speak, dress, comport themselves, and utilize expertise in ways that mark them as professionals. Seminary formation differs from other types in the scope and depth of the behaviors addressed. What in other schools is a person's "private life" was subject to the inspection of peers and faculty members. This fact also met students' expectations that priesthood was not a job but an entire way of life. However, living together with their class-mates and faculty members meant that seminarians had less of a haven where aspects of their identity didn't have to be man-aged in order to be ordained. In the area of sexuality, especially in light of the contemporaneous abuse scandals, students had good reasons to sequester potentially discrediting information about themselves. However, concealment of homosexual identities ap-peared to be part of a tacit agreement that students kept so that they were allowed to be ordained. I will consider this issue further later in this chapter.

St. Mark's Seminary became each student's physical home, providing not only room and board, but also emotional support from their peers. This fact deepens seminarians' institutional loyalties. As priests, they will be expected to see themselves as belonging to the institutional Church rather than the people they serve. As seminarians, they were dependent on the faculty and, to a lesser extent, their peers, for advancement toward their goal of priesthood. In addition, the seminary's activities provided the underpinnings for the religious symbolic universe that seminar-ians inhabited. This made seminarians highly dependent on the seminary and the Church for sources of satisfaction in their lives. The satisfaction of the most basic needs was contingent upon adequately performing the various aspects of the role of semi-narian. Presumably if their need for room and board, emotional support, the fulfillment of vocational aspirations, and a meaning-ful "world" were met, loyalty and commitment to the priesthood and the Church were deepened.

As Stark and Finke (2000:106) point out, the social capi-tal that seminarians build is a significant source of assistance, reference, and friendship for ministers and priests. This is es-pecially true for Roman Catholic seminarians, whose lives are spatially concentrated and dominated by the primary relation-ships formed with those who share their status. Because they lived together, St. Mark's seminarians formed a tighter social network than lay students, who were more likely to have sources of satisfaction in relationships outside the seminary. In their interviews, seminarians hoped that these relationships would be a source of continued emotional support after ordination. Seminarians' social networks would also be useful in advancing their ecclesiastical careers.

Seminarians' reliance on the social networks they formed in seminary for these sources of satisfaction builds loyalty to the Church. However, it may also have deleterious effects by contributing to a failure of priests to "police" themselves and develop professional standards of accountability. It has been alleged that priests have failed to report other priests who they knew were sexually abusing minors. When they were reported, bishops frequently failed to adequately deal with abusive priests. Bishops sometimes discounted victims' stories or accused victims of lying, while accepting the word of abusive priests.

While faculty members said that being able to relate positively to women was an important consideration in their evaluation of a student's fitness for ordination, the homosocial character of the seminary's exclusively male residential community provided far more opportunities to interact with, develop trusting relationships with, and derive emotional support from males than females. In addition, although there were female faculty members, formators and administrators were almost always men, making seminarians especially dependent on the authority of males in order to be ordained. Thus, though they did not share the isolation from women and laypeople that earlier generations of seminarians had experienced, males were both a primary source of emotional support *and* the most powerful authority figures in their lives. Students learned to be most comfortable with those who would share their status as priests. After ordination, they would continue to live and work in environments where males held the highest positions of authority. It is worth asking what effect these factors could have on the way in which newly ordained priests interacted with female parishioners, who usually outnumber men in parishes. Ruth Wallace's studies (1992,

2003) of laymen and laywomen and married deacons who headed Catholic parishes found that these ministers were more effective at "empowering" laity and developing collaborative, collegial relationships with parishioners. Priests' leadership styles tended to be less democratic and less open to the wishes of laity. Parishioners tended to identify more closely with lay ecclesial ministers who shared their own lay and married status.

The current dearth of priestly vocations also led St. Mark's seminarians to think of themselves as markedly different from other people. Especially because their calling required celibacy, seminarians admitted that they were frequently viewed by others with curiosity and sometimes, in the context of the clergy sexual abuse crisis, with suspicion.

That they were entering a profession with manifestly altruistic purposes and lofty ideals likewise added to seminarians' experiences of themselves as special or different from most people. This sense of specialness also was increased by the knowledge that their services would be in great demand once they were ordained. Students reported that they already were receiving encouragement from their home parishes and the parishes where they did fieldwork. Students spoke enthusiastically of their coming ordinations, knowing that Middlefield's cathedral would one day be filled with family and friends praising God and praising them for answering God's call to priesthood. Their day would come when men and women, a generation or more their senior, would address them as "Father" and kneel before them asking for their blessing.

On three occasions I observed a photographer taking pictures of seminarians for Fr. Moto's creative vocation campaigns. Seminarians' photos were widely displayed on posters, brochures, advertisements on buses, and even in movie trailers in theaters in metropolitan Middlefield. The archdiocesan newspaper frequently ran stories featuring St. Mark's seminarians. Entering the seminary made seminarians small-time "celebrities" due to Fr. Moto's vocation promotion media blitz. Moto said that his recent efforts were intended to present the image that seminarians were "normal, regular guys," not the sexual predators people had heard about from the media. All this attention added to the aura of specialness that seminarians developed.

The spatial and sexual segregation and shared timetable of activities reinforced this specialness by separating seminarians from their former lives and lay peers. Even in the post–Second Vatican Council seminary, contact with laity is markedly decreased as seminarians pray, eat, recreate, and study primarily with priests and other seminarians. However, being set apart has its costs. In *Married to the Church,* an ethnography of the 1969 graduating class of Milwaukee's St. Francis Seminary, Raymond Hedin (1995) argued that these priests internalized a "model of superhuman perfection" (106). Like the St. Mark's students, they also believed themselves somehow different from most men. One of Hedin's informants spoke to this issue:

> Perhaps the most damaging result of the residual notion of priestly difference, however, is that it tends to isolate my classmates from one another. Many of them do not speak openly of their problems to their peers, because they still cling to the assumption that other priests are immune even if they are not. (Hedin 1995:107)

As seminarians and priests, they internalized a model of priesthood in which they were expected to be saintly. Regarding their sexual struggles and lapses in celibacy, the men Hedin interviewed were hesitant to confide in one another. Failure in celibacy was literally "unspeakable." Because they were unable to admit their faults even to their own classmates, the saintly model they internalized led them to "induce much of their own considerable loneliness" (Hedin 1995:107). Priestly fraternity never developed for them, and other priests were more likely to be perceived as rivals (Hedin 1995:107). The tendency at St. Mark's to treat sexuality in an intellectualized fashion in conferences and during the month-long Intensive, where seminarians did not discuss their own experiences, meant students did not learn to openly share their sexual thoughts and feelings. Students did not learn to discuss their struggles with chastity except in nebulous, generalized ways. This certainly contributes to a culture of parish priesthood where men do not confide in one another but maintain a safe and secure, distant and secret life relative to other priests.

This case study found that St. Mark's students were idealistic in much the same way as those at St. Francis thirty-five years earlier. Both attended seminaries where Jesus was espoused as their model. Students like Luke and John particularly saw the seminary as a school for virtue that should encourage nothing short of perfection. More than Hedin's subjects, St. Mark's students were acutely aware of the failings of some priests whose tragic, heinous deeds were exposed in the clergy abuse scandal. From these priests, seminarians learned the costliness of a spoiled clerical identity (Goffman 1963).

Both seminaries were structured to form a holy, educated celibate clergy by reinforcing their aura of specialness and encouraged seminarians to set high standards for themselves in their pursuit of holiness. While the training of all professionals involves setting high standards, a drawback of the way formation was structured is that newly ordained priests may find themselves isolated and lonely, especially if they are not particularly adept at intimate relationships. However, Thomas Nester, in his study of Chicago priests, reported that priests had more close friends than most men (Greeley 2004a:32). Andrew Greeley also disputes that most priests live lonely lives, although he noted that a 2002 survey of priests found loneliness more of a problem for homosexual priests than for heterosexual priests (Greeley 2004a:56). Hoge's (2002) study of priests ordained in the 1990s found that many newly ordained priests had difficulty with the transition to parish life. Among the one in seven priests who resigned in their first five years after ordination, Hoge reported they were much more likely than their classmates to unfavorably rate how seminaries prepared them to handle loneliness and develop support networks (2002:14). Among resigned priests, the greatest post-ordination problems reported were living celibately (47 percent), loneliness (46 percent), and lack of privacy (36 percent) (Hoge 2002:25). Hoge (2002:18–19) concluded that unsatisfactory rectory living situations, marked by a lack of supportive bonds, contributed to a priest's decision to resign.

LEGITIMATING CELIBACY

St. Mark's students easily verbalized what they perceived to be the value of celibacy. These seminarians' convictions that celibacy would enhance their ministry surely made the requirement more palatable. To believe that celibacy would detract from their ministry would have provided little incentive to accept the practice and stirred dissonance regarding their vocations. For them, celibacy was unquestionably a symbol of undivided dedication to God and the Church. Students stressed the functional utility of celibacy as enabling priests' availability to their parishioners. However, if as priests they come to doubt the practical efficacy of celibacy, several St. Mark's students will be without a means to legitimate the practice. It is also questionable whether or not Catholic priests are more dedicated and actually work longer hours than their counterparts in other denominations. Whether or not celibate ministers actually serve in a more "single-hearted" manner is open to empirical debate and deserves more study. Two studies question the assumption that celibacy enhances a dedicated priestly ministry.

Don Swenson (1998) compared the number of hours worked by Canadian Catholic priests and married Evangelical ministers and attempted to measure the single-heartedness of their service.[41] Swenson did not find a significant difference in the number of hours worked or in the level of either group's pastoral commitment.

From a different environment, Eugene Gomulka (2001) found that Catholic military chaplains, who typically lived alone due to mandatory celibacy, were much more likely to be disciplined for serious offenses than their Protestant counterparts, who are usually married. Gomulka, while deputy chaplain of the U.S. Marine Corps, was responsible for supervising 250 chaplains from sixty faith traditions. He reported that although Catholics constituted less than 50 percent of the chaplains he supervised, they were more than 75 percent of the chaplains committing offenses that resulted in imprisonment or discharge. After examining the records, Gomulka (2001:17) concluded that chaplains who lived alone got into trouble more often than those who lived with a spouse. He found this to be true not only for chaplains, but for officers and enlisted personnel as well. Gomulka maintained that the military has long held marriage to be beneficial for reducing disciplinary problems. Marriage was not seen as a distraction from devoted service to a soldier's unit or country.

Gomulka speculated that chaplains who lived alone were more likely to have disciplinary problems because of loneliness and stress. I also would speculate that marital relationships add a degree of accountability and stability to chaplains' lives. More research needs to be done to understand how marital status can affect the likelihood of engaging in risky or problematic behaviors. However, the findings of Swenson and Gomulka do not invalidate the ideal of celibacy as undivided commitment and service. It may simply mean that these priests were weak candidates for priesthood, that their formation was lacking, or that celibacy is more difficult to live in the Marine Corps. Hedin (1995), in his interviews of priests ordained in 1969, found that few saw celibacy as enhancing their pastoral ministry. Often resentful of what they perceived as Church control of their personal lives, Hedin's informants took satisfaction in parish ministry, increased pay, and viewing themselves as professionals with specialized expertise.

Because the Church affirms married life, I was surprised by how many students saw spousal relationships as selfish — marriage was an impediment to attending to and caring for others equally. Of course the tendency to see a life committed to *agape* as incompatible with relationships involving *eros* is consistent with centuries of Catholic doctrine and practice. When the Church linked sexual renunciation to holy orders in the twelfth century by mandating celibacy, it shackled the ascetical practice to office and the Church's administrative structures. Whatever effects this had — and undoubtedly the effects were multiple and diverse — it essentially set priesthood apart from people. Connecting the office of priest with this hallmark of spiritual exclusivity and virtuosity enhanced the prestige of priesthood.

This "cachet" of celibacy may have been more valuable in the American Catholic Church, a nation of equal individuals where priests acquired special status. In the United States today, however, many Catholics are as highly educated as the parish priests who preach to them. Furthermore, professional ministry is no longer the privileged domain of priests, brothers, and sisters. Catholics experiencing a "call" to ministry can have satisfying lives as lay ecclesial ministers. St. Mark's lay ministry students frequently struck me as brighter, more socially adept, and more articulate than the seminarians. Middlefield's newly ordained priests are likely to serve on parish staffs with these laypeople, who are as intelligent and capable as they are. Except for presiding at sacraments, lay ministers fulfill all the roles that had been reserved to priests, including administering parishes.[42]

Especially in the post–Second Vatican Council Church of the past forty years, when laity study theology in larger numbers and serve capably in parishes, priests continue to be set apart from the laity only by their celibacy. In fact, even the laziest or most inept priest can still claim a degree of spiritual virtuosity and prestige by living apart and celibately. Thus, celibacy may be construed today more than ever as a seminarian's "trump card" of holiness and as an effort to recapture some of the status that priesthood has lost in recent decades. Students like Pat, who were modestly gifted and awkward in social situations, could wrap themselves in the cloak of celibacy and claim a measure of spiritual virtuosity for themselves. That celibacy frequently was seen by these men as a countercultural practice in a permissive, self-indulgent society also heightened priesthood's symbolic power, status, and appeal to students, while reinforcing a boundary with a negatively evaluated secular world. Their celibacy enabled students to see themselves as different, special, and superior to those who did not make this promise.

While Max Weber (Gerth and Mills 1946) viewed charismatic authority as opposed to all institutional routines, he maintained that "charisma remains a highly important element of the social structure, although of course in a greatly changed sense" (262). The juridical joining of the charism of celibacy to the office of priesthood in the twelfth century resulted from the Church's growing institutionalization and bureaucratization. Celibacy was "routinized," made a discipline and a subject of Church law. While most of St. Mark's students and faculty members viewed celibacy as a discipline rather than a charism, celibacy remained a symbol of spiritual virtuosity, now most frequently interpreted as undivided attention to Christ and his Church. As an element in the structuring of the Catholic Church and St. Mark's Seminary, celibacy continued to function as a boundary that legitimated priestly authority over laity and was a means by which seminarians internalized their difference from lay students. The tension between viewing celibacy as a charism (gift of grace) or discipline was experienced by students and marked the formation program's efforts to "routinize" or "reproduce" celibacy. Fr. Schrieter's efforts to incorporate the tools of psychology into St. Mark's formation program is a further "rationalization" of seminary formation for celibacy. More traditional students saw psychology as detracting from the specialness of the celibate, priestly calling.

HOMOSEXUALITY

The question of the numbers of homosexual seminarians and priests has been a source of much speculation in recent years. Though no accurate empirical data has been found to precisely gauge the sexual orientation of seminarians or priests, several authors have speculated that there is a larger proportion of homosexuals in American seminaries than in the population as a whole (Wolf 1989:60; Fox 1995:177; Sipe 1990:110; Cozzens 2000:98–99, 107–9; Wills 2000:193–94; Hoge 2002:3; Hoge and Wenger 2003:97–111).

The complexity of the question is added to by the fact that the categories "homosexuality" and "heterosexuality" are not unambiguous in how they are used and to what they refer. At the same time, the development of homosexual subcultures in American society since the 1960s has also made homosexuality more recognizable in seminaries and in the priesthood. Because there is more awareness of homosexuality in American society, it has become easier for seminarians to identify themselves as homosexuals, though this is an identification they understandably may be cautious about revealing because of the Church's teachings on homosexuality. The growth of homosexual subcultures has resulted in greater gay and lesbian visibility in business, government, and education, as well as in religious institutions.

The *Program of Priestly Formation* (1993), however, is remarkably silent on the issue of sexual orientation. Schuth acknowledged in her study that there was a concern regarding the possible high number of homosexuals in U.S. seminaries, but she does not say whether or how sexual orientation was addressed in seminary formation. As a former seminary rector, Donald Cozzens (2000) is able to offer credible insight into the alleged phenomenon. Cozzens acknowledges the emergence of homosexual subcultures within both the seminary and priesthood (2000:103), and he asserts that heterosexual men in an environment where such subcultures exist may experience "chronic destabilization" or feelings of self-doubt and that they do not "fit in" (2000:99–101).

In *Goodbye, Good Men: How Catholic Seminaries Turned Away Two Generations of Vocations from the Priesthood* (2002), Michael Rose asserts that orthodox, heterosexual men have been routinely denied admission to U.S. seminaries. Rose's work was based on interviews with disgruntled ex-seminarians, seminarians, and priests. Rose does not allow seminary administrators to respond to the allegations he reports. He maintains that "normal" men who were admitted to seminaries regularly encountered a homosexual ethos, lax discipline and morals, and the absence of solid Catholic teaching. Seminarians who objected to promiscuity and heterodoxy allegedly faced expulsion or were sent "Soviet-style" to psychologists for treatment. Rose's account paints a picture of U.S. seminaries rife with sexual impropriety and theological dissent. He described these seminaries as places where students are open about and even flaunt their homosexuality and sexual activity.

This was not at all the case at St. Mark's. While several students acknowledged past dating and romantic and sexual activity, none identified themselves as homosexuals. In a weekend workshop on celibacy and sexuality, no students acknowledged homosexual activity, though some students spoke of their own heterosexual activity. This doesn't mean there were no homosexual students (faculty indicated there were), but no students chose to talk about themselves in this way to me. Fr. Blatsky said that matters of sexual orientation are likely to be dealt with privately in spiritual direction sessions. Blatsky said that he has urged spiritual directors to bring up matters of sexuality in directions sessions and not wait for students to bring them up. Apart from the treatment of homosexuality in moral theology classes, students' homosexual thoughts, feelings, and behaviors were largely sequestered to the private spheres of spiritual direction, counseling, and confession.

Fr. Green reported that to his knowledge in his many years at St. Mark's, no student has publicly "owned up to a gay identity." He believed there was a "double standard" at St. Mark's. In formation discussions, students had acknowledged "sexual acting out" with women but never with men. Green asserted that such reticence regarding homosexual behavior "has handicapped our ability for realistic formation on sexual identity issues." He believed that "constraints around sexual orthodoxy" made discussion of homosexuality difficult for faculty and students. The result was that the school maintained a "don't ask, don't tell" policy about such matters. He wondered, "what kind of signal are we sending to a man, gay or straight? Is it that the only safe place to talk about who I am really as a sexual being is in a forum where it cannot be revealed publicly? Doesn't that very dynamic set up the conditions for shame or guilt?" He added, "So I don't know how you can expect them to have a healthy sense of sexuality where it is always surrounded in some context of shame or danger or caution."

Fr. Coughlin lamented a lack of openness at St. Mark's regarding sexuality and especially homosexuality. He believed the environment was such that a homosexual student would not likely reveal his orientation in any forum other than spiritual direction because it "might ultimately lead to their expulsion." Coughlin did not feel free to publicly identify himself as a homosexual and regretted that students knew of no publicly identified homosexual priests. He insisted that there were other gay priests in the faculty and administration. Faculty members freely acknowledged that there were homosexual students and appeared to hold no animus toward them.

Fr. Moto mentioned that homosexual candidates now are cautioned that while they can be admitted to the seminary, there is no assurance they will be ordained if the Vatican determines that homosexuals cannot be ordained. There were rumors of such a Vatican policy in the spring prior to the semester when these interviews were conducted (Williams and Cooperman 2002:B5). The policy was eventually instituted by the Vatican in November 2005 (Sacred Congregation for Catholic Education 2005). The rumored policy added to student reticence about identifying themselves as homosexual to other students or faculty. In any case, St. Mark's did not appear to be the "hotbed" of homosexuality that Rose's book might lead its readers to expect.

The norm that sequestered homosexuality to the custody of spiritual directors, confessors, and psychologists may have been prudent on the part of students and convenient for the administration. By making homosexuality "invisible," a potentially controversial matter could then be avoided. However, with Fr. Green, one might wonder whether sequestering the issue of sexual orientation was helpful to students' psychosexual development in the long run. Hedin noted the reticence of Milwaukee's 1969 ordination class to discuss their celibacy struggles with one another. The inability of homosexual-identified students to speak openly about themselves in formation conferences and retreats decreased the likelihood of students sharing with one another about these matters as priests.

The hierarchy has shown no willingness to soften its traditional teaching on homosexuality. Not only have they shown themselves to be wary of gay seminarians, the Vatican and U.S. bishops have spoken forcefully against recent proposed legal recognition of same-sex civil unions or marriage. Opposition to such legislation along with the potential exclusion of homosexuals from seminaries reinforces the "purity" of the Church set apart from a permissive secular culture that is seen to promote the "culture of death."

Whatever the actual sexual orientation of the perpetrators, most of the victims of clerical sexual abuse have been male children and teenagers. The crisis has drawn attention to the presence of homosexuals in the priesthood. For some people, this has resulted in the scapegoating of all homosexual priests and homosexuals as pedophiles. By further stigmatizing an already stigmatized group, a boundary was drawn between heterosexuals and deviant homosexuals, who allegedly are inclined toward abusing children.

In this case study, rules regarding bodily pollution and boundaries are viewed as a means of dealing with social disorder and resulting anxieties. When a group is threatened, concerns with bodily purity are intensified. Vatican anxiety regarding gay marriage and homosexual priests coincided with the alleged decline of the nuclear family, a moral panic regarding child abuse, and challenges to the policy of mandatory celibacy for priests. The clergy abuse scandal not only revealed the failure of bishops to protect children but also threatened the integrity and moral authority of the Church. The Church endangered children and was "polluted" by preying priests and negligent bishops. Amid this grave crisis, it is not surprising that the Church should seek to defend itself by reinforcing the boundary between itself and the "world." One means of doing this has been to focus on homosexuals. Their deviance is useful in a post–Vatican II Church seeking to negotiate its boundaries with the secular world. Durkheimian social theory suggests that in such instances, deviance is actually functional for groups and societies because it establishes norms for conduct (Erikson 1966). Talk of excluding homosexuals from seminaries reinforced a boundary between the Church's pure, faithful priests and impure, homosexual priests who have been corrupted by a sinful world, become morally lax, and preyed on children. Punishing and removing homosexual priests is seen to eliminate the source of pollution that caused the abuse crisis.

The norm at St. Mark's and all but one school I studied appeared to be that homosexuals can be ordained as long as their orientation is sequestered to the internal forum.[43] The school and its spiritual formation program did not have to deal publicly with faculty or students' sexual orientation. A public boundary between the Church and homosexuals was maintained and Church teaching on homosexuality was left unquestioned. In private contexts, homosexual students could be dealt with in a compassionate and pastoral manner and continue to be admitted to the priesthood. Whether this practice is a pastoral means of dealing with a thorny issue or a disservice to homosexual students who are denied opportunities to forthrightly deal with sexual matters is worth considering.

Eight

REMAKING SEMINARIES

IMPLICATIONS AND RECOMMENDATIONS

After the allegations of abuse made national headlines in 2002, Katarina Schuth requested materials from seminary rectors and formators used in formation for celibacy in their seminaries. She characterized the materials that many seminaries provided her with as describing "carefully planned comprehensive programs" (Schuth 2004:18). There is no question that seminaries have "beefed up" their celibacy formation in the aftermath of the abuse crisis. Formation for celibacy has become much more systematic and intentional than it was in the preconciliar days when little was said and celibacy was taken for granted. Given the effects of the clergy abuse crisis, formation for celibacy is likely to receive increased attention in the *Program of Priestly Formation*, currently being revised. Seminary formators now speak an educational jargon of goals, assessments, and desired outcomes. This change was the case at St. Mark's. However, the degree to which students personally integrated the matters covered in courses, conferences, and workshops remains in question. Even at an off-campus weekend retreat on relationships and celibacy, St. Mark's students shared little regarding the significance of what was said for their own lives.

Celibacy and affective maturity appeared to be topics to be exhaustively "covered" in the formation curriculum, but St. Mark's failed to create an environment where students could together discuss their sexual feelings and experiences. Though their treatment was greatly expanded and talked about more, celibacy and sexuality remained largely abstract and intellectual. St. Mark's administration was too confident that simply because matters relating to celibacy were treated in the formation program, students had therefore internalized what was taught to them. Students did not so much learn how to authentically live lives of celibacy as veil their sexual thoughts and feelings from others (and perhaps themselves).

As a vulnerable population subject to the scrutiny and evaluation of faculty members and their peers, students had reason to manage their public selves carefully. While students received psychological testing and evaluations before entrance to the seminary, there were no follow-up tests or interviews to objectively assess students' growth in affective maturation. Faculty bluntly admitted their frustration in addressing students' behavioral problems. In addition, older students with problems may be less amenable to behavioral change. So while seminaries have developed ostensibly comprehensive plans for celibacy formation, it remains an open question whether or not they are any more successful in forming holy, mature, celibate priests.

While St. Mark's students clearly evidenced a familiarity with the Church's official rationale for celibacy, my research suggests that formators wrestle with how to best cultivate the psychosexual maturity of these students. Faculty members believed that their school was doing better than in the past, but most were acutely aware of the inadequacy of formation for celibacy at St. Mark's. In conferences and workshops, sexuality was intellectualized and homosexuality was not dealt with in a forthright manner. This failing is compounded by Fr. Blatsky's concern that spiritual directors were not always successful in engendering an open discussion of sexual feelings and behaviors. Spiritual directors, frequently praiseworthy parish priests, had little specialized training in spiritual direction or human sexuality. The result was that (in Blatsky's words) some students "have held their cards very closely" and then have difficulties with celibacy after ordination. Though matters shared in spiritual direction were strictly confidential, with little tolerance for failure as seminarians in sexual matters students had reason to be cautious about discussing their sexual experiences. While seminarians spoke confidently of knowing their "boundaries" regarding relationships and sexual behavior, faculty members had a better grasp of the challenges that their students would face as priests. A "boundary" that St. Mark's students surely learned was to be overly guarded about discussing sexual thoughts, feelings, and behaviors, especially homoerotic ones.

Unless seminaries like St. Mark's find ways for students to more openly discuss their sexual feelings and experiences, it is likely that large numbers of recently ordained priests will continue to resign from active priestly ministry. Others may remain priests, but will violate their promise of celibacy and contribute to the current sexual abuse crisis within the Church. Diocesan seminaries should try to benefit from the experience of those religious orders who have dealt with sexual issues in a more open manner. While I will leave it to psychologists and spiritual directors to devise ways to enhance students' psychosexual maturity through more open and substantive discussion of sexuality and celibacy, I want to suggest changes in the way seminaries are structured to organize students' lives.

WHAT IS TO BE DONE?

It is worth considering if these students would have had a better sense of what celibacy and parish priesthood entailed if they had lived in a rectory during all their years in major seminary. Church leaders and seminary administrators should give consideration to reducing the number of years that priesthood candidates spend living together in a residential community with faculty members. Middlefield's candidates spent only their third year (parish internship year) living in a parish. This is already more time in parishes than most seminaries allow. Perhaps only the first year (if any) should be spent living together at the seminary. Under such an arrangement, candidates would enroll in classes at their seminary or a local university. However, parish priests, staff members, and parishioners would be their mentors in the parishes they resided in. Laypeople would be more actively involved in forming their priests. Seminarians would have a better appreciation of the gifts and wisdom of parish laity.

This change would end the quasi-monastic character of diocesan seminaries since the Council of Trent. It would likely make candidates' transition to post-ordination life and ministry easier.

While seminarians would remain members of an academic community, they could also derive their identity from their parish communities. Their prayer lives would be centered in parishes, and they would no longer pray just with those who aspired to be priests. Because they lived and prayed in a parish, other seminarians and faculty members would be less likely to be the source of their primary relationships. Seminarians could develop more supportive relationships with laypeople, who would become a greater source of social capital than their classmates. Students would have to take the initiative to develop supportive relationships both inside and outside the parish rather than seeking easy sociality from their dormitory mates. The present arrangement of having seminarians study, pray, and live in residential seminaries of between twenty and two hundred students does not make for an easy transition to post-ordination priests who usually live alone among the laity they serve. Nor does this arrangement allow students to "test" their celibacy in the circumstances that they will be living in as priests. Seminaries are predominantly male environments. Parishes are not. Students' ability to maintain "boundaries" would be more easily tested outside the highly ordered life of the seminary.

Those who rely too heavily on the seminary community for interpersonal relationships and their spiritual life may find rectory living a letdown. Most will reside alone within just a few years of ordination. Living alone also decreases priests' accountability and an element of oversight in priests' lives. The National Review Board for the Protection of Children and Young People (2004:88) in its report on the sexual abuse crisis cited the recommendation by some that dioceses establish living centers for their priests "to meet the twin purposes of fostering community and healthy intimate relationships and ensuring the oversight of priests." This recommendation appears to recognize the difficulties that Gomulka found among military chaplains who lived alone. While this possibility has been discussed in Middlefield, there has been little widespread enthusiasm from its presbyterate. The diocese is still considering establishing an "apostolic residence" where priests who choose to could live communally.

Of course, when it comes to reforming social institutions, the devil is not only in the details, but also in the unintended consequences of reforms. A proposal to have seminarians reside mostly in parishes would significantly alter the socialization process by which commitment to celibacy and the mission of the Church are developed. The change would reconfigure the carefully constructed and monitored "sacred umbrella" seminarians and faculty live under. Seminarians might come to identify more closely with the spirituality and attitudes of the laity of their parishes than the "official" version of Catholicism transmitted by the bishop and seminary faculty. It is not clear whether seminarians would internalize their "priestly difference" if they didn't have a lengthy period of preparation for priesthood in which they are "set apart" by their residential segregation, shared daily schedule, community life, and continual surveillance. However, I believe that laypeople would demand that seminarians become "good priests" and not expect them to be like them in every way. In addition, though lay support for celibacy is waning, laity continue to demand that their priests live lives of integrity and keep the promises they have made.

It is conceivable that if seminary formation were altered in this way, seminary life might not have the same appeal to the men now entering Catholic seminaries. The ability of St. Mark's to provide a distinctive subcultural identity for priesthood candidates helps explain the appeal to seminarians who evaluated most positively those elements of formation that excluded laypeople. In chapter 2 I noted that in the last two decades, priesthood candidates are less likely to have familial, social, and religious points of reference than did pre-1980s candidates (Schuth 1999; Hoge 2002). Applicants frequently had little sustained recent contact with the Church, but found life in the secular world wanting. Many recently had "conversion" experiences of some sort and had not found marriage partners. It is easy to understand why the priesthood, with its detailed role expectations, and seminaries, as highly organized, distinctive, culturally saturated subcultures, are appealing to men who fit this profile. These men, who had drifted from the Catholic "fold" before entering seminary, now seek to be "shepherds of the fold." In fact, dioceses, seminaries, and religious orders that stress the distinctiveness of priestly identity and stronger boundaries with the laity have been more successful in recruiting students. Traditional seminaries and dioceses (Stark and Finke 2000:169–217) and traditionalist religious orders such as the Legionaries of Christ (Berry and Renner 2004) have attracted larger numbers of candidates in the 1980s and 1990s by providing distinctive subcultural identities that stress the uniqueness and higher status of priests relative to laypeople. While these dioceses and religious orders impose greater demands, they are thought to also provide more rewards to recruits. However, research does not indicate whether these dioceses and groups have lower resignation rates. More study of the strengths and weaknesses of the "new breed" of seminarian and what kind of priests they are likely to be seems called for.

Hoge did find that today's younger priests are less likely than those ordained in the 1960s and 1970s to support changes that Vatican II introduced to the Church. Like St. Mark's students generally, they hold to a sacramental and cultic understanding of priesthood. According to Hoge and Wenger (2003), younger priests are more likely to "insist that the priest is distinct from the laity, and that emphatically includes ontological as well as institutional distinctiveness" (69). No such "traditional" trend has been found among young Catholics (Hoge and Wenger 2003:118; Davidson, Williams, Lamanna, Stenftenagel, Weigert, Whalen, and Wittberg 1997; D'Antonio, Davidson, Hoge, and Meyer 2001). In recent decades, because attitudes of seminarians about priesthood differ sharply from those of their Catholic peers as well as priests ordained in the 1960s and 1970s, as Hoge and Wenger found, polarization already exists within the Church between younger and older priests and is likely to grow between younger priests and laity (Hoge and Wenger, 2003:13, 132). They argue that "Catholics should prepare themselves for future tensions in parishes over roles, turf, and collaboration" (2003:133).

I have argued that what most characterizes diocesan seminary formation today is that seminarians learn what they are *not*. Catholic seminaries are organized around practices that enable students for priesthood to internalize their clerical difference, which is sealed by their ordination ceremony. Like the seminarians I came to know at St. Mark's, today's seminarians show a distinct preference for the activities that mark them as clerics and not laity. They thrive on the religiously saturated seminary schedule, strong prayer life, and segregated communal life. They look forward to wearing distinctive clerical garb. In themselves, these things are not bad. The professional training of lawyers and doctors is also intended to set them apart from their clients and confer a superior status. The training of other professionals can have a similar purpose in socializing them to see themselves differently than those they serve. The specialized knowledge and experiences of lawyers and doctors is a basis for the claims of authority they hold over their clients and patients. Their training leads clients and patients to follow the advice of professionals who are to have the interests of their client or patient in mind.

American Catholics no longer assume that "Father knows best." Not only must priests lead; today they are expected to minister collaboratively with laypeople. Not only do diocesan priests need supportive friendships for their personal lives; their parish ministry requires relational skills and communication so they can collaboratively promote the Kingdom of God with their parishioners. The students I talked with tended to rely on the "community life" they spoke highly of to compensate for an inability to make deeper friendships. Fr. Moto said that students in their thirties and forties entering seminaries today do not feel they would have difficulty forgoing marriage as priests. These candidates believe that if they were supposed to get married, they would have done so already. They have not found partners, so they consider themselves fitted for celibacy.

Seminaries need to make sure students are adept at developing friendships and effective ministerial relationships. Archbishop Lobble maintained that a celibate priest should be someone who would have made a wonderful husband and father. However, my suspicion is that today those who are equipped to be good husbands and fathers marry because of social expectations. I don't think it has always been the case. Fifty years ago such men may have accepted a call to the priesthood and celibacy as a worthy life. Today the seminary and celibate priesthood risks being a niche for men who are dependent, psychosexually stunted, and relationally immature. Without the ability to develop strong friendships and ministerial relationships, such men are bound to have difficulties in the priesthood and stir up problems in their parishes. Nor are they likely to be able to lead responsibly and in a collegial manner.

From a practical perspective, I doubt that there is much seminaries can do to teach students how to have satisfying, supportive friendships. Most enter the seminary between the ages of twenty-two and fifty, many years after their relational potential and abilities are set in early childhood. Seminaries simply should not accept candidates without a history of healthy relationships.

My research raises the question of how well the community life of the seminary prepares seminarians for diocesan priesthood. So important is identification with the presbyterate that Church law states "students are to be so formed that they are prepared for fraternal union with the diocesan presbyterate" (Roman Catholic Church 1983: Canon 245, no. 2). At St. Mark's, the students' experience of community met therapeutic needs, but did not appear to be rooted in preparing for a shared apostolate of doing the work of Christ and the Church. Seminarians derived consolation facilitated by their physical proximity while experiencing the trials of seminary life. It is not clear how they would support one another or collaborate effectively when facing the rigors of parish ministry. George Aschenbrenner has argued that "the physical presence of priests to each other in community is not the chief identifying characteristic of the [diocesan] presbyterate" (2002:132). Rather, diocesan priests are commissioned or sent to be dispersed among the laity they serve. However, St. Mark's was unsuccessful in developing a communitarian ethic in which students would see themselves intimately united with other priests and their bishops, engaging in ministry as a collective work. Indeed their sense of specialness and desire to spend large amounts of time in prayer cultivating a personal relationship with God could be detrimental to the collective work of the Church. Ministry and prayer risk being oriented toward a sense of personal fulfillment and not necessarily toward the Church's mission. To some degree this lack of a communitarian ethic as future members of a shared presbyterate results from the excessive individualism of American culture.

When asked what they looked forward to about the priesthood, students' response indicated a strong preference for those activities that were performed without collaboration with other priests, such as celebrating sacraments and providing pastoral care for parishioners. Few appeared to have any inkling how much of their ministry would involve meetings in which they would be expected to work collaboratively with other priests and the laity. More efforts should be made for seminarians to get to know and work alongside members of the presbyterate before they are ordained. This would occur if candidates lived in parishes most of their time before ordination while taking classes at a local seminary or university.

One day at St. Mark's I spoke with a parish priest who was the supervisor for a third-year student spending the year as his parish intern. The pastor was concerned that the student was inflexible in blocking out periods of the day in order to set aside time to pray. Several commentators have argued that some of today's seminarians and young priests exhibit an excessive individualism (Schuth 1999:88–89; Klein 1994; McDonough and Bianchi 2002). This tendency manifests itself in a preference for a "personalized spirituality" that places great stress on devotional prayer. On the other hand, a student's commitment to celibacy may be deepened if an intense habit of prayer is maintained. More opportunities for spiritual development, made possible by a lack of familial contacts, were central to the interest in priesthood of several of St. Mark's students. If this need is not met in the busy life of a parish priest, new priests could be inclined to resign from the priesthood. St. Mark's students also are "at risk" because of their lack of a communitarian sense of ministry as a sharing in a presbyteral order and ministry. The quasi-monastic organization of modern diocesan seminaries, while useful for internalizing certain attitudes and behaviors, could militate against a smooth transition to parish priesthood. It is important that vocation directors and seminaries make clear the active, pastoral orientation of diocesan priesthood to applicants and candidates. If candidates lived more years in parishes while taking classes, the nature of the parish apostolate would be clearer to them. Parish priesthood requires initiative with relatively little supervision or face-to-face contact with other priests. In addition, the intense experience of being set apart by their unique formation may lead seminarians to conclude that they are not only different from laypeople, but that they are also superior to them. Greeley (2004a), Hoge (2002), and Hoge and Wenger (2003) worry that clericalism among recently ordained priests could result in increased tensions between clergy and a highly educated and assertive laity.

It is also troubling that faculty members expressed so much frustration about the effectiveness of efforts to address students' problem behaviors. In one East Coast seminary I visited, where faculty gossiped cynically about their students' inadequacies, a "gallows humor" dominated the faculty dining room. After a priest is ordained, due to the Church's theology of priesthood and its severe shortage of priests, it becomes much more difficult to address a priest's shortcomings. Parish priests are not subject to regular performance reviews. Rarely are priests questioned regarding their post-ordination professional development. Catholics have rated the ministerial performance of their priests significantly beneath the ratings Protestants have given to their ministers (Greeley 2004a:92–95). According to Andrew Greeley, "A quarter of the Catholic people think that their priests do a miserable job on almost all their pastoral activities, and a sixth say that their priests are doing a fine job" (2004a:94). While priests who are found to abuse minors are now dismissed summarily, otherwise there is precious little accountability in the priesthood. Because of the shortage of priests, even the most inept associate pastor is likely to be promoted to a pastorate. I believe this lack of accountability, so clearly revealed by the clergy abuse crisis, to be among the most pressing problems facing the Church today and know of no simple remedies. However, because priests will continue to have such immense responsibilities and be expected to work without close supervision, it is imperative that bishops maintain the highest standards in admitting candidates to seminaries and holy orders.

In the long run, it surely would be counterproductive for the Archdiocese of Middlefield not to forthrightly address students' problems while they are in formation. However, administrators admitted that this was difficult at St. Mark's. While seminaries are unlikely to publicly admit lowering their standards or approving problematic students for ordination, the temptation to do so surely exists, considering the pressing personnel needs of dioceses. Yet nothing fuels anticlericalism like poorly trained or incompetent priests. Strong evidence already exists that there has been a decline in the academic preparedness of men to study theology at the graduate level (Schuth 1999; Klein 1994; Hoge 2002).

According to the National Review Board for the Protection of Children and Young People, the dearth of vocations in the 1970s and 1980s may have contributed to the ordination of men who were not psychologically well-suited for priesthood (2004:68). Fr. Wisher candidly maintained that more recently St. Mark's had "ordained too many mistakes." The shortage of priests is far worse than it was in the 1980s. So too may be the temptation to fill the depleted ranks with "warm bodies." This is a particularly frightening prospect that I believe seminaries have succumbed to. It is a problem that formators acknowledge privately, but have been reluctant to discuss publicly.

Further research about the academic and personal qualities and types of students currently being attracted to the priesthood would be useful for seminary administrators. Based on the types of candidates dioceses draw, Church leaders should then discern whether these candidates ought to form their identities primarily in the subculture of a diocesan seminary (closer to what Goffman [1961] termed a "total institution") or if candidates ought to be more thoroughly immersed in parish subcultures while doing coursework. Church officials also need to squarely address why better quality candidates are not being drawn to the priesthood today. Privately, many administrators bemoan the academic abilities, emotional immaturity, and vocational motivation of many of their students. They do not fear further sexual scandals as much as men who lack vision and zeal and are unable to relate to the lives of their parishioners. A searching discussion of why more Catholic young men aren't interested in serving as priests is sorely needed.

Blatsky's assertion that some students are ordained after keeping "their cards very closely" poses a central problem to seminary formators who seek to form all aspects of seminarians' lives. This problem results from the differing objectives of seminarians and formators confronting them with different problems. The challenge students face is tied to their status as seminarians. Their challenge is to be good seminarians, meaning they must pass their classes and be positively evaluated by the faculty. Faculty are very powerful in the lives of seminarians, and the relatively small number of students in most seminaries means that few of them are likely to escape the faculty's scrutiny. It is not surprising that students, subordinated to the power of faculty members, would engage in impression management in order to pass their annual evaluations. While the hierarchy has called for priests and seminarians to be transparent in light of the sexual abuse crisis, transparency could be detrimental from a student's perspective. That students managed their public identities for formators was clear. John and Luke indicated that they did not use the "v" word (virtue) and kept their disparagement of psychology to themselves. In the area of sexual identity, students were not free to identify themselves in formation conferences and thereby avoided the stigma of homosexuality if it applied to them.

The ability of students to keep "their cards very closely" is enhanced by the relatively short number of years that seminarians are in formation. Prior to the 1970s, most seminarians entered minor seminaries and underwent twelve years of formation. Today, many seminarians enter after graduating from college and spend only four or five years in major seminary. They are observed for fewer years, making more difficult an assessment of their character and abilities. Students intent on ordination can hide troublesome personality features and ideological tendencies. It may be worthwhile for dioceses to increase the number of years candidates spend in formation. This would allow more time to address problematic behaviors, as well as develop a habit of prayer and reflection. Dioceses without their own seminaries ought to arrange for lengthy internships in their own parishes that allow candidates to get to know the diocese and the diocese to know the candidates before ordination. In addition, formation must be seen as ongoing after ordination. In recent years much more attention has been paid to newly ordained priests' transition into first assignment and first pastorate (United States Conference of Catholic Bishops 2001). Without help after ordination, students whose priestly identity is tied to regimentation of a seminary schedule, its common prayer, and the support of its residential community are likely to feel lost, lonely, and ordinary, with no one to sustain their sense of specialness (Stanosz 2005a:23).

CONCLUSION

I have argued that the culture of St. Mark's encouraged students to see themselves as separate from the laity, whom they believed they were called to serve with Jesus Christ as their model. The bodily regime of celibacy was reproduced, as seminarians were set apart by their strong, shared religious experience and the social network they developed at St. Mark's. Celibacy was a distinguishing feature of students' identities and a symbol of their high vocation of service.

Historically, celibacy has contributed to Catholics viewing priests as extraordinary personages with special qualities. While it is frequently pointed out that priests at one time married and that celibacy is not of the "essence" of priesthood, celibacy's force as an organizing symbol linking Christ, the sacraments, and its administrative structures has been profound. Since Christianity's inception, the Church distinguished itself from "the world" by its sexual ethic. The requirement of clerical celibacy institutionalized this boundary with the world. A change in the policy also could alter the way the Church views itself in relation to the secular world.

I have suggested various ways that celibacy shapes the self-understanding of those who undertake the practice in seminaries, as well as how students and formators develop commitment to its practice. While the debate over mandatory celibacy continues, my research will contribute to understanding some of the ways that a change in the Church's policy could alter how seminarians view themselves and priesthood. So significant is celibacy to priesthood that a modification in the Church's policy would likely result in many changes in the way clergy exercise authority and interact with laity. The empirical findings of my research underscore how much is at stake in discussions of whether to continue mandatory celibacy of diocesan priests, as well as how much room there is for improvement in the training of seminarians to live celibate lives.

Appendix A

INTERVIEW
QUESTIONNAIRE GUIDE
FOR SEMINARIANS

- How did you come to have an interest in priesthood and enter the seminary?
- How do you understand your promise of celibacy? What does it mean to you and your priesthood?
- How important or essential is it to priesthood?
- Do you personally find it more of a legal requirement or more of an integral part of and an enhancement of your priesthood?
- Have you dated much or been married?
- What helps you believe that you are able to live celibately as a priest?
- What have you experienced positively and negatively in your seeking to live celibately while seminarians?
- What is most appealing about the celibate lifestyle to you?
- What has been most challenging about trying to live celibately?
- Does any part of celibate living ever make you uneasy?
- What do your family and friends think of your becoming priests, especially living celibately?

Appendix B

INTERVIEW
QUESTIONNAIRE GUIDE
FOR ADMINISTRATORS, FACULTY,
AND THE ARCHBISHOP

- Is there a particular "curriculum" for celibacy?
- What modes of formation are used (conferences, courses, group discussion, required reading, spiritual direction, counseling)?
- What kinds of books and approaches (theological, spiritual, moral, psychological, legal) figure prominently in formation for celibacy?
- What has been most effective in helping candidates explore sexuality and celibacy?
- What particular difficulties are candidates most likely to encounter in preparing for celibacy?
- What are considered indicators of capacity for celibate commitment and what modes of assessment of candidates are used (when, by whom, and how)?
- What is your perception of candidates' realism, maturity, and honesty regarding sexuality and celibacy?
- What concrete behavioral expectations are there for candidates?
- What changes in the formation for celibacy have occurred since Vatican Council II, and what are the reasons for these changes?
- What joys and challenges do formators experience in working with men preparing for a celibate commitment?

Appendix C

VARIOUS REASONS PRO AND CON FOR MANDATORY CELIBACY

Celibacy has been required of priests in the Western Church since the twelfth century and has been invested with a variety of meanings before and since by Catholics. In addition, different official and unofficial rationales for the practice and legislation have been offered over time. Below is a partial listing of popular, current arguments for and against mandatory celibacy for diocesan priests commonly heard in the United States. These reasons can be heard from laity and clergy in sacristies, church basements, and barrooms. Several of them were mentioned by the seminarians and priests I interviewed.

In favor of mandatory celibacy:

1. Since seminarians do not date or have wives, more time is available for their spiritual, academic, and pastoral formation.

2. Christ is presumed to have been celibate, and therefore celibacy is fitting for priests.

3. A life of prayer and companionship with God is made possible to a greater degree by remaining unmarried. A priest belongs only to Christ.

4. Living without marriage and sexual activity, a priest is an eschatological sign of what life will be like in heaven.

5. Celibacy brings greater focus with less distraction to a priest's life and ministry.

6. Without family obligations, a priest can devote more time to the Church's ministry and his parishioners' many demands.

7. Priests are uniquely approachable and likely to be impartial in offering support and counsel to husbands and wives.

8. Parishes would have to pay married priests more so that they could support their families.

9. In a sexually indulgent U.S. culture, a priest's celibacy is a sign that people can live happy lives unmarried and without genital sexual activity. Thus, celibacy is countercultural in a praiseworthy fashion.

10. Celibacy gives priests a unique, mysterious, otherworldly, charismatic quality.

11. A celibate clergy adds distinctiveness to the Catholic Church.

12. Unmarried priests are able to live the gospel in a more radical manner and take unpopular stands because they do not have to worry about downward mobility and the inability to provide for a family.

13. Because remaining unmarried is a great sacrifice, only the most devoted men are ordained priests.

14. If celibacy were optional, further challenges would be posed to the Church's teachings on homosexuality, divorce, remarriage, artificial birth control, and the ordination of women. Some gay priests would likely demand partners and perhaps the right to marry. Some priests' marriages would result in divorce. Some of these priests would seek to remarry. Plus, priests and their wives would consider using artificial birth control. Pressure to ordain women would likely increase.

In favor of making celibacy optional:

1. Celibacy is a charism or gift that should not or cannot be legislated. Some men believe themselves called to service in the Church as priests but do not believe that they have the charism of celibacy.

2. If celibacy were optional, it would be lived better by those with the charism, since they would be doing so more willingly.

3. Some of the apostles were married. For many centuries, many diocesan priests married. Compulsory celibacy is a discipline and not a doctrine of the Church. The rule can be changed.

4. A small number of Anglican priests who were married before they converted to Catholicism are able to function as married Roman Catholic priests. It is hard on morale and an injustice to not allow other Catholic priests to marry.

5. Priests, wives, and their families could provide good examples for the family lives of their parishioners.

6. The experiences of marriage and parenthood would serve priests well as counselors, confessors, and homilists.

7. Since only men who are not in intimate relationships with women are allowed to hold most administrative offices in the Church, celibacy distances the Church from the experiences of women.

8. An unmarried priesthood maintains the priesthood as a "men's club" and perpetuates patriarchy, women's subordination, and women's exclusion from sharing fully in society.

9. Without wives and children, celibates may lapse into forms of irresponsible, selfish, immature bachelorhood. Some celibates never "grow up."

10. Priests who are unhappy as celibates may engage in unchaste, destructive sexual behaviors. Priests who live celibacy poorly are prone to loneliness, depression, alcoholism, and pedophilia.

11. The celibate priesthood has become a predominantly gay calling. Optional celibacy would attract more heterosexual men to the priesthood and increase the proportion of heterosexual priests.

12. More priests are a pastoral necessity, especially to assure that the faithful are able to receive the sacraments. If celibacy were optional, more men would respond to a call to priesthood.

13. The requirement of celibacy has led to a smaller pool of candidates for seminaries, leading seminaries to be less selective in their admission standards. Making celibacy optional would result in candidates for priesthood who are more spiritually, psychologically, and intellectually capable.

14. The experiences of married priests can bring more realism to the treatment of sexual morality and gender issues in the Church. This realism could bring forth a more compelling articulation of its traditional teachings. On the other hand, optional celibacy could also lead to changes in the Church's teachings regarding homosexuality, divorce, remarriage, birth control, and women's ordination.

Some of these arguments are empirical assertions worthy of psychological and sociological research. For instance, are celibate priests more devoted to their parishioners than their married counterparts? Are they more courageous in preaching the gospel? Or are celibate priests more prone to alcoholism and depression than married ministers? Far too little research has been done on these questions. It should be kept in mind that priests in other times and places are likely to have different experiences living celibacy. In different times and places, celibacy is likely to have different effects on priests' lives and a different impact on the culture.

Moreover, these two lists suggest how multifaceted the discussion about compulsory celibacy really is. No amount of research can settle the argument. Though only partial, these lists indicate that much is at stake and that a change in legislation would lead to other unknown changes. Unintended consequences are likely to result from changing the legislation. Unintended consequences are also likely to result from maintaining compulsory celibacy.

NOTES

1. Ambrose, Cyprian, Tertullian, Jerome, and Augustine all reflect this tendency in varying ways.

2. In the Eastern churches, many priests are married.

3. This document was promulgated on October 28, 1965. The reference is to Austin Flannery's 1975 edition of the documents of Vatican II.

4. Eschatological (adjectival form of *eschaton*) refers to the last or final days of the coming of Christ.

5. The psychological concept of "self-actualization" originated with the highly influential work of psychologist Abraham Maslow and was widely disseminated as part of popular U.S. culture.

6. In 1965, 1,575 priests were ordained in the United States. In 1998, only 490 priests were ordained (Froehle and Gautier 2000:117).

7. Research that has studied factors relating to recruitment to priesthood, numbers of ordinations, and reasons for resignation include the work of the following: Richard A. Schoenherr and Andrew M. Greeley (1974); Andrew Greeley with Joan L. Fee, William C. McCready, and Teresa A. Sullivan (1981); Dean R. Hoge, Raymond H. Potvin, and Kathleen M. Ferry (1984); Richard A. Schoenherr and Lawrence A. Young (1993); Richard A. Schoenherr (2002); Dean R. Hoge (2002).

8. Among the journalistic accounts of the current sexual abuse crisis, including how U.S. bishops responded, are Jason Berry, *Lead Us Not into Temptation: Catholic Priests and the Sexual Abuse of Children* (1992); Jason Berry and Gerald Renner, *Vows of Silence: The Abuse of Power in the Papacy of John Paul II* (2004); the Investigative Staff of the *Boston Globe*, *Betrayal: The Crisis in the Catholic Church* (2002); and David France, *Our Fathers: The Secret Life of the Catholic Church in an Age of Scandal* (2004). The *National Catholic Reporter*, a lay-edited weekly independent newspaper, has been in the forefront of covering abuse allegations and episcopal responses since the 1980s, even when other media outlets did not extensively publicize abuse allegations.

9. A diocese is a territory established by the pope and headed by a bishop, who is its chief pastoral and juridical leader. A province is a regional cluster of several dioceses, centered on an archdiocese. Archbishops have some supervisory responsibilities for the dioceses in their province. Bishops are accountable to the pope for the governance of their dioceses. A parish is a stable community of Catholics usually established locally as a geographical territory within a diocese. Bishops appoint priests called "pastors" for the pastoral care of Catholics within a parish.

10. The word "seminary" is derived from the Latin *seminarium*, or "seed plot."

11. The Council of Trent did not address the training of religious order priests.

12. By rationalization, Max Weber meant "the disenchantment of the world," a term borrowed from the German poet Schiller, to refer to a process where more and more aspects of modern life are subject to the laws and statutes of technical reason.

13. Besides the works of Brown (1988), Douglas (1966, 1970), Beaudette (1998), and Giddens (1991) referred to in this chapter, an enormous number of studies have addressed the body and asceticism from differing disciplines and perspectives. Michel Foucault (1978), especially his *The History of Sexuality*, vol. 1, has been influential in viewing the body as produced by the discourses that classify and regulate it. In *The Civilizing Process* vol. 1: *The History of Manners*, historical sociologist Norbert Elias ([1939] 2000) argued that concealment of bodily propriety, individualization, and human affect are not natural characteristics, but result from social and historical developments. The historical study *Holy Feast and Holy Fast: The Religious Significance of Food to Medieval Women*, by Caroline Walker Bynum (1987), examines the dietary asceticism of that period. Much of the attention that the Church directs toward sexuality today was given to food practices in the past. Bynum uses historical materials to show how medieval women exercised agency and cultivated a relationship to the divine by their food practices.

14. The concepts of primary and secondary socialization are widely used concepts in sociology. Secondary socialization is distinguished from primary socialization, the first social education of the child within the family institution. A child first learns the roles and attitudes of parents that induce the acceptance of an objective social order as "reality."

15. Durkheim argued that "social facts," as the object of sociological inquiry, are patterned regularities that cannot be explained by reference to individuals' experiences, representations, or motivations. Constituted by social practices, social facts constrain the behavior of the individuals who internalize the "reality" of these external phenomenon.

16. Some of the documents of the Second Vatican Council that addressed the status of the laity and the Church's relationship to the world are discussed in chapter 2.

17. The *Program of Priestly Formation* is addressed more fully in chapter 2.

18. These works include Peter Berger, Brigitte Berger, and Hansfried Kellner, *The Homeless Mind* (1973); T. Luckmann, *The Invisible Religion* (1967); Daniel Bell, *The Cultural Contradictions of Capitalism* (1996); Eli Zaretsky, *Capitalism, the Family, and Personal Life* (1976); Robert Bellah et al., *Habits of the Heart* (1986); and Arnold Gehlen, *Man in the Age of Technology* (1980).

19. Denis de Rougemont, *Love in the Western World* (1940); Edward Shorter, *The Making of the Modern Family* (1977); Phillipe Aries, *Centuries of Childhood* (1962); Norbert Elias, *The Civilizing Process* ([1939] 2000); Charles Taylor, *The Sources of the Self* (1989); Peter Gay, *The Bourgeois Experience: Victoria to Freud*, vol. 1, *The Education of the Senses* (1984); William M. Reddy, *The Navigation of Feeling: A Framework for the History of Emotions* (2001); Richard Sennett, *The Fall of Public Man* (1974).

20. Highlighting this literature J. M. Barbalet, *Emotion, Social Theory, and Social Structure: A Macrosociological Approach* (1998); Deborah Lupton, *The Emotional Self: A Sociocultural Exploration* (1998); Simon J. Williams, *Emotion and Social Theory: Corporeal Reflections on the (Ir)Rational* (2001); Jeff Goodwin, James M. Jasper, and Francesca Polletta, *Passionate Politics: Emotions and Social Movements* (2001); Jack Katz, *How Emotions Work* (1999); Ann Swidler, *Talk of Love: How Culture Matters* (2001); Eva Illouz, *Consuming the Romantic Utopia: Love and the Cultural Contradictions of Capitalism* (1997).

21. An ordinary is a bishop with personal jurisdiction over a territory, as distinguished from an auxiliary bishop, who assists the ordinary bishop of a diocese.

22. Seminaries use differing titles for describing the various necessary administrative functions. I have used the most common titles. These are described in the *Program of Priestly Formation* (NCCB 1993: nos. 458–83).

23. According to the *Program of Priestly Formation*, the distinction between the external and internal fora is to be observed in seminaries. The relationship between a student and his spiritual director is internal forum, meaning that it is privileged and confidential. Spiritual directors may not share the content of direction sessions with anyone. Student evaluations are conducted in the external forum (NCCB 1993: nos. 311, 482–83). Church law prohibits directors of novices and seminary rectors from hearing the confessions of their students (Roman Catholic Church 1983: Can. 985). This permits rectors to be uninvolved in internal forum matters.

24. Diocesan seminary programs are usually four or five years long, depending on the school. In addition, those without an adequate background for graduate theological study may spend one or two years in a pre-theology program (philosophy and an introduction to theology) plus additional time in an ESL program (English as a Second Language).

25. While all priest faculty alternated between clerical dress and their "civvies," faculty were somewhat more likely to wear clerical clothing when teaching class and in some other formal situations. The year after my interviews were conducted, Archbishop Lobble requested that priest faculty members wear clerical clothing when teaching class and that they vest and concelebrate when attending Eucharist.

26. I declined to attend Fr. Schrieter's session on celibacy for fifth-year students. One of the two students could not attend on the scheduled evening, so Fr. Schrieter was going to meet with him individually over a meal, but I felt my presence would be intrusive.

27. My personal schedule did not permit me to stay the third day of the workshop.

28. See Jozwik (2004) for a not atypical story of a seminarian who professed to be religiously indifferent till he had an intense religious experience at Medjugorie that led him to return to the practice of Catholicism. Another trip to Medjugorie led him to turn down a professional football career because he believed God called him to the priesthood. Indeed, without Mary's reported apparitions or John Paul II's appearances at World Youth Day rallies, many previously religiously uninterested Catholic men likely would not have found their way into Catholic seminaries in the 1980s and 1990s.

29. "Particular friendships" referred to friendships with other seminarians. These natural attachments were commonly seen as an obstacle to growth in perfection and perhaps to seminarians' chastity. They were devalued as natural because they were based on natural motives, such as the appreciation of something that one finds attractive in another person. According to Dubay (1954), seminarians should renounce such relationships in favor of one based on charity, which is the supernatural love of God. Natural attachments discriminate and do not treat others equally. Detaching oneself from others and overcoming particular attachments was a necessary condition for the attainment of perfection (Dubay 1954:87–91; see also Jordan 2000:171–75).

30. Dr. Stephen Rossetti is a psychologist and priest of the Syracuse diocese. Rossetti is also the president and chief executive officer of St. Luke's Institute, a psychiatric hospital for priests and male religious in Silver Spring, Maryland.

31. The practices engaged in to internalize this rationale are addressed in chapter 6.

32. How homosexuality is dealt with at St. Mark's is treated more extensively in the final chapter.

33. It should be noted that a few lay students did not participate in Catholic practices and culture when off campus. Since the 1980s there were usually two or three Protestant students at St. Mark's. They attended classes and earned degrees at St. Mark's, but did most of their spiritual formation elsewhere.

34. C.P.E. refers to Clinical Pastoral Education, a hospital chaplain training program that seminarians take in the summer following their second year, just prior to their nine-month parish internship.

35. Prior to admission to the M. Div. program, some students completed an English as a Second Language program and a pre-theology (philosophy) program.

36. As the seminary's spiritual director, Fr. Blatsky did not evaluate or vote on whether students should be able to return the following year. Fr. Blatsky's relationships with students were considered "internal forum" and therefore privileged and confidential. Faculty members who were students' individual spiritual directors did not vote on students they were directing.

37. Frank went on leave at the end of the fall 2002 semester. Larry did not return for the fall 2003 semester. Ken, a student who was not formally interviewed for this project, went on leave at the end of his parish internship in May. Ken told me he did not intend to ever return to his studies for the priesthood. The circumstances of the fourth student's departure are unknown to me.

38. In 1972, Pope Paul VI replaced the minor orders of porter, reader, exorcist, and acolyte with institution into the ministries of reader and acolyte.

39. Smith developed the concept in reply to Peter Berger (1967), who described the "classical task" of religion at a macro level as "constructing a common world within which all of social life receives meaning binding on everybody" (133). Berger maintained that this unified shelter of meaning, or "sacred canopy," that upholds the social order as a sacred order is threatened by the pluralism of the modern world. Several years later, Christian Smith (1998) replied to Berger that believers do not need to construct an overarching, protective canopy in which to meaningfully situate them in the world. Instead, under the pluralism of modernity, "sacred umbrellas . . . small, portable, accessible relational

worlds — religious reference groups" suffice for believers to construct their faith-sustaining worlds (1998:106).

40. Curiously, though I looked in the chapel many times, I never observed students praying alone at other times of the day. This may have indicated a preference for communal prayer forms over praying alone. Another possible explanation is that students preferred to offer their individual or "private" prayers in the presence of peers and faculty members. In either case, being seen not only by God but also in the company of others is an element of the practice.

41. The sample of 80 Catholic priests was drawn from two western Canadian dioceses and from priests involved in Catholic Charismatic Renewal. The 1,294 Protestant ministers (most of whom were married) were members of 22 conservative denominations. The celibate clergy did not spend any more significant time with their parishioners than did the married clergy. Priests did average 9.07 more minutes in prayer daily than did the Protestant clergy. The study also sought to operationalize "giving oneself entirely to God" through two measures to determine how salient their faith was in their lives (Swenson 1998:40). The study also sought to measure if clergy gave themselves more to their parishioners. Swenson found no significant differences in the salience of faith or the pastoral commitment between the two groups. The fact that Swenson studied Canadian priests from only two dioceses and only Evangelical clergy means that his results cannot be easily extrapolated into generalizations about clergy elsewhere.

42. Ruth A. Wallace's *They Call Her Pastor: A New Role for Catholic Women* (1992) and *They Call Him Pastor: Married Men in Charge of Catholic Parishes* (2003) describe the ministry of laywomen and laymen and deacons who are "pastoring" as directors and administrators of Catholic parishes.

43. One seminary I visited early in my research had an outright ban on admitting homosexual students.

BIBLIOGRAPHY

Aries, Phillipe. 1962. *Centuries of Childhood: A Social History of Family Life.* New York: Vintage Books.

Arksey, Hilary, and Peter Knight. 1999. *Interviewing for Social Scientists.* London: Sage Publications.

Aschenbrenner, George. 2002. *Quickening the Fire in Our Midst: The Challenge of Diocesan Priestly Spirituality.* Chicago: Loyola Press.

Barbalet, J. M. 1998. *Emotion, Social Theory, and Social Structure: A Macrosociological Approach.* New York: Cambridge.

Baum, Cardinal William. 1986. "Letter to the Bishops of the United States Concerning Free-Standing Seminaries." In *Norms for Priestly Formation.* Vol. 2:221–40. 1994. Washington, DC: National Conference of Catholic Bishops.

Beaudette, Paul. 1998. "'In the World but Not of It': Clerical Celibacy as a Symbol of the Medieval Church." In *Medieval Purity and Piety: Essays on Medieval Celibacy and Religious Reform,* ed. M. Frassetto, 23–46. New York: Garland Publishing.

Becker, Howard S. 1960. "Notes on the Concept of Commitment." *American Journal of Sociology* 66:32–40.

Becker, Howard S., Blanche Geer, Everett C. Hughes, and Anselm L. Strauss. 1961. *Boys in White: Student Culture in Medical School.* Chicago: University of Chicago Press.

Bell, Daniel. 1996. *The Cultural Contradictions of Capitalism.* With a new afterword by the author. New York: Basic.

Bellah, Robert N., Richard Madsen, William M. Sullivan, Ann Swidler, and Steven M. Tipton. 1986. *Habits of the Heart: Individualism and Commitment in American Life.* Berkeley: University of California Press.

Berger, Peter L. 1969. *The Sacred Canopy: Elements of a Sociological Theory of Religion.* New York: Doubleday.

Berger, Peter L., Brigitte Berger, and Hansfried Kellner. 1973. *The Homeless Mind.* New York: Random House.

Berger, Peter L., and Thomas Luckmann. 1966. *The Social Construction of Reality: A Treatise in the Sociology of Knowledge.* New York: Doubleday.

Berry, Jason. 1992. *Lead Us Not Into Temptation: Catholic Priests and the Sexual Abuse of Children.* New York: Doubleday.

Berry, Jason, and Gerald Renner. 2004. *Vows of Silence: The Abuse of Power in the Papacy of John Paul II.* New York: Free Press.

Bleichner, Howard P. 2004. *A View from the Altar: Reflections on the Rapidly Changing Catholic Priesthood.* New York: Crossroad.

Borhek, James T., and Richard F. Curtis. 1974. *A Sociology of Belief.* New York: Wiley.

253

Briggs, David. 2001. "Isolated Life Takes Toll on New Priests." *Religion News Service. www.pulpitandpew.duke.edu/newpriestlife.html.*

Brown, Peter. 1987. "Late Antiquity." In *From Rome to Byzantium,* vol. 1 of *A History of Private Life,* ed. P. Veyne. Cambridge.

———. 1988. *The Body and Society.* New York: Columbia University Press.

Bruni, Frank. 2003. "John Paul Announces 31 New Cardinals." *Milwaukee Journal Sentinel,* September 29, A1, A8.

Bynum, Caroline Walker. 1987. *Holy Feast and Holy Fast: The Religious Significance of Food to Medieval Women.* Berkeley: University of California Press.

Caceres, Peter. 2000. "The Production of Knowledge on Sexuality in the AIDS Era: Some Issues, Opportunities, and Challenges." In *Framing the Sexual Subject: The Politics of Gender, Sexuality, and Power,* ed. Richard Parker, Regina Maria Barbosa, and Peter Aggleton, 241–57. Berkeley: University of California Press.

Canary John F., and Louis J. Cameli. 2002. " 'Goodbye' a Bad Tale." *Seminary Journal* 8:2.

Carroll, Jackson W., Barbara G. Wheeler, Daniel O. Aleshire, and Penny Long Marler. 1997. *Being There: Culture and Formation in Two Theological Schools.* New York: Oxford University Press.

Chaves, Mark. 2003. "Religious Authority in the Modern World." *Society* 40:3.

Cornwell, John. 2001. *Breaking Faith: Can the Catholic Church Save Itself?* New York: Penguin Compass.

Cozzens, Donald B. 2000. *The Changing Face of the Priesthood.* Collegeville, MN: Liturgical Press.

Crosby, Michael H. *Celibacy: Means of Control or Mandate of the Heart?* Notre Dame, IN: Ave Maria Press

Cuneo, Michael W. 2001. *American Exorcist: Expelling Demons in the Land of Plenty.* New York: Doubleday.

D'Antonio, William V., James D. Davidson, Dean R. Hoge, and Katherine Meyer. 2001. *American Catholics: Gender, Generation, and Commitment.* Walnut Creek, CA: Alta Mira Press.

Davidson, James D., Andrea S. Williams, Richard A. Lamanna, Jan Stenftenagel, Kathleen Maas Weigert, William J. Whalen, and Patricia Wittberg. 1997. *The Search for Common Ground: What Unites and Divides Catholic Americans.* Huntington, IN: Our Sunday Visitor Publishing Division.

De Rougemont, Denis. 1940. *Love in the Western World.* Princeton, NJ: Princeton University Press.

Dolan, Timothy M. 2000. *Priests for the Third Millennium.* Huntington, IN: Our Sunday Visitor.

———. 2002. "Reestablishing the Culture of Vocation." Presented as a public lecture at Marquette University, October 30.

Donovan, Gill. 2003. "Seminarian Enrollment Drops While Lay Ministry Rises." *National Catholic Reporter,* May 16, 2003, 8.

Douglas, Mary. 1966. *Purity and Danger: An Analysis of Concepts of Pollution and Taboo.* New York: Routledge.

———. 1970. *Natural Symbols: Explorations in Cosmology.* New York: Routledge.

Dubay, Thomas. 1954. *The Seminary Rule: An Explanation of the Purposes behind It and How Best to Carry It Out.* Westminster, MD: Newman Press.

Durkheim, Emile. [1915] 1965. *The Elementary Forms of Religious Life.* New York: Free Press.

Elias, Norbert. [1939] 2000. *The Civilizing Process.* Trans. Edmund Jephcott. Malden, MA: Blackwell Publishers

Erikson, Kai. 1966. *Wayward Puritans.* New York: Wiley.

Ference, Thomas P., Fred H. Goldner, R. Richard Ritti. 1971. "Priests and Church: The Professionalization of an Organization." *American Behavioral Scientist* 14:507–24.

Festinger, Leon, Henry W. Riecken, and Stanley Schachter. 1956. *When Prophecy Fails.* Minneapolis: University of Minnesota Press.

Finke, Roger, and Kevin D. Dougherty. 2002. "The Effect of Professional Training: The Social and Religious Capital Acquired in Seminaries." *Journal for the Scientific Study of Religion* 41:103–20.

Foucault, Michel. 1977. *Discipline and Punish: The Birth of the Prison.* New York: Vintage Books.

———. 1978. *The History of Sexuality.* Vol. 1, *An Introduction.* New York: Random House.

Fox, Thomas C. 1995. *Sexuality and Catholicism.* New York: George Braziller.

France, David. 2004. *Our Fathers: The Secret Life of the Catholic Church in an Age of Scandal.* New York: Broadway Books.

Froehle, Bryan T., and Mary L. Gautier. 2000. *Catholicism USA: A Portrait of the Catholic Church in the United States.* Maryknoll, NY: Orbis.

Gautier, Mary L., ed. 2001. *Catholic Ministry Formation Directory.* Washington, DC: Center for Applied Research in the Apostolate.

Gay, Peter. 1984. *The Bourgeois Experience: Victoria to Freud.* Vol. 1. *The Education of the Senses.* New York: Oxford.

Geertz, Clifford. 1973. "Thick Description: Toward an Interpretive Theory of Culture." In *The Interpretation of Culture.* New York: Basic Books.

Gehlen, Arnold. 1980. *Man in the Age of Technology.* Trans. Patricia Lipscomb. With a foreword by Peter L. Berger. New York: Columbia University Press.

Gerth, H. H., and C. Wright Mills, eds. 1946. *From Max Weber: Essays in Sociology.* New York: Oxford University Press.

Giddens, Anthony. 1990. *The Consequences of Modernity.* Stanford, CA: Stanford University Press.

———. 1991. *Modernity and Self-Identity: Self and Society in the Late Modern Age.* Stanford, CA: Stanford University Press.

———. 1992. *The Transformation of Intimacy: Sexuality, Love, and Eroticism in Modern Societies.* Stanford, CA: Stanford University Press.

Gill, James J. 2002. "Seminaries Await Vatican Visitation." *America,* July 15–22, 10–13.

Goergen, Donald. 1975. *The Sexual Celibate.* New York: Seabury Press.

Goffman, Erving. 1961. *Asylums: Essays on the Social Situation of Mental Patients and Other Inmates.* New York: Doubleday Books.

———. 1963. *Stigma: Notes on the Management of Spoiled Identity.* Englewood Cliffs, NJ: Prentice Hall.

Goldner, Fred H., R. Richard Ritti, and Thomas P. Ference. 1977. "The Production of Cynical Knowledge in Organizations." *American Sociological Review* 42:539–51.

Gomulka, Eugene. 2001. " 'Home Alone' in the Priesthood — Why Did Catholic Chaplains Get into More Trouble More Often Than Protestants?" *America*, August 27–September 3, 17–19.

Goodstein, Laurie. 2002. "At Seminary, New Ways for a New Generation." *New York Times*, March 9, A1, A19.

Goodstein, Laurie, and Sam Dillon. 2002. "31 Bishops Removed Abusers, Survey Says." *New York Times*, August 18, A1.

Goodwin, Jeff, James M. Jasper, and Francesca Polletta. 2001. *Passionate Politics: Emotions and Social Movements.* Chicago: University of Chicago Press.

Greeley, Andrew M. 1972. *The Catholic Priest in the United States: Sociological Investigations.* National Opinion Research Center study. Washington, DC: United States Catholic Conference.

———. 1995. *Religion as Poetry.* New Brunswick, NJ: Transaction Publishers.

———. 2004a. *Priests: A Calling in Crisis.* Chicago: University of Chicago Press.

———. 2004b. *The Catholic Revolution: New Wine, Old Wineskins, and the Second Vatican Council.* Berkeley: University of California Press.

Greeley, Andrew with Joan L. Fee, William C. McCready, and Teresa A. Sullivan. 1981. *Young Catholic Adults.* New York: Sadlier.

Hedin, Raymond. 1995. *Married to the Church.* Bloomington, IN: Indiana University Press.

Heinz, Martin. 2004. "My Soul-Shattering Experience in the Seminary." *New Oxford Review* 71:27–31.

Hoge, Dean R. 2002. *The First Five Years of Priesthood.* Collegeville, MN: Liturgical Press.

Hoge, Dean R., Raymond H. Potvin, and Kathleen M. Ferry. 1984. *Research on Men's Vocations to the Priesthood and Religious Life.* Washington, DC: United States Catholic Conference.

Hoge, Dean R., and Jacqueline E. Wenger. 2003. *Evolving Visions of the Priesthood: Changes from Vatican II to the Turn of the Century.* Collegeville, MN: Liturgical Press.

Illouz, Eva. 1997. *Consuming Romantic Utopia: Love and the Cultural Contradictions of Capitalism.* Berkeley: University of California Press.

Investigative Staff of the *Boston Globe*. 2002. *Betrayal: The Crisis in the Catholic Church.* Boston: Little, Brown.

Jenkins, Philip. 1996. *Pedophiles and Priests.* New York: Oxford University Press.

John Paul II. 1993. *Pastores Dabo Vobis.* In *Norms for Priestly Formation.* Vol. 2:263–346. 1994. Washington, DC: National Conference of Catholic Bishops.

Johnson, Luke Timothy. 2001. "A Disembodied 'Theology of the Body.'" *Commonweal*, January 26, 11–17.

Jordan, Mark D. 2000. *The Silence of Sodom: Homosexuality in Modern Catholicism.* Chicago: University of Chicago Press.

Jozwik, Tom. 2004. "Seminarian Chooses Priesthood over NFL." *Catholic Herald*, January 13. Special Vocations Section. 1.

Kanter, Rosabeth Moss. 1968. "Commitment and Social Organization: A Study of Commitment Mechanism in Utopian Communities." *American Sociological Review* 33:499–517.

Katz, Jack. 1999. *How Emotions Work*. Chicago: University of Chicago Press.

Kauffman, Christopher. 1988. *Tradition and Transformation in Catholic Culture: The Priests of Saint Sulpice in the United States from 1791 to the Present*. New York: Macmillan.

Kennedy, Eugene C., and Victor J. Heckler. 1972. *The Catholic Priest in the United States: Psychological Investigations*. Washington, DC: United States Catholic Conference Publications Office.

Kissling, Frances. 2000. "The Catholic Church's Achilles' Heel." *Conscience* 20, no. 4:27–28.

Klein, Terrance W. 1994. "U.S. Culture and College Seminaries." *America*, June 18, 16–21.

Loftus, John Allan. 1999. "Sexuality in Priesthood: *Noli Me Tangere*." In *Bless Me Father for I Have Sinned*, ed. Thomas Plante, 7–19. Westport, CT: Praeger Books.

Luckmann, Thomas. 1967. *The Invisible Religion*. New York: Macmillan.

Lupton, Deborah. 1998. *The Emotional Self: A Sociocultural Exploration*. London: Sage Publications.

McBrien, Richard P. 1994. *Catholicism*. New ed. New York: HarperCollins Publishers.

———. 2002. "Obligatory Celibacy Is Not Cause of the Sexual Crisis." *Catholic Herald*, September 5.

McCarthy, E. Doyle. 1996. *Knowledge as Culture: The New Sociology of Knowledge*. New York: Routledge.

McDannell, Colleen. 1995. *Material Christianity: Religion and Popular Culture in America*. New Haven, CT: Yale University Press.

McDonough, Peter, and Eugene Bianchi. 2002. *Passionate Uncertainty: Inside the American Jesuits*. Berkeley: University of California Press.

McSweeney, William. 1980. *Catholicism: The Search for Relevance*. New York: St. Martin's Press.

Mead, George Herbert. 1934. *Mind, Self, and Society*. Chicago: University of Chicago Press.

Morris, Charles R. 1998. *American Catholic: The Saints and Sinners Who Built America's Most Powerful Church*. New York: Vintage.

Murphy, Brian. 1997. *The New Men: Inside the Vatican's Elite School for American Priests*. New York: Riverhead Books.

National Conference of Catholic Bishops (NCCB). 1987. *Handbook for Vocation and Seminary Personnel*. Washington, DC: United States Catholic Conference.

———. 1993. *Program of Priestly Formation*. 4th ed. Washington, DC: United States Catholic Conference.

National Review Board for the Protection of Children and Young People. 2004. *A Report on the Crisis of the Catholic Church in the United States*. Washington, DC: United States Conference of Catholic Bishops.

NCCB. See National Conference of Catholic Bishops.

Paul VI. 1967. *Sacerdotalis Caelibatus*.

Reddy, William M. 2001. *The Navigation of Feeling: A Framework for the History of Emotions*. New York: Cambridge University Press.

Roman Catholic Church. 1976. "Admission to Candidacy for Ordination as Deacons and Priests." In *The Rites of the Catholic Church*, 740–50. New York: Pueblo Publishing.

———. 1983. *Code of Canon Law*. Latin-English ed. Washington, DC: Canon Law Society of America.

———. 1997. *Catechism of the Catholic Church*. 2nd. ed. Washington, DC: United States Catholic Conference

Rose, Michael S. 2002. *Goodbye, Good Men: How Catholic Seminaries Turned Away Two Generations of Vocations from the Priesthood*. Cincinnati: Aquinas Publishing Ltd.

Ruether, Rosemary. 2000. "Sex and the Body in the Catholic Tradition." *Conscience* 20, no. 4:2–12

Sacred Congregation for Catholic Education. 1985. *Ratio Fundamentalis Institutionis Sacerdotalis*. In *Norms for Priestly Formation*, vol. 2:15–60. 1994. Washington, DC: National Conference of Catholic Bishops.

———. 2005. "Instruction Concerning the Criteria for the Discernment of Vocations with Regard to Persons with Homosexual Tendencies in View of Their Admission to Seminary and to Holy Orders."

Schneiders, Sandra. 1986. *New Wineskins: Re-imaging Religious Life Today*. New York: Paulist Press.

Schoenherr, Richard A. 2002. *Goodbye Father: The Celibate Male Priesthood and the Future of the Catholic Church*. New York: Oxford University Press.

Schoenherr, Richard A., and Andrew M. Greeley. 1974. "Role Commitment Processes and the American Catholic Priesthood." *American Sociological Review* 39:407–29.

Schoenherr, Richard A., and Lawrence A. Young. 1993. *Full Pews and Empty Altars*. Madison: University of Wisconsin Press.

Schuth, Katarina. 1999. *Seminaries, Theologates, and the Future of Church Ministry: An Analysis of Trends and Transitions*. Collegeville, MN: Liturgical Press.

———. 2000. "Preparing Tomorrow's Priests" (Karen Sue Smith, interviewer). *Church*. Fall, 19–23.

———. 2004. "Seminaries and the Sexual Abuse Crisis." *America*, March 22, 16–18.

Second Vatican Council. 1975a. *Lumen Gentium*. In *Vatican Council II: The Conciliar and Post Conciliar Documents*, ed. Austin Flannery, 350–426. Newport, NY: Costello Publishing Company.

———. 1975b. "*Presbyterorum Ordinis*." In *Vatican Council II: The Conciliar and Post Conciliar Documents*, ed. Austin Flannery, 863–902. Newport, NY: Costello Publishing Company.

Sennett, Richard. 1974. *The Fall of Public Man: On the Social Psychology of Capitalism*. New York: Random House.

Sheldrake, Philip. 1993. "Celibacy and Clerical Culture." *The Way Supplement* (Summer): 26–36.

Shorter, Edward. 1977. *The Making of the Modern Family*. New York: Basic Books.

Sipe, A. W. Richard. 1990. *A Secret World: Sexuality and the Search for Celibacy.* New York: Brunner/Mazel.

———. 1995. *Sex, Priests, and Power: Anatomy of A Crisis.* New York: Brunner/Mazel.

Smith, Christian. 1998. *American Evangelicalism: Embattled and Thriving.* Chicago: University of Chicago Press.

Stanosz, Paul. 2005a. "Seminarians Today." *Commonweal*, August 12, 19–23.

———. 2005b. "Gay Seminarians." *Commonweal*, December 16, 8–10.

Stark, Rodney, and Roger Finke. 2000. *Acts of Faith: Explaining the Human Side of Religion.* 2000. Berkeley: University of California Press.

Sweeney, Terrence. 1992. *A Church Divided: The Vatican versus American Catholics.* Buffalo, NY: Prometheus Books.

Swenson, Don. 1998. "Religious Differences between Married and Celibate Clergy: Does Celibacy Make a Difference?" *Sociology of Religion* 59, no. 1:37–43.

Swidler, Ann. 1986. "Culture in Action: Symbols and Strategies." *American Sociological Review* 51:273–86.

———. 2001. *Talk of Love: How Culture Matters.* Chicago: University of Chicago Press.

Taylor, Charles. 1989. *The Sources of the Self: The Making of the Modern Identity.* Cambridge, MA: Harvard University Press.

Thomas, Judy L. 2000. "Concern Growing about the Number of Priests Who Have Died of AIDS-related Illnesses." *Kansas City Star*, October 15.

Turner, Bryan S. 1992. *Regulating Bodies: Essays in Medical Sociology.* New York: Routledge.

United States Conference of Catholic Bishops. 2001. *The Basic Plan for the Ongoing Formation of Priests.* Washington, DC: United States Conference of Catholic Bishops.

———. 2002. *Charter for the Protection of Children and Young People.* Washington, DC: United States Conference of Catholic Bishops.

Wallace, Ruth A. 1992. *They Call Her Pastor: A New Role for Catholic Women.* Albany: State University of New York Press.

———. 2003. *They Call Him Pastor: Married Men in Charge of Catholic Parishes.* Mahwah, NJ: Paulist Press.

Walsh, James, John Mayer, James Castelli, Eugene Hemrick, Melvin Blanchette, and Paul Theroux. 1995. *Grace under Pressure: What Gives Life to American Priests.* Washington, DC: National Catholic Educational Association.

Weigel, George. 2002. *The Courage to Be Catholic: Crisis, Reform, and the Future of the Church.* New York: Basic Books.

White, Joseph M. 1989a. *The Diocesan Seminary in the United States: A History from the 1780's to the Present.* Notre Dame, IN: University of Notre Dame Press.

———. 1989b. "How the Seminary Developed." In *Reason for Hope: The Futures of Roman Catholic Theologates*, ed. Katarina Schuth, 11–29. Wilmington, DE: Michael Glazier.

———. 1995. "Seminary" in *The HarperCollins Encyclopedia of Catholicism*, ed. Richard P. McBrien. New York: HarperCollins.

Williams, Daniel, and Alan Cooperman. 2002. "Vatican Considers Barring Gays from Priesthood." *Milwaukee Journal Sentinel,* October 12, B5.

Williams, Simon J. 2001. *Emotion and Social Theory: Corporeal Reflections on the (Ir)Rational.* London: Sage Publications.

Wills, Garry. 2000. *Papal Sin: Structures of Deceit.* New York: Doubleday.

Wittberg, Patricia. 1994. *The Rise and Fall of Catholic Religious Orders: A Social Movement Perspective.* Albany: State University of New York Press.

Wolf, James G., ed. 1989. *Gay Priests.* San Francisco: Harper & Row.

Wolfe, Alan. 2001. *Moral Freedom: The Search for Virtue in a World of Choice.* New York: Norton.

Zaretsky, Eli. 1976. *Capitalism, the Family, and Personal Life.* New York: Harper Colophon.

Zullo, Jim. n.d. "Educating Seminarians for Healthy Sexuality." In *Ripe for the Harvest: A Resource for Formation Advisors.* 2nd ed. Edited by James Walsh. Washington, DC: National Catholic Educational Association Seminary Department.

INDEX

Of Related Interest

Mark S. Massa, S.J.
ANTI-CATHOLICISM IN AMERICA
The Last Acceptable Prejudice

Now in paperback!

Since 2003, when it was first published, this astonishing study of the distinctiveness of Catholic culture and the prejudice it has generated has been hailed as a "stimulating" (*Journal of Religion*) and "eye-opening chronicle" (Catholic News Service) with "an explosion of creative insight" (Andrew Greeley).

Now with major study guide!

0-8245-2362-8, $19.95 paperback

Howard Bleichner
VIEW FROM THE ALTAR
Reflections on the Rapidly Changing Catholic Priesthood

"*View from the Altar* is a must-read for all who are interested in understanding the causes of the scandal of sexual abuse by members of the Catholic clergy.... I am grateful to the author for handling this sensitive topic with both raw honesty and brotherly compassion.... *View from the Altar* reminds us that spirituality must be at the core of seminary formation." —*America*

0-8245-2141-2, $19.95, paperback

crossroad

Of Related Interest

Edward P. Hahnenberg
MINISTRIES
A Relational Approach

This comprehensive text for every student, minister, and teacher offers excellent scholarship and a visually enhanced presentation of the concept and practice of ministry. Dr. Hahnenberg sheds light on the various aspects of modern ministry offering a prophetic vision of the church as ordered communion.

0-8245-2103-X, $24.95, paperback

Please support your local bookstore,
or call 1-800-707-0670 for Customer Service.

For a free catalog, write us at

THE CROSSROAD PUBLISHING COMPANY
16 Penn Plaza, 481 Eighth Avenue
New York, NY 10001

Visit our website at
www.crossroadpublishing.com
All prices subject to change.

crossroad